Chinese kinship

Chinese kinship

Paul Chao

Professor of Social Anthropology
William Paterson College

Kegan Paul International
London, Boston and Melbourne

First published in 1983
by Kegan Paul International Ltd
39 Store Street, London WC1E 7DD,
9 Park Street, Boston, Mass. 02108, USA,
296 Beaconsfield Parade, Middle Park,
Melbourne 3206, Australia
Broadway House, Newtown Road,
Henley-on-Thames, Oxon RG9 1EN
Set in Press Roman by
Hope Services, Abingdon, Oxon,
and printed in Great Britain by
Redwood Burn Ltd,
Trowbridge, Wiltshire

Library of Congress Cataloging in Publication Data

Chao, Paul, 1919-
Chinese kinship.
Bibliography: p.
Includes index.
1. Family – China.   2. Kinship – China.   3. China –
Social life and customs.   I. Title.
HQ684.C47 1982   306.8'5'0951   82-13200

ISBN 0-7103-0020-4

To my brother Benedict Kuang Ch'i

Contents

Preface

Professor Paul Chao writes *Chinese Kinship* in the line of the Chinese tradition; it is in this tradition that cultural complexes, such as family structure and kinship in relation to religious, political and economic organizations, are expounded by analysis of concepts and supported by historical documents. For the anthropological study of kinship is indispensable as a supplement to important historical work on basis of written documents. Professor Chao has made, in the main, a study of kinship in China of all known periods. He has taken the points of view of social anthropology and has also given a history of his topic. In China, there was in one period a custom of preferred or prescribed marriage between a man and a daughter of his maternal uncle. In all known periods to this date there has been a custom of forbidden marriage between members of the same surname. Such customs as these have close analogies in some preliterate societies whose social histories were unknown. In discussing his study of such a preliterate society in the Trobriand Islands the social anthropologist Bronislaw Malinowski once said that 'he preferred his work to a study of a European society.' But he found European societies were too complex. It is probable, however, that it was the method of fieldwork needed in the study of simple societies without recorded histories which appealed to him. In discussing Kinship in China, Professor Chao has confronted the complexity of the problem and has dealt with it adequately.

The president of Lingnam University in Canton, where I taught social anthropology at one time, married a woman of his own surname. I think that in the sequence the old custom of forbidden marriage between members of the same surname survived the revolution of 1911.

I learned in China that the sentiment between a man and his mother's brother's daughter was closer than that between him and his father's sister's daughter or between him and his remote cousins on his and their father's side. Professor Chao reports that in certain parts of China cousin marriage is restricted to mother's brother's daughter and mother's sister's daughter. This matrilateral cross-cousin and parallel-cousin marriage is practised with the accompanying prohibition of marriage with father's sister's daughter. But until I read Chao's work on kinship I did not know that the difference in the sentiment between cousins of opposite sex today was in part a survival of a preferred or prescribed marriage of a man to his mother's brother's daughter of a definite historical period.

Professor Chao is the author of *Women Under Communism – Family in Russia and China*, published by General Hall in 1977. I think, therefore, that he needs no preface from me; but he is kind enough to wish me to write something of the kind. In China I took a party of students to use a method of fieldwork in the study of the Yao, a preliterate people with the blessings of the Bureau for civilizing the Yao. But I believe that, although there are a few preliterate peoples in China, there are records of them over a long period in the literature. I do not know how detailed these literary records are. I think that if Professor Chao will tell us some day, it may be of interest to know. He is a painstaking and serious student of his subject, who is well read in the Chinese literary classics, a domain in which I, for my part, have no competence.

Social anthropologists, many of whom have been Europeans, have written of a custom of forbidding marriage between couples related by common descent on one side of their families from a remote ancestor. As many of them have noticed exogamy amongst some preliterate peoples and not amongst some literate peoples, and not amongst Europeans, they have assumed that it was especially a primitive custom. Probably it was a custom with an early origin. However, there is no evidence that it was once European. As far as we can be guided by evidence, the inclination is that it was not. It appears that in European societies the rules about degrees of consanguinity were a barrier to marriage on both sides of families. There is a similar regulation in some preliterate societies. In contrast, a group of people related by common descent on one side of their families from a remote ancestor has been called a unilaterally enlarged family or a clan or a gens or a surname. In some preliterate societies it is believed that the remote ancestor from which a clan or a gens was descended was a bird, and its members were forbidden to kill or to eat that species of bird. Such a belief has been called totemic.

In this book Professor Chao says that the patrilineal category includes agnatic third cousins and rising and falling four generations in the direct line of descent. The official patterning of mourning portrays the diminishing intensity of relationships between agnates according to proximity. In ancestor worship, tablets kept in the domestic shrine are those of the deceased father, grandfather and great grandfather; tablets remain by right in the possession of primogeniture. When the family division takes place, a domestic shrine will become the ritual centre for a number of agnatically related families.

In many societies, cousins who are the children of a brother and a sister pair by their respective spouses are distinguished from cousins who are the children of brothers or the children of sisters. Social anthropologists call the former kind cross-cousin and the latter, parallel-cousin. The Chinese distinguish cousins of the same surname, called inside (t'ang agnatic) cousins from all other cousins, called outside (piao non-agnatic) cousins. But for more detailed study about this and other features of the reckoning of kinship in China it gives me great pleasure to recommend this book by Professor Chao to the reader. For *Chinese Kinship* will be counted as a landmark in the development of the anthropological theory of kinship. It is not written by an outsider looking at the kinship system in a strange land; it contains research conducted by a citizen upon his own people. If self-knowledge is the most difficult to gain, then an anthropology of one's own people is the most valuable and worthy achievement and contribution.

Reo F. Fortune
Cambridge

Foreword

Professor Paul Chao has given us in this book an outstanding example of sociological–anthropological work done on a people by one of themselves, the self-observation of a culture seen from within rather than from outside. But Chao has not been content with observations made during one particular time-slice, he has gone back to the classics of the literature in order to add the element of historical development, and for this he has mobilized a deep sinological learning, testimony of his admirable education in classical Chinese scholarship. It is important for the reader to recognize these two roots of his exposition: the personal experience of traditional Chinese life, on the one hand, and the historical study of the origins and early forms of those traditions, on the other. I certainly know of no similar book which does just this.

So alive for Paul Chao is traditional Chinese family life that he often uses the verb 'is', when with regard to contemporary China it may not be quite the *mot juste*, but the reader must introduce the necessary personal adjustment. Paul Chao is certainly not unconscious of the vast changes which have occurred in the Chinese social and family life of today, as we know from another of his books on the position of women in socialist China, but here he is concerned to delineate a set of patterns which lasted for more than two thousand years down to the time of his own youth. In a sense, therefore, he is the Cecil Sharp of the Chinese family, preserving for posterity a clear account of how it all began, and what it was like to grow up in the midst of it. What good fortune for the world that one inside person noted it all down, and was capable of telling the story, both historically and pragmatically.

As a historian of science I must just add that since science and

Foreword

society are inseparable, there is much in Paul Chao's book which will
be helpful to those concerned with the social and economic background
of Chinese science and technology. The sixty-four dollar question for us
always is, of course, why distinctively modern science should have
developed in Europe, and in Europe only, at the time of Galileo and the
Scientific Revolution; and many of us do not believe that intellectual
factors alone will explain the difference. Social, fiscal and economic
factors are going to have to be called in as well, and may even have to
take the main burden of explanation. Thus here, with Chao, the alerted
reader notices at once the absence of primogeniture among the Chinese,
that feature of occidental life which led Dr Johnson to exclaim that it
was the foundation of all stable property relationship; feudal essentially,
of course, but also of enormous importance for incipient capitalism.
Once again the bureaucratic feudalism of China seemed weaker, but was
actually much stronger than the military-aristocratic of Europe.

Again, much fascinating material is found in Paul Chao's book about
the honeycomb-like courtyard of the great extended Chinese family
home. It was dying out fast from 1911 onwards, and during my time in
China through the war years, I only entered such a home once – at
Ta-t'ung in Szechuan, where I had gone to view the cave-temples still
rarely visited. So many Westerners know China only through the great
novels such as the *Hung Lou Mêng* and Chao's exposition will bring a
great deal of those descriptions to life for them. Lastly, there is much
in his book on the ching t'ien system, the nine fields with the well in
the midst of the centre one. He works it in to his discussions of the
ideal family of traditional China, but in truth nobody still knows
whether it was a theoretical construct of Mencius or the feudal-
bureaucratic theoreticians of later ages. All in all, however, Paul Chao's
contribution is going to be helpful far beyond the realm of the professional anthropologists, for it throws a deal of light on many aspects of
Chinese life which are highly important for historians of science and
technology, especially on what may have been limiting factors for
their development.

Dr Joseph Needham, FRS, FBA
Director, East Asian History of Science Library,
Cambridge

Acknowledgments

The publication of this book was made possible largely by a grant in aid from the Pacific Cultural Foundation, the Republic of China.

The author and publishers would also like to thank the following: Philo Press, for permission to quote from *The Chinese Village Plays*, based on Franklin C. H. Lee and Chang Shih-wen, *The Ting Hsien Yang Ke Hsüan*, edited by Sidney D. Gamble, published by APA-Philo Press, Postbox 806, NL-1000 BW Amsterdam, Holland, 1970.

Introduction

This work deals in the main with Chinese kinship from the anthropological point of view, which is couched in ancestor worship and filial piety. It is not based upon fieldwork, but on historical documents. What motivated me to take up this subject was the advice and guidance of Professor M. Fortes and the Department of Social Anthropology at the University of Cambridge. Their advice and comments have helped to provide me with additional points of view on the crucial and interesting materials that throw light on ancestor worship and make it even more illuminating, in relation to filial piety within the Chinese kinship system.

While this study was in progress I came to see, in the materials collected, the significance of the sociological role of kinship systems in relation to ancestor worship and filial piety, political, economic and recreational activities. This constitutes one of the mechanisms of Chinese social stability. What I have written cannot be regarded as a comprehensive study; this would have been quite impossible, considering the amount of material there is in the long history of China, but it provides a basis for understanding the traditional social complex which has interested anthropologists for many years. Also, it helps to clarify and correct some errors that writers have made on account of their ignorance of the Chinese language. More than once missionaries in China have written about filial piety and ancestor worship by hiring Chinese interpreters; unable to read the classics, they pretended to be versed in them and so furnished an incorrect translation.

Furthermore, the present subject appealed to me because it concerned many problems, such as the lineage, clan, village organization, the concept of the soul, the social importance of ancestor cults and filial piety and various aspects of social life that have rarely been tackled before, and for this purpose I have used original Chinese texts as a basis for the study.

Here we are concerned with the domestic organization of traditional Chinese society. Social bonds are based on genealogical relations, but it is patrilineal descent that gives one membership of a lineage. Membership of the patrilineage becomes membership of an exogamous group. Ties of kinship and marriage constitute domestic groups, which, however, have no permanent basis either in time or in space. For each domestic or family group is formed with age and sex; it grows, expands with maturity, splits through marriage and disperses; but the norms or moral codes that the domestic group inherits are permanent features of its social organization. Dr Fortes wrote:

> Domestic organization has two aspects. Its form derives from a paradigm or cultural norm sanctioned by law, religion and moral values. Its structure is governed by internal changes as well as by changing relations, from year to year, with society at large.

It is due to the substitution of one generation by the next, and to marriage, that the domestic group undergoes change. In Chinese traditional society the domestic group or family usually lasts for two or three generations. Grandparents and children with their spouses and their children bound to one another by direct kinship ties live in one household. The household head is the most senior by age and generation. Although age and generation correlate, it can happen that a junior in age may be higher in generation. In this case the index of generation prevails over that of age. The importance attached to seniority is due to the fact that it possesses authority and wisdom and is entitled to respect. The function of the head is primarily to achieve domestic harmony, cohesion and stability.

Ancestor worship is of great interest in itself, and is related to a primitive religion which should be of interest to students of theology, of comparative religion and of social anthropology. Among the main features of the ancestral cult which will be discussed in detail are the concepts of the soul in various religious forms. Although there is a considerable amount of literature on the concept of the soul, its definition is still ambiguous because of the lack of a word in the Chinese language which corresponds to the ideas conveyed by the English word 'soul'. This difficulty is not simply a matter of language and definitions, but also involves the personal judgment of believers. Christians think differently about the concept of the soul from the Chinese who are not Christians. (I have tried to compare the concept of the soul in Western thought and Chinese philosophy.) As this is partly a study of Chinese religion, I have described those ceremonies which took place during ancestor worship and have indicated those parts which had religious significance, explaining how they concerned the Chinese kinship system.

Since the clan organization, ancestor worship, dwelling pattern and village structure were not uniform in North and South China, I have attempted to make a comparative study of their differences, particularly in dwelling forms, by consulting former works written for the most part by Chinese scholars on the subject. They are: Fei Hsiao-tung, *Peasant Life in China: A Field Study of Country Life in the Yangtze Valley* (Central East China); Dr Martin Yang, *A Chinese Village; Taitou, Shantung Province* (North China); Lin Yueh-hua, 'An Enquiry Into the Chinese Lineage-Village from the Viewpoint of Anthropology', in I-hsü Village, Fukien province (South China), published in *She Hui Hsüeh Chieh*, no. 9, 1936; D. H. Kulp, *Country Life in South China: The Sociology of Family in Phoenix Village*, Kwangtung province (South China). These works have provided me with valuable materials on social structure in North, Central East and South China. Literary sources for the study of Chinese kinship in the past have not yet been fully exploited and brought to light. A few years ago Dr Hu Hsien-Chin in *The Common Descent Group in China and its Functions* whetted our appetites for the provision of literary evidence on Chinese kinship, especially lineage organization in China and its functions. Apart from the above sources, Freedman's *Lineage Organization in South-eastern China* has proved very useful.

With regard to the 'time' basis of this study, I have attempted to clarify the kinship system which bears on filial piety and ancestor worship from the 'Chou' period up to the Ch'ing dynasty. I have had to use whatever materials I could lay my hands on to collect and fit pieces together so as to make a picture of Chinese kinship. The data, however scattered they may be, do not prevent us, in principle at least, from building a model of Chinese social structure, which is common, though not totally uniform, in the whole of China and persists over all Chinese dynasties. What has strengthened this endeavour has been the continuing practice of anthropologists of studying 'the whole' of a society of 'culture'. (See C. Wright Mills, *The Sociological Imagination*, New York, Oxford University Press, 1959, pp. 136-7. He says: 'The traditional subject matter of . . . anthropology has been the total society; or, as it is called by anthropologists, "the culture".')

In fact, notwithstanding its long history, Chinese culture, which is based on the principle of filial piety, proves to be rather homogeneous. Staunton wrote in the preface to *Ta Ch'ing Lü Li*:

> [The vital and universally operating principle – the duty of submission to parental authority] may be traced even in the earliest [Chinese] records; it is inculcated with the greatest force in the writings of the first of their philosophers and legislators; it has survived each successive dynasty, and all the various changes and revolutions which the state has undergone; (it continues to this day powerfully enforced, both by positive laws and by public opinion.) (Sir G. R. Staunton, translator's preface to *Ta Ch'ing Lü Li,* London, 1810, pp. XVIII–XIX.)

Likewise, in his foreword to Ch'ü's book *Law and Society in Traditional China*, A. F. P. Hulsewe says of Professor Ch'ü's basic assumption that:

> during the last two thousand years Chinese society was static. The historian will be inclined . . . to disagree, but on second thoughts he will realize that in spite of all growth and change . . . the fundamental conditions which determine the structure of Chinese society remained unchanged. This is clearly shown by recent development in family law and in criminal law.

A noticeable part of this study consists of the Chinese documents which are not available in English, and of well-known stories, myths and history which shed a strong light upon the complex social structure. It is the presentation of the stories that has justified our approach to a study of Chinese kinship from the point of view of anthropology, and that constitutes my main original contribution in this field. I have taken care to set out the exact reference of every passage from the classics according to their original Chinese sources. This is, in my opinion, of great importance as it shows the authenticity of sources.

I owe so much to my teachers in social anthropology at Cambridge University: to Professor M. Fortes who gave me help and encouragement, and to Dr E. R. Leach and Jack Goody from whom I gained an insight into problems not previously explored in depth. I gratefully acknowledge the help, advice and guidance of Dr Reo Fortune; I am greatly indebted to him for his kindness in writing the preface. I wish to thank kindly Dr Joseph Needham who has found time to read the manuscript and write a foreword. His profound and broad knowledge of Chinese culture has been second to none. I am indebted to Dr David Davies who has taken his valuable time in reading through the text. I am also grateful to the other teachers of the Department of Social Anthropology whose lectures I attend and who aroused and sustained my interest in carrying on the research. I take the opportunity to express my thanks to Dr M. I. Scott of the Chinese section of Cambridge University Library for having kindly and willingly helped me in my quest for Chinese books for consultation. And last, but not least, I appreciate the painstaking efforts of Mrs V. Williams who has seen to the editing and final typing of this manuscript.

Chapter 1

The nature and the development cycle of the Chinese family

> The typical family, a group consisting of mother, father and their
> progeny, is found in all communities, savage, barbarous and civilized.
>
> B. Malinowski

In describing the life process of an individual and then the family
system we must set out the following stages: birth day, the full month
and the first year after birth, weaning, the formation of playmates,
going to school, adulthood, marriage, fatherhood, old age, death and
burial. In my village, Pai-tang, when a child is born, there is a ceremonial
feeding called 'kai-kou' which consists of opening the baby's mouth and
giving it a few drops of water.

The whole family is happy but is kept busy. Some, for example, are
sent to announce the good news to fellow lineage members, to the
child's mother's family, and to other relatives and friends. The third
day after the birth the family is obliged to give a banquet to which
fellow lineage members and other relatives and friends are invited. All
those who offer congratulations on this happy event bring presents
according to their relationship to the child. The maternal grandmother
has to send a gown, a pair of trousers, swaddling clothes and some food
for the nursing mother. Fellow lineage members and neighbours send
only food, such as rice, noodles, glutinous millet and eggs, and some
brown sugar, cakes and pastries, as these foods are considered to be the
most nourishing for the mother.

The child's father chooses a name for the baby which is traditionally
known as his 'milk name'. For the first few years of a child's life, he
bears a baby or a milk name. This is generally chosen with reference to
the time of his birth or to some personal peculiarity. For example, the

milk name 'liu chin' (six pounds) is chosen because this is his weight at birth. The milk name is retained until the boy or girl goes to school when his/her personal name is chosen.

At this point we should notice the difference between the life history of a boy and that of a girl. When a female child is born, the procedure is similar to that carried out for a boy, except that a girl, when young, lives with her parents and, when she grows up, will marry and be incorporated as a member of her husband's lineage. The life of a girl changes in terms of space as well as time, while that of a boy undergoes change only in the dimension of time.

The individual and society are essentially closely knit: they stand, in a sense, for two aspects of the same thing. The individual cannot exist outside society, likewise the society cannot function without individuals, its component elements. It follows, that if we are to study the family and kinship, we should on no account neglect the study of the individual.

In studying the individual we use the biosocial method which serves to describe both the individual's life and his relationship with others, proceeding from the most intimate to the more remote relations. For example, after the birth of each baby, the closest relationship will be with the parents, especially mother and child; when parents have more children, there will be the relationship of siblings (co-family relationships), which develop into play-group (outside the family) relationships. When these siblings themselves come of age and marry there will be the relationship of man and wife, of younger brother and elder brother's wife, of sister and brother's wife, of wife and husband's brother's wife and relationships with the maternal kinship. When brothers have established families and have children there will be the relationship between father's brother and brother's son and between paternal parents and son's children.

With succeeding generations, branches are further subdivided as their numbers grow, and this brings about the relationships of members of the same branch and the same sub-lineage until the relationship includes a large group of 'kin' membership which is in the same lineage and which shares descent from the same ancestor. Further subdivision will involve membership of distinct lineages descended from different ancestors. In the kinship system the family is a composite of individuals. In studying the family our attention must be called not only to the broad outline of its organization, but also to the contents of its structure. It engages as a group in everyday activities and has various functions, economic, juridical, legal, moral, religious and recreational, all of which will be put forward in the last section of the first chapter and fully described in the fifth chapter.

Before discussing the domestic group and its development, we have to clarify some of the kinship terms. 'Kin' includes persons descended from a common ancestor, while 'kith' involves friends by vicinity or neighbourhood.[1] 'Gens' refers to the ancestral functions, while 'clan' is an exogamous group of the same surname, the members of which claim descent from a common ancestor. A 'household' is constituted by the joint occupancy either of a single large dwelling or of a cluster of adjacent compounds, and is used in connection with the economic functions of domestic groups. 'Generation' is the perpetuation of the family line.[2]

The total domestic organization is the family.[3] Etymologically, the character 'chia', 'farmhouse' (see the Glossary) is composed of two ideograms: the top part like a roof symbolizes house or chamber, whereas the lower part stands for pig. Likewise, the character 'chia' shows that all homesteads are originally farms, for the roof has a pig underneath it. These ideograms have no undertone of contempt. In the Chou dynasty sheep and pigs were sacrificial objects. In the absence of an ancestral temple commoners offered pigs in sacrifice in their house. In this sense the term 'chia' also suggests the religious ritual.

The Chinese family is the cornerstone of the social structure. Its first phase is the nuclear or elementary family, which develops in successive generations into the joint or extended family, which includes a large number of elementary families.[4] Here we are interested in the developmental cycle of the family system and are describing it in the light of the internal system of the domestic group and in its relation to the external system of social structure at large. The internal system is regarded as including the domestic group and the family, between which there is a distinction in the direct sense.[5] While the nuclear family is formed by the direct bonds of marriage, filiation and siblingship, the domestic group is constituted by kinship, descent and other legal and emotional bonds. Again, it is marriage that unites two people and legitimizes their function in procreation. This is the first phase during which the nuclear family takes shape. In this phase the children depend upon their parents from the economic, emotional and legal points of view, but they enter into the patricentral nuclear family units. The nuclear family is the incipient and basic form of the family, consisting of a nucleus of a married couple and one or several dependent or unmarried children. Sometimes after the death of her husband, the wife lives with her children without joining another unit and, correspondingly, a widower may live with his son without a woman in the house. In such

Figure 1.1 *The nuclear family (as seen by the observer from the outside)*

circumstances either the widower will remarry or the son will marry at the youngest possible age so that a normal function of the group can be restored.

The second phase is the period of dispersion or fission. The term 'fission' connotes the process of internal subdivision. This phase marks the beginning of the stem family. It begins with the marriage of the eldest child and continues until all the children are married. But one of the married sons lives with his parents until their death. Other sons break away from their parents and form a nuclear family upon marriage; they establish their own family, set up their own cooking and cultivate their portion of the land. The married sons and their wives and children

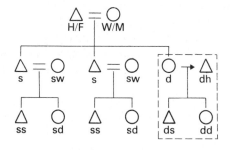

Figure 1.2 *The stem family*

continue to perform many common functions, such as ancestor worship and participation in the family council, even though they live in separate households.

Being described as an enlarged nuclear family, the stem family brings about the fusion and fission of the domestic group. The 'stem' may refer to what Professor Fortes terms 'segmentation', a state of internal subdivision within a group, that is, in our case, a nuclear family, and to 'fission,' the process of internal subdivision, as, for example, the dispersion of the original group, the parent couple.[6] With regard to the question of which of the married children moves out of their original home, this depends on individual families and the decision of the parents. If there are two or more children in the family, the eldest son, when he marries, will move out if the parents are still living. If the division of the family occurs after the death of the father, the elder son will occupy the old house and the younger son will move out with the mother. If there is only a daughter in the family, her marriage and her residence with the husband mark the phase of dispersion of her natal family.

Thus we see how the domestic group plays its part in the developmental cycle of the family. This group as a unit retains the same form, but its members in their social relations and activities undergo a regular sequence of changes which culminates in the dissolution of the original unit and its replacement by one or more units, i.e. the families of married children. This is because the form of domestic organization is stable in so far as it is derived from a cultural norm sanctioned by law, religion and moral values, but its structure is governed by internal changes as well as by changing relationships, from year to year, with society at large.[7] For example, the partition of family or parental property results in the dissolution of the original family, but it gives rise to the establishment of new, separate, nuclear families among the married siblings and subsequently of a family of orientation. Failing male issue in any of the nuclear families, a concubine serves as a mechanism for reproducing a male child and perpetuating the family line.

The most important form of property is land, which belongs to all generations; it lays the foundation of the family. People and land are the two pillars of the farming family. When a family is said to be broken up or dissolved, it implies the partition of land.

Another factor of the internal structure of the domestic group is residence. Apart from kinship and descent, economic, legal and emotional

10

bonds determine the disposition of residence, such as the nuclear-family type, the stem-family type and the joint-family type, with a class of mixed types. It should be kept in mind that these so-called types are only phases in the developmental cycles of a single, general, nuclear type.

Let me revert to what I have mentioned previously about marriage, kinship, inheritance, succession and so forth, which are the significant events in the life of the domestic group. It is clear that the domestic group and the unilineal descent group are intertwined, the former, being the source from which the latter is incessantly replenished, grows and expands. This means that different persons in the domestic group by generation, filiation, kinship and descent, are incorporated into the structure of the unilineal descent group to generate the modes of collocation or 'juxtaposition' (a linear series) and segmentation (a merging series), characteristic of the lineage system. This continuing process expands into the joint family phase, a phase which is important in analysing the family structure in traditional China.

The joint family[8] consists of parents, their unmarried children, their married son or sons and the son's wives and children. In other words, a family is described as a joint family when two or more lineally related kinsfolk of the male sex, with their spouses and offspring, reside in a single homestead and are jointly subject to the same authority or to a single head. In the joint family either the father is the head, or one of the brothers; in the latter case usually the eldest, presiding over his unmarried and married brothers, with their wives and children. The successor to headship of a joint family should be the first son of the principal wife, even when there happens to be an older son from a concubine. The next successor will be the second son of the principal wife. Only in default of sons of the principal wife could the son of a concubine be the heir of the family.

It should be borne in mind that a joint family was an ideal form of family in feudal times, though the nuclear family was the fundamental unit of the family structure.[9] During the Chou dynasty such families were on the wane. Later, legislation reduced the size of the family. Shang Yang, for example, statesman and philosopher of the Ch'in dynasty (fourth century BC) imposed a tax on families in which several sons lived in one household.[10] In the same period the need for intensive agriculture prompted duke Hsiao of the Ch'in state to break up the extended or joint noble family for the purpose of abolishing their opposition to the imperial order.[11] However, the Han dynasty

11

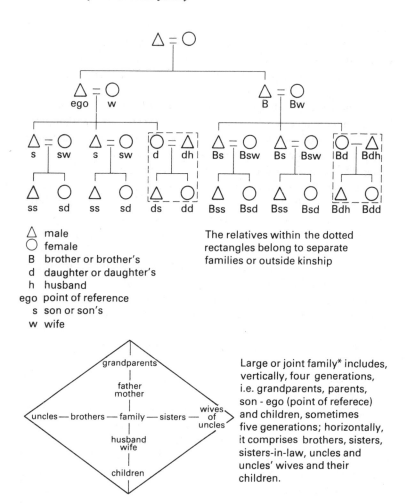

△ male
○ female
B brother or brother's
d daughter or daughter's
h husband
ego point of reference
s son or son's
w wife

The relatives within the dotted
rectangles belong to separate
families or outside kinship

Large or joint family* includes,
vertically, four generations,
i.e. grandparents, parents,
son - ego (point of referece)
and children, sometimes
five generations; horizontally,
it comprises brothers, sisters,
sisters-in-law, uncles and
uncles' wives and their
children.

*Mai Hue-t'ing, *The Problem of Reforming the Chinese Family System*,
Shanghai, 1929, pp. 53-4, 57.

Figure 1.3 *The joint family*

(206 BC-AD 220) abrogated the law and made an attempt to restore joint families. From the T'ang to the Ch'ing dynasties, decrees and laws encouraged joint families. Since all the sons were entitled to equal shares of their father's real estate, they had not much incentive to stay together after his death. Consequently, in a majority of cases the average family of a Chinese household was not a large one. For instance, in the early Han dynasty the size of the average family ranged from five to six persons; in the T'ang period (seventh to tenth century) from five to six, and under the Yüan and Ming dynasties (thirteenth to seventeenth century) the average size was under six.[12]

In brief, in view of the long stability of the Chinese cultural tradition, heritage and of the stability of family life, we can therefore draw a diagram which illustrates five phases or stages in the development of the domestic group (see Figure 1.4). This graphic model can be applied equally to the whole of China proper, considering the influence of the Han culture complex in the North, Central East and South China. These phases can be explained as follows:

Phase I is the nuclear or elementary group - there is husband, wife and children.

Phase II emerges, when one of the sons marries. Each marriage of a man adds to the membership of the elementary group. When elementary or conjugal families multiply, the family enters the second phase and it becomes a compound; when the daughter marries out, this causes the incipient fission of the natal domestic group.

Phase III appears when the married sons have their own children, but still live with their parents and unmarried brothers and sisters.

Phase IV begins when all the sons are married, and have their children and move out, with just one remaining in the natal family with his parents. This phase is also called the stem family. It is the result of the fission of a joint family. Some of the married sons leave their parents' home after having stayed with them in a joint family; one of the sons with his wife and children continues to live with his parents until their death. Every branch of the family, however intricate its ramifications are, is always connected with a parent-stem.

We have phase V when the parents are gone and all the sisters are married out; in this case the brothers will usually separate from each other. If they can keep the family group from breaking up, it has then reached the fifth phase. However, when it breaks up, a number of elementary or nuclear families of the first phase reappear. Each one of them comes into existence with the birth of the first child in marriage and it continues

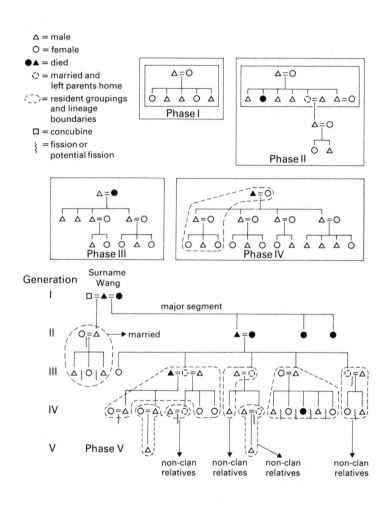

Figure 1.4

14

to grow through the birth of other children. Although a joint family of five generations is ideal, very few families are able to reach this phase. When a family has grown into a very large group, a few male members of this group would often emigrate to a different locality and establish an independent household; this grows and develops in the same way as the original family or domestic group with which it always retains ties.

Again, in the fifth phase there may be a concubine and a wife, but only one father, and a mother with her own children forms a separate unit of the domestic group.

Domestic group, agnatic and cognatic kinship: the component units of the household

We now describe the structure of the family from its constituent parts in a logical and natural order and in the context of both physical and genealogical aspects, both in traditional and contemporary China.

Several houses or chambers make up a dwelling-unit or home,[13] each with a house head. A dwelling consists on average of three rooms. The central room is larger, comparatively speaking, than the rest, and serves for family gatherings, as a sitting-room, a reception room and a dining-room when the weather is bleak and boisterous. The two rooms on either side of the central room are, as a rule, occupied by the two family units of the household. Each of these rooms contains one or two beds. The married couple and their young children share one bed, while an older child would have a separate bed in the parents' room or sleep in the central room. In a larger house, however, a boy or girl might move to his or her grandmother's room.[14]

A household may be either a large dwelling or a group of dwellings with or without a common courtyard. A homestead is a single habitation, the occupants of which constitute a household,[15] consisting of the parents, their young children or unmarried children.

The pattern of dwelling is fairly uniform. In his study of Kai-hsienkung village, Wukiang, Kiangsu province in Central East China, Fei Hsiao-tung describes the household as the basic territorial group. The writer presents a similar household in North China on the basis of his personal observation. Dr Yang has drawn the plan of a household in Taitou village, Shantung province, North China, which is similar.

In his study of Phoenix village near Chaochow in northern Kwangtung province, D. H. Kulp provides a small amount of material on household

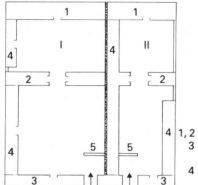
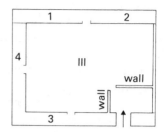

1, 2 Bedrooms of family members.
3 Rooms for hired labourer and farm
implements, also granary.
4 Shed for the family's animals.

1 Main house where parents, unmarried
daughters and the first married son live.
2 Middle house where the second married son lives.
3 Front house where hired labourers live; also for farm implements.
4 Small house for keeping domestic animals.
5 Spirit wall or 'yung-pei'.

Source: Martin C. Yang, *A Chinese Village: Taitou, Shantung Province*,
London, 1948, p. 39.

Figure 1.5 *I and II Two houses of rich peasant families; III The house
of an average peasant family*

composition. The units he describes as 'economic families' correspond
to what I have called the household. Kulp says:[16]

> Members of the economic family may all live under one roof, under
> several roofs joining one another, in houses somewhat separated in
> the village, or far apart as in Chaochow, Swatow, or even the South
> Seas. (So long as there is no imbalance between the incoming and
> outgoing funds and so long as the whole group is administered by a
> certain head or 'chia-chang', the persons living under these arrange-
> ments belong to an 'economic family'.) Ordinarily an economic
> family is composed of a mature man, his wife or wives, his parents or
> frequently his mother and his children, and the wives of married
> sons with their young children.

His description of the 'economic family' covers not only a family in a house, but also what 'household' means in relation to the economic function of domestic groups. According to Spencer,[17]

> the arrangement of the house in South China is much the same as that in the North, with the enclosed courtyard in front and spaces between each additional section of the house. In these courtyards children may play while their mothers work at the sorting of beans for drying, at sewing, or at preparing vegetables for cooking.

The setting-up of dwellings may be traced back many dynasties and shows little variation as a result of the prevailing agricultural economy throughout almost the whole of China. The dwelling-house plans show the houses of urban inhabitants, rich peasants and average peasants in the Northern, Central, Central East, South and South West China (see Figure 1.5).

With regard to the family structure there are ramifications. When several elementary families make up a compound,[18] the head of the family is also the head of the compound as well. In addition, there are cases where two families belonging to different branches are in one compound. Several compounds make up a branch of 'chih', or 'fen', each with a branch head; several branches make up a sub-lineage 'fang'; several sub-lineages make up a lineage 'tsung' or 'tsu', with a lineage head. The terms 'lineage' and 'clan' have been used indiscriminately, although in fact the latter adds something to the former. A 'clan' refers to the group of descendants in its entirety, that is, it embraces whole patrilineal groups of families, while 'lineage' means an unspecified division of a clan.[19] The ramifications of branches and lineage can be demonstrated (see Figure 1.6).[20]

The family (chia), as has already been said, is the basic economic unit of which the oldest in the highest generation (pei) is the head. Family units are reckoned by kitchens,[21] whereas compounds are counted according to dwellings or households. It should be kept in mind that a family is not equivalent to a household. The members of a family may be temporarily absent or may wish to be incorporated for a time into another working unit without affiliating themselves to a new kinship group. As a consequence, those who live even for a long time in the same house and participate in most of its economic activities are not naturally considered members of the family. There are three common ways in which non-family members may live in a household. First, the member may be a guest and make a definite monthly payment over

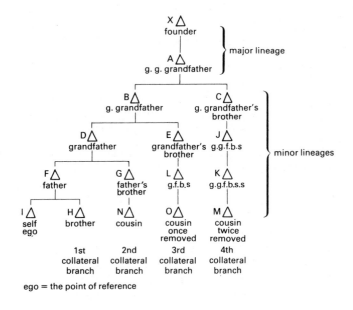

Figure 1.6

a long period of residence. A doctor practising in the village resides in a house of the medicine shopkeeper. Second, a child who has lost his own parents may be brought up and nursed in a house; his relatives make some contribution to the cost of nursing him. Third, employment provides a way of introducing to a household a working member under a definite contract to work on the farm. The worker is provided with accommodation in his employer's house.

Branches or segments are counted by lines of descent. Agnatic cousins belong to a common line of descent from the paternal grandfather, though they may occupy an abode in different compounds, or a small unit within the same compound. A larger family often splits into smaller units but continues to share the same compound. Bearing this situation in mind helps to dispel any misconceptions about the apparent size of what appears as one family. Above the branch are further branches in which the line of descent springs from the same patrilineal great-grandfather or from the same patrilineal great-great-grandfather down to the point of sub-lineage ramifications. Branches have no longer remained in one single organization; nevertheless each branch still recognizes the others as being related through a remote or founding ancestor. A small clan forms one integral unit, whereas large clans involve several ramifications articulated by such terms as: (1) 'fang', meaning home, house or chamber, room; 'pai', branch; 't'ing', courtyard; (2) 'hu', mouth or household meaning house or 'shih'; 'tsai', wealth; 't'ien', land; 'ting', head; (3) 'men', door or gate conveying the idea of a famous name or family; (4) 'chih' and 'fen', both meaning branches. At times some branches break up through migration, poverty, or death during disaster, while other branches may grow in size and prosperity; such branches can proliferate into several sub-branches. In terms of structure and function there is, in fact, no difference between a branch and a sub-branch, seeing that they share equal responsibilities in regard to ancestral rites, common welfare activities, and control of the members' conduct.

Lineage is related to the term 'tsung', the characteristics of which are 'following', 'branch', 'tribal rules', 'religious or ancestral hall', 'temple' and 'sacrifice'; 'tsung' also means 'honour'. Whoever officiates as host to the ancestors deserves to be honoured by the members of his lineage. Lineage is a collective name standing for the major lineage and the minor lineages. Lineage includes no deeper than five generations. It represents a consanguineal kin group, comprising those persons who trace their common relationship through patrilineal links to a known ancestor. Usually the smallest corporate segment of a lineage consists of unilinearly related persons of the male forming the core of a joint family. Also included in the lineage are married siblings of the opposite sex who may reside elsewhere. Evans-Pritchard defines a lineage as a 'group of living agnates, descended from the founder of that particular line; it also includes dead persons descended from the founder'.[22] Lineage is a relative term, since its range of reference depends on the particular person who is selected as the point of departure in tracing descent.[23]

With the 'tsung' institution during the Chou dynasty (*c.* 1100–220 BC), the line of descent was strictly patrilineal, and this determined not only the transmission of the clan name, but also the transmission of office and property. In the tsung units there was one ta-tsung, or major lineage (major segment) and four hsiao-tsung, or minor lineage (agnatic descendants). The major tsung comprised all descendants who claim to to be direct lineal descendants from a 'pieh tzŭ', that is, a son other than the eldest or heir selected. The direct descendants from

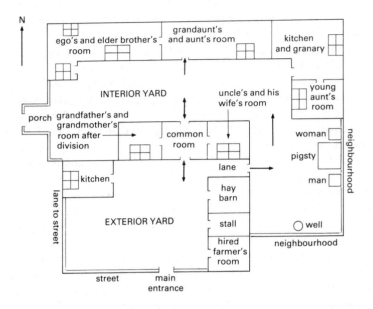

Figure 1.7 *The plan of author's household, Cheng-ting, Hopeh province, North China.*

the great-great-grandfather, great-grandfather, grandfather, and father were those who were separated after five generations. The 'tsung' from father to great-great-grandfather together constitute the four minor tsung. The son who became the founder of a new line naturally became the first ancestor of his sons and grandsons and formed in turn a major tsung. His collateral descendants in each successive generation formed minor tsung.[24] The tsung system is shown in Figure 1.9. Williamson's description of the Polynesian political and kinship system can shed some light on the Chinese tsung lineage system.[25] The Polynesians say that their kinship system originated from China 2,000 years ago. The tsung lineage system disintegrated with the decline and chaos of the feudal system and then came the period of social organization dominated by the family units, namely, the Imperial Period (*c.* 250 BC–AD 1900). The tsung lineage system is of general import and great importance in relation to succession, legal aspects of primogeniture, the inheritance of rank and ancestral cult.

Side by side with the lineage are the cognatic ch'in, who are thought of as being connected by sentiment, that is, 'emotional' ties with the rise of the family and comprise those relatives who are entitled to mourning rites. Paternal kinsmen are those within nine generations and five collateral grades. Lang has described the whole links of kinship as 'comprising twenty-one categories including lineal ascendants, lineal descendants, brothers and their wives, sisters, uncles and their wives, cousins and their wives.'[26] Paternal kinsmen are distinguished as living under one roof and as constituting an economic unit, which is a typical Chinese family (an extended or joint family). Foremost among maternal relatives are grandparents, uncles, aunts, and first cousins for whom various grades of mourning insignia are worn. Included in the kinship circle are the relatives of the wife, her parents, grandparents, uncles, sisters and brothers.

Paternal relatives are considered nearer than maternal relatives and the relatives of the wives. The mourning period for paternal grand-parents is one year, while for maternal grandparents only five months; for paternal uncles one year, and for maternal uncles only five months. Mourning for the relatives of the wife is no longer than three months. Here again, the mourning for the father's unmarried sister, ego's unmarried sister, unmarried daughter, and brother's unmarried daughter, is one year, and, after their marriage, the mourning period is decreased to nine months. Thus the marriage of clan relatives to another clan has extended their bond to their original clan and therefore with ego.

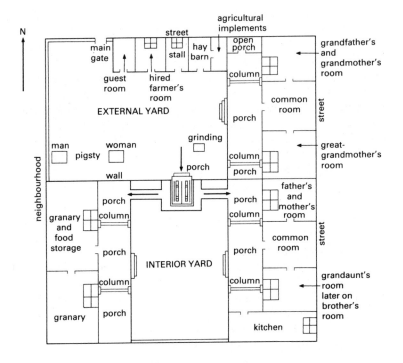

The clan organization

The term 'tsu', clan, means 'ts'ou', to collect; the term 'chu' stands for 'assemble'. The term 'tsu' conveys the meaning that love and affection flow together and collect. In the ascending line, 'tsu' includes the great-great-grandfather in the collection, whereas in the descending line it reaches the great-great-grandson. Thus 'tsu', clan is the group known in Roman law as 'agnates' as distinct from 'cognates' which include all blood relatives, whether on the male or female side.[27] According to

Figure 1.8 *The plan of the author's household.*
It is to be noted that there are no windows open to the street both for secrecy and security. The exterior and interior yards are walled up so that direct access is impossible. The porch provides only for an entrance to the interior yard. However, the door of the porch is closed daily and locked during the night.

It is conventionally required of unmarried girls and young couples to live in the rooms within the interior yard. Guests and visitors are by custom barred from entrance to the interior yard. This represents the prescribed pattern of the household set-up.

Hired farmers must always live in one of the rooms of the exterior yard, close to the stall so that they can easily attend horses and mules.

The great-grandmother and grandfather and mother live in the same compound because it is incumbent on the latter to serve the former. Also ego's grandfather and mother have no right to require the service of their son and daughter-in-law (ego's father and mother) as long as the former's father or mother is alive.

Again ego's mother's room is in the compound as the kitchen enables her to be engaged solely in the cooking tasks and the rest of the domestic chores. Unless it is very necessary, she is not permitted to interfere with the business in the exterior yard.

Shang Shu, 'if one house enjoys good luck a hundred houses share it'. When alive they feel affection for one another, while in death they grieve for one another. They follow the method of combining in a body to form a tsu, that is, nine groups of kindred, four kin on the father's side, three kin on the mother's side, and two kin on the wife's side. 'Nine' means in Chinese 'chiu', profound.[28]

A clan is a group organized by and composed of numerous component families which trace their patrilineal descent from a common ancestor, first settled in a given territory. Men throughout their life and

Figure 1.9 *In this diagram Wen wang, Wu wang, Cheg wang, K'ang wang are all emperors and grand tsung of the 'chi' surname; duke Chou, T'ang shu, Tan tze are all dukes, and their status is inferior to that of emperor. They have branched off from minor tsungs. Duke Chou passes his title and rank in succession to Pai ch'in, and K'ao. Similarly T'ang shu passes his rank in succession to other dukes. This diagram entirely coincides with that of Williamson.*

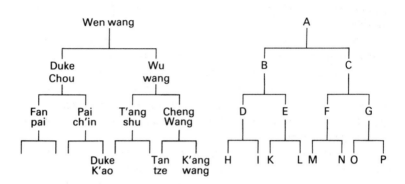

The original ancestor chief of the tree is A, and he and each of his descendants have two sons, and the succession passes to the elder son. Occasionally the succession goes to younger sons, brothers, nephews or other relatives, but such variations do not affect the general principle. Succession is patrilineal as well as by descent.

A passes in succession to B, D and H, each of whom will in turn have a rank as high as that of A. None of the younger sons will be the possessor of any title until he becomes the head of a social group. C, E and I when they become the heads of groups, may be recognized as titular chiefs; each of them is the son of a holder of the original title; but, being heads of cadet branches only, their rank will not be so high as that of A and of B, D, and H successively as holders of the original title.

Descendants of B are considered higher in social rank than those of C because they are titular ancestor A. The descendants of D and F will be senior to those of E and G, and so on for subsequent generations. According to the tsung system, C, the younger son of A, E, the younger son of B and I, the younger son of D all have an equal status and rank and are all minor tsung.

women until their marriage belong to their father's clan; a wife becomes a member of her husband's clan. It should be borne in mind that the clan system in traditional China is not identical with those of other societies, though it comprises both the nature of the clan existing in other societies and the nature of the Chinese joint family.[29] As a consequence, many authors prefer to refer to it by its original Chinese term 'tsu' or by the descriptive term 'the common descent group'.[30]

In its historical evolution, the clan has developed in four phases: (1) In the feudal period (1122–222 BC) clan organization was restricted to a few great families of lineage groups of alleged aristocratic origin, and in this sense it was called the 'shih'. For example, the lineage group Wang and Hsieh were of such an origin, and they found that the clan system gave them prestige and power. They won from the centralized state the legal status of 'shih-tsu', successive clan or 'wang-tsu', esteemed clans.[31] The clan of noble origin, one hundred names in number, was in contrast with the 'black-haired' people, or lower-class people.[32] This older stage of the patriarchal exogamic clans of the nobles was characterized by the distinction of 'hsing' and 'shih',[33] and the extension of the clan organization to the whole of the people began with the older Chou dynasty,[34] and ended by the conclusion of the Chou period. The 'shih' organization reappeared through increasing contact with non-Chinese people from the third to sixth century AD when a vast territory north of the Yangtze River was overrun by uncivilized people from the northern steppes.

The bulk of Chinese migration brought forth the institution of the shih tsu, the degenerated form of which is the 'men fa', the caste-like institutional system of official recruitment. In conjunction with clan organization the rule of primogeniture empowered the head of the leading lineage, called the 'tsung', with control over the whole clan.[35]

(2) As primogeniture was a significant factor in the feudal period, it disappeared with the decline of this period, though the eldest son has continued to take precedence over his younger brothers. However, all sons have equal inheritance rights. The clan organization altered its form in such a way that its members thought of the clan as giving them social prestige and providing for their protection and power. (3) This form of clan organization reached its climax during the Six Dynasties (AD 618–906).[36] (4) The clan organization revived during the Sung dynasty (AD 960–1278) when the scholars advocated the clan system as being conducive to family stability. The clan thus revived, but with some different characteristics to those of the clan in the past. It was no

longer confined to the upper-class or noble families; on the contrary, it included families from every strata of society, though the ruling class valued it more highly than the lower classes.

A clan is not to be identified with lineage, though a close parallel may be established between them. While lineage consists of all the descendants in one line of a particular person through a determinate number of generations, i.e. patrilineal agnatic descent from a known common ancestor,[37] the term 'clan' is used for a group having unilineal descent in which all the members regard one another as kinsfolk.[38] Lineage is the extension of the family, but each clan is composed of a series of lineage relationships demonstrable at each level, that is to say, the lineage at various levels extends from the nuclear family to what is known in Chinese as the 'tsu', the equivalent of a maximal lineage. However, it is to be noted that the Chinese clan is no longer a localized group, but consists of all individuals with the same surname. It is therefore a widely dispersed collectivity. The clan in China has no other function than that of defining exogamy,[39] though among overseas Chinese associations based on clanship it provides the possibility for local lineages to form larger political units. In traditional China[40] the clan partakes of the nature of the Chinese extended family. However, the family and clan are not identical. In contrast to the family, which is an economic unit whose members live together, the clan is a unit[41] embracing a number of families each of which constitutes a family, i.e. husband, wife and children. The domestic affairs of each family are managed by their respective family head without interference from the clan head. The clan seems akin in the context of its structure to the 'maximal lineages' among the Tallensi.[42] The maximal lineage is the most extensive group of people of both sexes, all of whom are related to one another by common patrilineal descent traced from one known founding ancestor through known agnatic antecedents.

Although everyone with the same surname[43] belongs to the same clan and is assumed to be descended from one ancestor, the effective clan is a much narrower group, usually including only those whose origin has been traced to the same village, i.e. all the members of the economic family and the whole paternal kinship. Clan relatives are denominated by the Chinese terms 'tsung ch'in', or 'tsu jen', clansmen. All clan relatives belonging to the same clan possess the same clan surname. The paternal relatives descended from males through males are differentiated from those descended from females through males. This is carried out by differentiating the father's brother's sons (t'ang hsiung ti) and their descendants from father's sister's sons (piao hsiung ti) and their descendants. Brother's sons (chih) are differentiated from sister's sons (wai sheng),[44] son's sons (sun)[45] from daughter's sons (wai sun) in ascending, descending and collateral lines. This bifurcation is necessary because ego's father's sister, ego's sister and daughter or any other female relatives who have married into other clans, and their descendants, belong, on the basis of patrilineal descent, to different clans.

From the historical point of view, early in the feudal period, under the Chou dynasty (*c*. 1100–256 BC), the clan flourished. At the close of the feudal period, village communities began to emerge, composed of neighbours who were not clansmen. During the imperial Ch'ing dynasty, further dissolution of clan communities appeared; private ownership of land was established in villages which were inhabited by members belonging to individual economic families and not to the clan. In respect of spacial distribution, the clan organization is significant in rural areas, while in cities it is weak, as the city is barely regarded as a 'home' at all. Moreover, the clan is strong in South China, which includes the provinces of Fukien and Kwangtung and Kwangsi. In Central China the clan is well developed and maintained; in North China it is not dominant. In Yang's description of the village of Taitou, Shantung province, all the better houses are in the central part of the residential area. This area is divided into four main sections according to the four clans in the village. Eight-tenths of the whole area is occupied by the P'ang clan, the second section is occupied by the Ch'en clan; the third by the Yang clan, and the fourth by the Liu clan. A few isolated families of each clan have settled among families of other clans, who are regarded as strangers, even after many generations of residence in the village.

The 'outside' clan organization of kinship relations

The differentiation between paternal grandparents (tsu) and maternal grandparents (wai tsu), paternal uncle (po), older brother or shu, younger brother and maternal uncle (chiu), paternal aunt (ku) and maternal aunt (yi) is the feature of the kinship system based on exogamous social groupings. But the descendants of father's sisters, mother's brother and mother's sisters are non-clan relatives; they are referred to by the term 'piao', outside.[46] The cousins, 'ku piao', 'chiu piao', and 'yi piao' are the three first degree 'piao' relationships of the Chinese kinship system.[47]

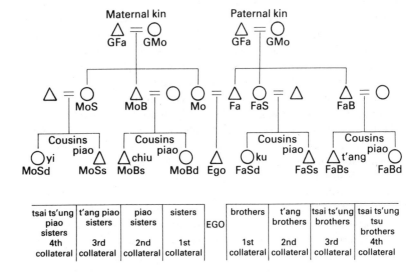

Figure 1.10

The development of the term 'piao' deserves our attention. According to the *Erh Ya* and the *I Li*, father's sister's sons and mother's brother's sons were both designated by the term 'sheng', through cross-cousin marriage. Being parallel cousins, mother's sister's children were denoted as ts'ung mu hsiung ti, for males, and ts'ung mu tzu mei, for females. During the first two centuries AD, when cross-cousin marriage fell into abeyance, father's sister's sons were designated as outside (wai) or 'wai hsiung ti'[48] and mother's brother's sons as inside (nei), or 'nei hsiung ti'.[49] During the first two centuries AD mother's sister's sons were designated by the term 'yi' or 'yi hsiung ti', though 'ts'ung mu hsiung ti' was still used. From the fourth to the seventh centuries AD confusion arose involving father's sister's, mother's brother's and mother's sister's descendants.[50] This resulted in the fact that those relatives of clear affiliation all belonged to the non-clan group. During the T'ang dynasty, the 'chung', meaning 'middle' or 'inside', fell into disuse, and the term 'piao' alone was applied to all these relatives.[51]

The generation category

We now enter upon another cultural universal generation. Generation arises from the basic concept of procreation. Etymologically the word 'generation' means 'to beget a child', and thus designates the physiological function of the male and the female in bringing a child into the world. This implies the creation of a tie of physical consanguinity. On the basis of their birth people are ranked in various degrees of generation. Moreover, in the Chinese kinship system the word 'generation' suggests 'inheritance' (ch'uan, transmission), 'history' and 'rivalries' (tieh, family pedigree), and 'descendants' (tso, posterity or offspring).

The criteria of age, sex and seniority, and the cycle of individual life and kinship create a network of relationships between parents, children, siblings, and others, in which one is born. In the kinship system, ego's ascending generation comprises parents, his uncles, aunts and grandparents and so forth through ascending lines of ancestry; ego's descending line includes sons, daughters, nephews, nieces and grandchildren. Since marriage is normally contracted between persons of the same generation, affined relatives are aligned by generation in the same manner as consanguineal relatives. Under normal circumstances genealogical depth and durability extend over three or four, and at the most five generations. This category of relationships is illustrated in Figure 1.11. The columns stand for lineage and collaterals, while the horizontal

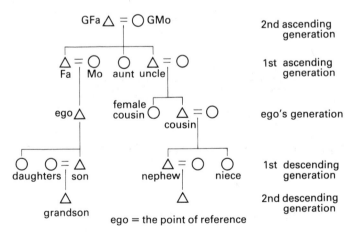

Figure 1.11

29

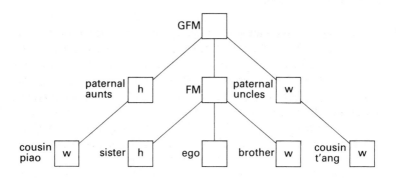

Figure 1.12 *This diagram shows that to maintain the distinction between the clan and non-clan groups the terminology must be bifurcated in such a way that paternal relatives descended from males are differentiating the father's brother's sons (t'ang) and their descendants from father's sister's sons (piao) and their descendants.*

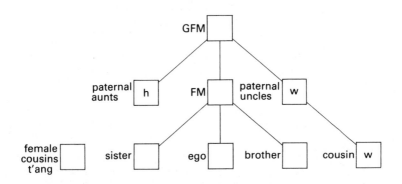

Figure 1.13 *The Code of the Ch'ing dynasty*

rows represent generations. The generation categories are expressed by the application by ego of 'generation' modifiers: (1) the term 'piao' is used as a modifier for lineal kin, whereas a number of modifiers such as 't'ang', 'tsai ts'ung', and 'tsu' for ego's generation, indicate the collateral lines descending from the grandfather, great-grandfather and great-great-grandfather, respectively; (2) the term 't'ang' (hall or ancestral hall) is used for ego's father's brother's sons and daughters; (3) the term 'piao' (outside or external) is used for: (a) ego's father's sister's sons, (b) ego's mother's brother's sons, and (c) ego's mother's sister's sons. The opposition of t'ang and piao brings about a dichotomy of cousinship. It is due to 'cousins' belonging to the ego's group or outside ego's group or to having the same surname or a different one that cousins call one another 't'ang' or 'piao'.

'Cross-cousin' stands for the descent of ego's father's sister (ku piao), mother's brother (chiu piao). 'Parallel cousins' are children of two siblings of the same sex, i.e. children of brothers or children of sisters; but children of brothers call one another 't'ang', while children of sisters call one another 'piao'. These modifiers are adapted from nuclear terms, since the lineal relatives are referred to as absolute indexes of measure. Figures 1.10, 1.11 and 1.12 show the generation of 'ego' in relation to his siblings and collateral relatives.[52]

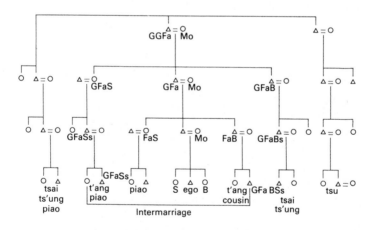

Figure 1.14

In Figure 1.13 we are concerned with substituting female cousins 't'ang' (the left cell of the diagram) and 'piao' who, being cognates, married their cousins 't'ang', for they have no kinship relationships. The above cell is for both cousins and female cousins (cousines in French). But these female cousins should not be daughters of the first collateral, i.e. the daughters of ego's paternal aunt, but daughters of ego's father's father's sister's son. These female cousins are of the same generation as their cousins, i.e. sons of ego's father's brother. This is illustrated in Figure 1.14. In this case, 't'ang piao' is symmetrical to tsai ts'ung (c), not to t'ang (b), and tsai ts'ung piao (d') to tsu, not to tsai ts'ung (c).

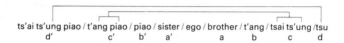

ts'ai ts'ung piao / t'ang piao / piao / sister / ego / brother / t'ang / tsai ts'ung /tsu
d'　　　　　c'　　 b'　　a'　　　a　　 b　　c　　d

Figure 1.15

Again in terms of symmetry, all women born in their natal family are connected with their brothers. Also the relations of mourning grades are established according to symmetry.*

female cousins　　　　　　　　cousins
tsu / tsai ts'ung / t'ang /sister / ego /brother /t'ang / tsai ts'ung / tsu
V　　IV　　III　 II　　　　 II　　III　　IV　　V

Figure 1.16

Although seniority does not invariably constitute a higher grade in the kinship system, seniority and generation run parallel with each

* According to M. Granet, the numbers II, III, IV, and V indicate that ego wears mourning dress for one year for II; for nine months for III; five months for IV and three months for V. M. Granet, 'Catégories matrimoniales et relations de proximité dans la Chine ancienne', *Annales Sociologiques*, September, 1/3, 1939, p. 161. Cited by A. Rygaloff, 'Deux points de nomenclature dans les systèmes chinois de parenté', *L'Homme*, October/December 1962, p. 58.

other for the most part and bring an element of distinction. Seniority is a biological constant. Children being born in succession, the distinction between elder and younger children emerges. In feudal times the eldest member of the oldest generation bore the title of 'elder'. He enjoyed a kind of pre-eminence, but it was only by his right as trustee for the group that he retained the vague authority which he exercised. When he died, a younger member took his place without any succession in the true sense of the word.[53] After the feudal period, Confucius and his disciples still emphasized respect and deference not only towards aged parents, but to all old people.[54] The basis of this Confucian ethic is the belief that the old man represents an accumulation of wisdom. The young man is expected to imitate, not oppose him.

Under the influence of Confucian ethic, Chinese society pays great respect to seniority, and thus primogeniture was, for a time, of the first importance in defining rank, succession, inheritance and other rights and responsibilities in political, economic and juridical relations, as with European aristocracies and among the Ashanti and Tallensi in Africa. For example, in feudal times only the eldest son of the first ancestor of a line by his legal wife could inherit his father's fief and offer sacrifice. Later, the first-born son had a legal right to an extra portion of the joint property,[55] as a special recognition of his age status. In parental-filial relationships children were bound to show respect to their parents, especially the father, but there was more familiarity allowed with uncles, aunts and grandparents. As in African societies, the contrast between restraint in the presence of a father or his brother and the freedom of joking with a grandfather is striking. This structural principle is conducive to equilibrium and stability in social relations in Chinese society and African societies alike.

Again, a newly married wife is at the beck and call of her husband's mother, but with growing age and the birth of male children she becomes, in turn, the matriarch of her kin group. Generation is an important principle of social organization (and social structure) among the Chinese, as among many peoples; the long generic lists in the New Testament[56] furnish an obvious instance of its importance in a quite unrelated culture.

One of the salient features of generation is the position of 'head' in the ramified segments of lineage. As has been pointed out before, the family, the branch, the sub-lineage and the lineage each have a head, who is the oldest member to act on behalf of his respective group. The head, as such, is neither elected nor appointed, but comes to his position as a result of natural succession. That means that among the male members of each kinship category, the member of the senior generation who is also the oldest of that generation naturally becomes the head. Seniority in terms of generation is more important than seniority in terms of years. For instance, X is twenty-five years old, while his uncle Y, his father's younger brother, is only twenty. Although Y is younger than X, he enjoys a superior status by virtue of belonging to the same generation as X's father. Obvious difficulties can occur in this system. Sometimes a boy in his teens or a child of seven or eight is the head of his lineage, and in these circumstances it is customary for a village head to assist the child. This choice is determined by age alone, ignoring the 'generation' criterion; the chosen head is the oldest male member of the lineage, sub-lineage, branch or family. The integrity with which the established custom is followed ensures that the organization is perpetuated, unchanged.

Since the social structure is maintained by the principle of generation, one of the greatest threats to its integrity is the 'inter-generation' marriage. To prevent this, a Chinese is forbidden to marry outside his own generation. This rule, however, was grossly flouted in ancient times. The Han emperor, Hui Ti (194–88 BC) married his older sister's daughter.[57] The T'ang emperor, Chun Tsung (705–10 AD) contracted marital alliance with his paternal grandaunt's daughter.[58] As emperors they were excused for having infringed the rule, though they were condemned as being incestuous by later historians and moralists.[59] The generation rule was more stringent during the Chou dynasty, but it was as early as the third and fourth centuries AD that the generation indicators in personal names were added. The T'ang Code (*c.* 600 AD) prohibited marriages between the relatives of different generations.[60] The enactment of the law reflects the desire to preserve the generation strata of relatives and prevent their breach. If the generation distinction is abrogated by marriage, the position of the relatives connected with it would concomitantly be broken up.

We have previously described marriage, kinship, descent and inheritance as the activities within the internal system which are particularly the domain of the domestic group, and those in the external system with which the domestic group is linked in its political, economic, juridical, ritual and religious aspects. The interests of the society at large and those of the domestic group are interlinked. This is exemplified by such rules as those of exogamy in the regulation of marriage and prohibition of incest, and by the participation of political authorities in funeral ceremonies, decisions about inheritance and taxation, and ritual performance; for it is through political, economic, ritual and juridical institutions in the external system that the function of the domestic group can be performed and its interests guaranteed.

It is interesting to show the historical development of village organization. In the Chou dynasty the Ching Tien System', called the 'system of Sages', was introduced, and it aimed at establishing agricultural co-operation and a political system of administration and of taxation. 'Ching Tien' (well land) means fields laid out symbolically like the character 'Ching' (well).[61] The 'Ching Tien' system and village organization are illustrated in Figure 1.17.[62]

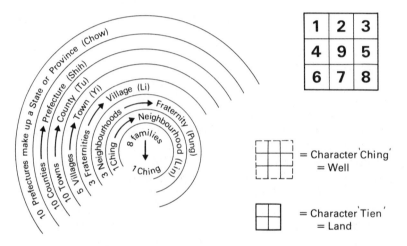

Figure 1.17

The Ching Tien system in relation to the social structure at large in China

In the year AD 614 a new agricultural system was developed under the T'ang dynasty. Holders of land were divided into nine categories.[63]

In Yang's study of the village of Taitou,[64] he describes the village as a unity with a life of its own. Unlike the family, a primary group, the village is a secondary group, embracing smaller groups or units, such as clans and neighbourhoods, the associations of families on the basic of social, economic, school affiliation, political aspect and religious functions. The village may comprise one or several clans.[65] If a village is a group bound by consanguinity it is a 'lineage' village. The village 'I-hsü' (Foochow, Fukien province), which Dr Lin has investigated, is a case where all the inhabitants are the descendants of a common ancestor.

While in South China many fairly large villages are composed of families belonging to one clan, in North China most villages contain two, three, four or even more clans. Taitou, for example contains four clans.

(1) Politically, the wide-ranging village organization consists of its village-defence programme, in which every family is urged to take part. The able-bodied men are registered and organized into a number of teams. The village takes up special functions that cannot be performed by individual families; the heads arbitrate in disputes and look after public property; also they are responsible for local defence and for the execution of administrative orders coming from the government. The collective protection of crops is another aspect of village organization. A hired crop watcher guards against the damaging and stealing of crops by animals and thieves.

(2) Education is highly valued and is considered a stepping-stone to raise the family to a higher social position. Children are taught to read, write, understand the content of land deeds, and recognize the different kinds of paper money. Ideally, the children at least learn calligraphy, the use of the abacus, and the terms of farm products, farm implements and domestic utensils.

(3) The chief mechanism of social control is public opinion. Some people may pursue and indulge in immoral conduct with impunity; nevertheless, most people frown on lax behaviour and are likely to sever their relations with dishonourable families. As for religion, apart from the ancestral spirits, most peasants worship the kitchen god, as he is thought to be the supernatural guardian and inspector of the household. The pleasure or displeasure of the god which is the criterion of human behaviour depends on the observance or the breach of certain taboos, such as the trampling underfoot or the wasting of rice, or the touching of anything on the platform of the kitchen god by women during menstruation. In such circumstances religion constitutes another mechanism of social control in village life.

Another aspect of social control is that the village organization is based on neighbourhood. A number of families living in close proximity to one another are apt to form a larger territorial group. This formation depends on their common interests. Natural damages and calamities such as floods, droughts and famine, and the threat of encroachment by outsiders do not affect individuals only, but all those living in a locality. Also the need for relaxation, amusement and recreation is another factor which creates neighbourliness.

Neighbourliness is in many cases more important than clan consciousness. In Yang's *A Chinese Village, Taitou*, a family of the P'an clan has closer relations with 'neighbouring' Yang families than with their own clansmen. Frequent contact in daily life brings families together and results in the formation of a number of neighbourhood groups in a village. Likewise, in his *Peasant Life in China*, Fei reports that when a boy is one month old, his mother will bring him to see neighbours even before visiting her own father's house. She and the boy are courteously received and entertained. When they leave, their neighbours will give him a gift of cakes.[66] Thus a fortuitous group of adjacent households will combine for daily contact and mutual help.

The foregoing description has laid out two levels of social structure: one is the internal system which covers the developmental cycle of the structure of the family in the domestic sphere. This includes the ramifications of the family in the network of relationships by kinship and affinity; the reciprocal rights and obligations as well as legal and emotional ties among agnates and cognates are expressed in the domestic group. The lineage system is built up on the agnatic line of descent and provides the framework of corporate groupings, whereas interpersonal kinship ties are recognized between cognates of all degrees through either or both parents. The other is the eternal system of domain, where the domestic group is linked with the total social structure (the village) in its political, economic, juridical, religious, ritual and recreational aspects. In the second chapter we shall describe 'intra-family' relations which are observed in two cultural factors: parental authority and filial piety. Our next discussion is what might be called the warp of social relations in the lineage in terms of filial piety and in the context of 'intra-family' relations in village organization.

In Figure 1.18 each circle represents a kinship group. The solid lines represent the lineage or clan and the joint of the extended family. Likewise, the broken lines represent large and small kinship organizations. The elementary family is biological, or procreative, the groups embracing the parents and their children. The matrimonial group denotes a married couple without issue or children. A joint family or extended family which may include two or more lineally related kinsfolk is an economic unit whose members share a cooking stove and are communal. The

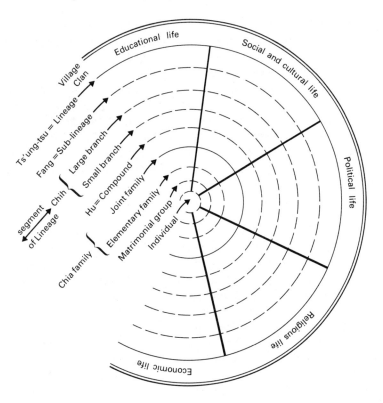

Figure 1.18

matrimonial group is capable of forming an elementary family, while several elementary families living either in a single dwelling (household) or in an aggregate of dwellings (a homestead) make up a joint family. The combination of several joint families share a common residence, under the same roof.[67] The remaining categories can proceed in a similar fashion; the straight lines crossing the broken lines demarcate the various aspects of life – educational, social, political, religious and economic. Like warp and woof, these aspects of life are all interrelated and interdependent, a most important factor.

Also the different grades of the circles and the dots between the straight, diagonal lines represent cultural hinges, to use Dr Lin's terminology, the dots and the lineage circle falling within the confines of the political sector can be interpreted as representing corporate units with political functions. A similar interpretation is applicable to the rest of kinship categories. The domestic bonds in a segmentary lineage system play an important role in the lives of individuals. Similarly, the dots within the economic sphere represent the established norms of succession and inheritance. Again, as there is a closer interdependence of large segmentary lineage systems and the various aspects of life, the latter, in relation to the minor segments of the kinship system, have decreasing relationships and effects, correlated to individual interests, rights, duties and values. These are illustrated in Figure 1.19.[68]

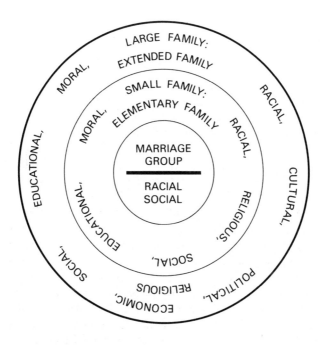

Figure 1.19

Figures 1.18 and 1.19 serve as a framework of the social structure of the family. With regard to the function of the maximal lineage and its segments in conjunction with the various aspects of life, a detailed discussion will be presented in the last chapter.

Chapter 2

The family in kinship structure

Blood is thicker than water. The old adage says.

The elementary families of orientation and procreation exist among the Chinese and constitute the nuclear elements around which extensive and elaborate kinship relations are formed. The families of procreation and orientation are fundamental factors in the formation of the personality of ego in his kinship system or cluster. He is born in his family group but oriented by it to the kinship organization. He is related, for instance, to his father in his patrilineal clan, and in an affined relation to his mother's clan.

The basis of the Chinese families of orientation and procreation is the strict incest taboo: that is, sexual relations among the members of the two elementary families are absolutely forbidden. This taboo is strengthened by prohibited degrees and by exogamy which prescribes marriage to be contracted with persons of different surnames,[1] and accordingly creates the family of procreation out of extra-familial personalities. It must be borne in mind that the nodal relationship in a Chinese family is that between father and son, and other kinship relationships may be said to be projected from it. If a father has four sons, each son with his own children would form a distinct line or branch of descendants in the family; its members cluster on the four different lines by lineal descent. What underlies the father-son reciprocal relationship is that the father's status is the expression of the generation of children or offspring and thereby of the creation of family. At the moment when a son is born, the father witnesses the beginning of a new generation within his family, and this establishes the essential element in the filio–parental relationship.

40

Within ego's own generation and his family of orientation there may
be brothers and sisters. Ego and his brothers enjoy an identical status in
the social structure, being in the same patrilineal line. The primary
differentiation index is the distinction in terms of birth order, that is,
between older and younger brothers. The brother and sister recipro-
cation is another part of the foundation of the kinship system. There is
a considerable degree of equivalence between brothers and sisters on
the basis of their generation and line of descent. From the structural
point of view, the 'horizontal' generation lines of brother and sister
cross out the 'vertical' patrilineal lines at the same point; yet because of
their sexual difference they are not entirely equivalent. The sister, when
young, lives with her father, and when she grows up, marries a man outside her kinship group and lives with her husband and his lineage.

In brief, in his family of orientation, ego's relationship with his
mother's kin is less strong than with his father's; this still holds in his
family of procreation. In terms of the complete kinship system, all
vertical patrilineal lines of descent are in direct familial structural continuity with ego's elementary families of orientation and procreation.
The total kinship system is considered as a group of interlinking
elementary family units, each of which has certain social elements
which set up an intercellular unity and an independent system of
relationship. The Chinese family structure is the basic groundwork of
their large social organization. In its micro-form it consists of limited
elementary families, and in its macro-form it embraces the whole range
of kinship system of which a large number of elementary families are
component parts. The web of the relationship among the members of
the family is dealt with in the rest of this chapter.

Father–son relationship

Addressing or vocative name[2]	papa or tieh	milk name of son
Reference name	fu	tzu

Included in this category are two varieties of this relationship: (1) the
natural father, and (2) the adoptive father. A distinction is made
between the natural father and his son and his adoptive son. The usual
behaviour between the natural father and his son does not hold good
for the behaviour between the father and his adoptive son.

The son, once he has become a major, is under the obligation of fulfilling the innumerable duties of piety which affiliate him to his father. Among the duties, marriage is the most fundamental; it is the starting point of the family - the procreation of legitimate children. No man or woman can satisfy his or her filial piety without marriage, and thus only a married son can act as a pious son. Although among men marriage must not be entered into before thirty years of age, in the majority it is ratified at twenty. The head of the family must have a wife, considering his charge of an ancestral temple where the tablets of husbands and wives are juxtaposed. If he is bereaved of all his wives when he is less than seventy years of age, he is obliged to marry again; if he has passed seventy, he must retire, and transfer the charge of the temple to the religious chief.[3]

In short, the son endeavours to share the paternal life in every way, happy when the father is well, and sad when he is ill, eating when the father has a good appetite, fasting when he has not, the son will be utterly desolate at the death of his parents. It behoves the son to see that the father can die a good death.[4] The eldest son takes the responsibility for the funeral rites. As death shuts out the deceased from communion with the living, so does mourning shut out the pious son. He lives in seclusion, his right to speak is greatly restricted, and he eats only with reluctance. These are marks of the severity of the son's bereavement. The death of a father is therefore felt with great sorrow by the children, and as among many people, for example, among the Murngin, the death of a son is a great social loss to the father, since there is no one to succeed him.[5]

Furthermore, in treating the relations between parents and children it is, I think, important to point out that a Chinese child is not born into the family alone, but is born into a wider circle than the family in that all the members who share the homestead of the father take an interest in the child from the moment of his birth. The Chinese say that the bonds between parents and children can never be severed. This moral principle is indispensable to the Chinese social structure. The customs and laws of the Chinese society, imbued with the spirit of Confucianism, conferred upon the Chinese father, the head of the family, great power and authority. Hence the principal control within the family rests with the father's authority, which requires of the children filial piety and an active devotion to the parents: this is required of sons particularly, for they remain in the family, while daughters are married out into other clans. Nevertheless, as filial piety puts no limitations on sex, the marrying out of the daughters does not dispense altogether with filial piety.

The character 'fu' (father) means 'chü' (a square), that is, the father teaches his son the rules and measures. Again, according to the earliest Chinese dictionary, *Shuo Wen*, the character 'fu' means a model, a head of the family who educates. It is 'fu' formed by a hand holding a stick which symbolizes the head's coercive power and authority. The character 'tzǔ' originally means 'descendant' or 'child', etymologically 'to engender', i.e. engender without end.

The head of the family officiates in traditional China in all ceremonies, such as ancestor worship, marriage and funerals; he is entitled to all family property and to its disposal. Yet in contrast to conditions prevalent in ancient Rome, where the *pater familias* has '*jus vitae et necisque*', the Chinese father has no absolute power over the life and death of his children, unless he is grossly insulted and attacked. It is to be noted that parental authority varies with various dynasties. In the period of Tsung fa,[6] a father had the power of life and death over a son. When Fu-su (210 BC), a prince of the Ch'in dynasty, was absent from the court, his father, the first emperor of Ch'in (221-207 BC) ordered him, through his younger brother, to commit suicide; Fu-su was advised by his younger brother to escape, but he said: 'When a father commands his son to die, how can a son dare to implore?'[7] However, this power of life and death was reserved as the right of the sovereign only. The logic is given in *Pai Hu Tung*:[8]

> Why should a father be executed for killing his son? Human beings are most important in the nature of heaven and earth; they are produced by heaven merely through the medium of their parents. And the king provides a living for them and educates them. Therefore the father can have no claim on them.

In *Hou Han Shu*, two murder cases were reported to a magistrate; the one was that a man was beaten to death by a robber in a southern city, while in a northern city a man was killed by his mother.[9] In anger the magistrate said that it was repugnant to heaven and human nature to kill a son. He ordered an investigation of this case and the mother was punished. Also in *Hou Han Shu*, some cases were reported in which parents were prosecuted for infanticide.[10] These facts lend support to our assumption that a father was not vested with the right to kill his son directly.[11] The sons are punished either for defying the authority of their parents or for failing to conform to moral or ritual custom and especially filial piety and parental respect.

43

It is an established custom that a son is destined to show his father filial respect, and the father readily asserts his authority and exercises discipline to ensure this in the event of any defiant behaviour of his son; hence to curse or scold a parent is stigmatized as unfilial and as such is considered to be a gross crime. Filial piety among the Chinese is a binding moral principle and arises from the fact of bringing a child into the world. Filial piety was not introduced by Confucius although he reasserted and reappraised it. The *Hsiao Ching* (*The Classic of Filial Piety*) says: 'Among five punishments inflicted for three thousand articles [crimes], no crime is more grave than that of filial impiety'.[12] The *Chou Li Chu Shu* (*Records of the Rites of the Chou dynasty*) regards impiety as one of the crimes for the eight punishments.[13]

According to the law of Han (dynasty), an unfilial son was beheaded and the head was exposed to the public.[14] From the time of Northern Ch'i (AD 550-77) and Sui (AD 589-618) to the Ch'ing dynasties, filial impiety was categorized as one of the ten unpardonable offences.[15] The law of Han and Sung decreed that a son who strikes his father should be beheaded and his head exposed on a pole. Similarly, in the laws of T'ang, Sung, and Ming and Ch'ing dynasties beheading was the usual penalty for this crime.[16] In the Ch'ing dynasty's criminal code strangling was introduced.[17]

The punishment for killing a parent by accident was not so severe as for killing him by mistake. The laws of the T'ang, Sung, Ming and Ch'ing dynasties lay down that the wounding of a parent by accident should be punished by imprisonment for three years, while punishment for the killing of a parent by accident is banishment to a distance of three thousand 'li'.[18] This increase in severity stemmed from the principle that regulates the father-son relationship. The law declares that though an accident happens without intention, a child should always be respectful and careful towards his parents and ensure that an accident does not happen. Therefore among 'ordinary' people the sentence may be commuted, but a son or daughter must be punished by imprisonment or banishment, whether or not the accident is due to his or her negligence. This rests on the principle that a minister or a son is allowed neither to claim an accident before his sovereign or father nor plead an accident in extenuation of his punishment.[19] Further, even if a parent dies from an accident which has not been directly caused by any fault of the child, the latter is still held responsible. The law of the Ch'ing dynasty stipulates that if a parent falls in the course of beating or scolding his son and dies therefrom, the son must receive punishment according to the law of 'disobeying instructions and causing a parent's suicide and must be detained in prison for strangling'.[20]

The following stories shed light on the law:

> Ch'en Wen hsüen scolded his son when the latter brought him a cup of cold tea. The father poured the tea on the ground and took a stick to beat his son. The son, however, dodged his stick, and Ch'en lost his footing, fell and struck his head; he died from this accident.[21]

> In his father's refusal to grant a request for straw, his son, Chiang Pa gave three bundles to the man requesting it. When Chiang Pa's father was drunk, he scolded his son for this action. The son argued with his father and made him so infuriated that he was struck by his father. Chiang Pa ran away, and his father took out a small knife and pursued him. Because he was drunk, he stumbled over the straw, and the knife pierced his breast from which he was wounded and died.[22]

These cases imply that the offences are not very grave on the ground that the children are not the direct cause of the tragic outcome. The law rules that the perpetrator of the killing must be punished regardless of his justification; it does not distinguish between a son's direct or indirect involvement in the death of his father. This holds although authorities are conscious of a child's innocence and a father's stupidity and irrational behaviour. The law allows of no circumstances in which a son can be exonerated from the obligations of filial obedience; it is intrinsically embodied in filial piety. Confucian ethics is thought of as the mandatory tenet that a son should obey and never show resentment, let alone impious conduct. In the father-son relationship, right and wrong are judged from this position: I am wrong because I am my father's son; what he says or does is right because he is my father.

In brief, the father possesses the supreme authority within the family in the feudal period. His will is a command with which every member is under obligation to comply. In support of the Confucian insistence on filial piety Ssu-ma Kuang (1019-86) wrote: 'All the inferiors and the younger ones must consult the head of the family in regard to every event, large or small. How dare an inferior do anything without obtaining permission from his parents?'[23]

Of the human relations within the family, those of father and son are central. Now we must answer the question: Is there a conflict between father and son in the Chinese family? If the answer is affirmative, what are the cohesive forces maintaining the stability of the family? It is well known that in the Chinese patrilineal descent system the power vested in the head of the family is a counterpoise to fissiparous tendencies and is the genesis of the centripetal force which maintains the solidarity of family organization. Kinship preserves the stability of the family structure to the extent that the living depend on their ancestors and are dutiful both to those still living, and to those of the future who will, in turn, depend on them. The values symbolized in the concept of patrilineal descent create the centripetal force of stability and continuity in the organization of the family and of the social structure at large. The lineage system serves to unite the ancestors, the living, and the yet unborn in a uniform integrated sequence, actualized at a given time in determined corporate groups.

We can see that parental authority is indispensable to the existence and continuity of the organization of the family and the entire social structure. Fatherhood or paternal status stands for lineage eldership. But paternal authority never dies; although a 'real' or 'physical' father does, the theme continues. For as long as a man's descendants exist, they are dependent upon the dead; it is in this sense that ancestorhood is fatherhood immortally projected in spite of the death of the father. Addison postulates that the Chinese believe that ancestors exercise a providential care over all their descendants. Their spirits are able to work good or evil according to the treatment they receive. The main motive for sacrifice, therefore, is to obtain protection and prosperity, to secure temporal goods, and to avert the calamities which must ensue upon neglect.[24]

Fatherhood and sonship exist in polarity. They are bound to each other in mutual dependence, though they are embedded in ambivalence. Confucius failed to make them live completely in harmony. The ambivalent father-son relationship puts sons at a disadvantage, being under the paternal authority, on the one hand, and bound to support their father, on the other. The severe and rigid discipline no doubt weighs down the solidarity of the relationship between father and son. The Chinese father and son rarely touch each other after the son's childhood and express themselves in somewhat formal terms, if at all. Although respect, fear and avoidance are proper terms in which to describe the father-son relationship, there also exist their mutual solicitude, and the son's fondness for and dependence upon his father.

However, despite the existence of solidarity and cohesion between father and son,[25] certain considerable strains also coexist between them; these are conspicuous among the gentry or wealthy families, though they are certainly not lacking among the peasants. Among the gentry, whose property is in the form of large land holdings and other capital ownership, the family head will be able to assert his parental authority until an advanced age, but there will be a shift of authority in the management of the family.[26] In the poor peasant family, on the other hand, the son will continue to serve his father, but gradually assuming family authority. The son is more individualistic and independent of his father, and he comes into his own status. It is the father who makes untoward demands upon his son, refuses his desires, finds fault with his daily conduct and takes a firm hand with him, much to his chagrin.

It is interesting to note that the strains in the father-son relationship are more bitter and more enduring among the gentry than among the peasants in the Chinese family. The burden of the material obligations of the father varies between the gentry and peasant fathers. It seems that economic factors do not create serious problems among the gentry;[27] though the material obligations repeatedly become a centrifugal force in an upper-class family. The fact that an extravagant father dissipates the family property and thereby undermines the economic foundations of the family looms large in straining his relations with his sons and may even provoke revolt on their part.[28]

The father's training of the son is a more intricate matter than his material support. Among the peasants the major part of the training falls to the father, while among the gentry the father delegates much of it to teachers. In Confucian ethics moral training is integral to the learning process, and therefore teachers hold the responsibility for inculcating moral ideas as well as for the advancement of learning. One aspect of learning among the gentry consists in the complex code of 'li' (etiquette), which paves the way for the 'gentleman'. But for the peasants no similar discipline is imposed; and the obedience and respect of a peasant son are sufficient to conform with the 'li' and to serve many purposes.

Again, conflicts between father and son were not rare among the nobles in the feudal period and were often generated by sexual rivalry. For instance, the system of concubinage prevailing among the nobles tended to create the father-son cleavage hypothesized by Freud. It is attested by historians that feudal lords took their wives' sisters and nieces as concubines, thus including among their sexual objects women of their son's generation. The *Tso Chuan*[29] says that fathers had illicit relations with their sons' wives and that sons approached their fathers' concubines. Granet propounded the theory that the father-son conflicts contained both sexual rivalry and the relics of matrilineal family system

47

in which father and son were thought to be estranged. These rivalries are illustrated in the imperial annals and in a popular novel.

Father–son antagonism is depicted in the popular novel of imperial China *Hung Lou Mêng* (*The Dream of the Red Chamber*). The antagonism of Chia Cheng and his son, Po-Yu, described in *The Dream of the Red Chamber* is illuminating of the opposition in the father–son relationship. The father's hatred was at such a height that he let his son be beaten almost to death.[30] Paternal authority was too austere to be resisted. Po-Yu, however, resigned himself to such an uncouth treatment without expostulation. For all his father's cruelty, the son expressed his antagonism only indirectly. Chia Cheng, the father of Po-Yu, was a circumspect official, a Confucian rationalist, and immune from superstition, but was imbued with supernatural ideas. Po-Yu was said to have been born with a magic stone in his mouth and devoted to the negative wisdom of Buddhist and Taoist mysticism; as a result, he left his wife in the lurch together with the child she was expecting and, to his father's chagrin, abandoned his brilliant career for a mysterious call to become a Buddhist monk.

Although this father–son conflict existed, it was never overtly revealed in *The Dream of the Red Chamber*. It is to be noted that although Chia Cheng exercised his paternal authority out of bounds, it remained unchallenged. Neither his son, Po-Yu, nor the author attempted to discredit him or represent him as a detestable character; instead, his son obeyed him because he was his father. Despite the repugnant behaviour of a son towards his father, in the Chinese family system filial piety is embedded in social structure and important in social relations. It is the socially prescribed expression of filial devotion and feelings that is not always desirable and involves destructive as well as constructive elements.

The mechanism of reducing the conflict in the father–son relationship

Our next problem is how to maintain parental and filial trust and affection in face of the conflict in the father and son relationship. The trust and affection which are based on the incessant reciprocity of parental solicitude, fondling and filial dependence against the centrifugal impetus generated in their relationship; it is a question of strengthening family solidarity.

First, inheritance of, or succession to, the family property provides a medium through which family stability can be reinforced. In traditional China not only was property such as land, house and livestock inherited but also individual crafts and skills such as brewing, weaving, drug-making, and painting were obtained or acquired through the father–son relationship. However, for crafts the general rule prescribes that they should be transmitted only to male heirs, and not to daughters and daughters-in-law,[31] for fear that they should fall into the hands of out-side kinsmen. If a son expects to be a legal heir to any of the crafts, it is imperative for him to obey the family's rules and live up to the family's traditional mores. Since family property or any craft is a hallmark of the achievements of many forbears, sentiments are inherent in it. It is the duty of heirs to improve their heritage so that failure to keep family property in its integrity, or any division of it, would bring disgrace to the heirs. If circumstances have become adverse to such a degree that a partition is unavoidable, the family property should be arranged and apportioned along the line of the father–son relationship.

Second, the glory of living descendants honours their ancestors and is an imposing sanction for venerating ancestors at the higher levels of the lineage, i.e. in the ancestral halls.[32] Any external sign of hostility between father and son would show a lack of 'corporate' spirit and would be a source of discontent to their benevolent ancestors. This would necessarily ensure that father and son remained on good terms.

Third, piety is rooted in the relationship of father and son. It is incumbent on the son to obey and respect the father and support him. Confucius preached unremittingly the duties of filial piety and even raised the practice of this piety to the plane of the official worship of Heaven, which he thought would suffice to become a religion. He said that 'to serve one's parents as one would Heaven, that is the law of filial piety'. Furthermore, the concept of sacrifice adumbrates the idea of piety. Sacrifice is the fulfilment of human relations and the foundation of moral teachings, for it reminds us of our origin. The sacrifice is an essential element of ancestor worship, which seems to minimize the conflict between father and son. Death, while depriving the father of his physical existence, at the same time elevates fatherhood above the mundane realm and its commitments. It provides sons with the occasion to undergo as moral injunctions the ritual exigencies that metamorphose fatherhood into ancestorhood.

On the basis of filial piety any external sign of hostility between father and son or filial impiety has been regarded as a despicable infraction of public morality. This ethic lends support to the theory that the relationship between ancestors and their living descendants is a good one, so that there is no need for ancestors to use coercive force in controlling the behaviour of descendants. Living descendants owe to their ancestors a debt for the gift of life and for sustenance; they pay them respect and support them during their life. This duty does not come to a stop when death has removed their elders from among the living. They must continue to revere and succour their forbears by respecting their graves and making sacrifice to their tablets. This is the way children pay their forbears reverence and respect in the cult of ancestors.

Father and daughter relationship

Addressing or vocative name:	pa or papa or tieh	nü erh[33] or hsiao nü or milk name
Reference name:	fu or fu ch'in	name of daughters

In feudal times when a girl was born in a noble family, she was laid on the ground.[34] She was not brought up for public life and for war, but for the labour and service in woman's apartments. A girl of ill-omened appearance, red or hairy, was exposed in an open field[35] and left to die. When a girl augured good fortune she was lifted from the ground where she had been laid to learn humility. The father did not allow the little girl to be presented to him. Between him and the girl there appeared to be no performance of any rite of approach. Her name was given by the mother. As soon as she was capable of speaking, she was destined to submission by learning to say 'yes' in the humble tone befitting women. The *Li Chi* states: 'When he was able to speak, a boy was taught to respond boldly and clearly, while a girl, submissively and low.'[36]

At the age of seven, when sexual bans came into play, the girl was not allowed to sit on the same mat as her brothers nor eat with them.[37] In the tenth year, complete seclusion was imposed on the girl. This restriction was concurrent with instruction in the work, language deportment and virtue required of women. She also initiated herself into the art of preparing and serving the ceremonial repasts which were offered to the ancestors. The *Li Chi* reads again:[38]

Her duenna taught her the arts of pleasing speech and graceful
manners . . . to furnish garments, to watch the sacrifices, to supply
the liquors and sauces, to fill the various stands and dishes with
pickles and brine, and to assist in setting forth the appurtenances
for the ceremonies.

The girl was declared major at her marriageable status, and a new name
was conferred on her in the course of the ceremony in which she was
obliged to alter the customary mode of hair-style in connection with
using a head-pin.[39] The noble girl when betrothed had to live in complete confinement or seclusion; no men might see her save for the
gravest reasons. The Chinese word for the habitation of a woman is
'kwei', which is composed of two parts: a jade and a door. The Chinese,
having much respect for womanhood, consider feminine purity as something sacred, comparing the woman to flawless jade. The *Li Chi* says:
'When a young lady is promised in marriage and unless there be some
great occasions, no male enters the door of her apartment.'[40]

When the betrothed girl was handed over to her husband it did not
mean that the father's authority was completely transferred. The
husband became simply a guardian, and the transference of guardianship to the husband did not in any way conclude the father's rights nor
even his responsibility. The prescribed formulas used by the father and
mother of the bride, when the bridegroom came to fetch her, implied
no transference of the father's authority. For example, the parents,
particularly the father, admonished their daughter as she entered upon
her new status of wife and daughter-in-law not to do anything which
would forfeit the good reputation and honour of her own natal family.

It is said that daughters asked their father to guard against an ambush
laid by the husband;[41] and asked their mother 'Who is the nearest,
father or husband; who ought to be dearest?' 'Anyone can be made a
husband, but we can only have one father,' replied the mother.[42] Thus
after the marriage, while the wife was in her husband's house and
service, she ought to think how she might serve her parents. After the
marriage, wife and husband seemed to live in ambivalence, that is, in a
state of armed peace, each endeavouring to deprive the other of prestige
for the benefit of their own family. In the *Shih Chi* (*Historical Records*)
it is recorded that Tsai Chi and her husband, duke Huan Kung (657 BC)
prepared a boating party and, observing an old custom, amused themselves by making the boat keel over. The wife, the daughter of Prince
Tsai, was expert at rowing and swimming and agitated the boat so
boldly that her husband was frightened and asked her to stop it, but

his wife refused to listen to him. After they were on shore, the husband was irritated and sent his wife back to her family, though he did not repudiate her. Yet her parents took offence and married their daughter to someone else. The duke Huan Kung was offended in learning of the news and sent troops to fight Prince Tsai and defeated him.[43]

The foregoing description shows the father–daughter relationship among the nobles in feudal times. Now we consider the father–daughter relationship in traditional China, which covers the period from the T'ang to the Ch'ing dynasties and the Republic until the advent of the Communist regime.

When a girl was born she was put in the care of her mother and she was entirely dependent on breast milk for nourishment. If the mother failed to produce milk, the baby was fed by a neighbouring woman. The father held himself rather aloof. When the next baby was born, the first girl, aged perhaps two or three years by then, was usually cared for by her grandmother rather than sharing her father's bed as a boy did. By the age of six she began to lend her mother a hand to look after the younger sister or brother. At thirteen years, she set out to learn to sew, cook, spin, and to perform many other domestic arts. By fifteen she became even more needed by her mother.

While the relation of mother and daughter became more intimate, that of father and daughter was distant. A good deal of respect was imposed on the daughter in both peasant and gentry families. In peasant families the fathers might see their daughters more than did upper-class fathers, and a close relationship between them could develop. The position of the family head was far less rigid in the peasant family than in other classes, and the father would be more ready to establish an informal face-to-face relationship with family members than the father in upper-class families. In the latter, the father felt genuine and strong affection for his daughter, especially if she lived up to the standardized model of a 'good' girl. The clever and beautiful girl who merited her father's fondness was common in Chinese poetry, novels and stories. The 'Rainbow Girl', Jui-Hung, heroine of one of the modern and strange stories, a seventeenth-century collection, allowed herself to be captured and raped with the aim of finding her father's murderer and seeking vengeance upon him.[44] In the T'ang dynasty the famous girl soldier, Hua Mu-lan, joined the army as a substitute for her old father.[45] She was inspired by filial piety rather than by patriotism.

Intimacy and affection supersede avoidance, but the affection between father and daughter has to be submitted to restraint from the standpoint of the girl's training. Negligence in proper training would affect the solidarity of the daughter's family in a time of prosperity.

Further, if an adult girl is reproached for her misbehaviour, the person who bears the responsibility is the mother. Thus when a father sees the villagers frowning at his daughter's conduct, he does not bring an accusation directly against her, but against her mother; the latter could not be exonerated from blame on the pretext of being unaware of the reprehensible conduct of her daughter, but must apologize to the father, for it is incumbent upon her mother to discipline her daughter.

The father's knowledge of his daughter in both upper-class and peasant families is acquired through the mother. The daughter's marriage is, as a rule, arranged by the mother, although obviously the father, who has the right to dispose of his daughter in marriage as he pleases, has to be kept informed and be consulted. After the marriage arrangement is successfully made, the mother is responsible for the preparation of the wedding, but she has to bring home to the father an ample dowry. Before marriage the father exercises authority over his daughter with regard to her morality through his wife, and this is what tempers conflict between father and daughter. A kind father is reluctant to exert his full rights against his daughter's wishes and desires even in connection with her marriage. Although the daughter would inevitably leave her father's house to marry and bear children for another clan, the father's affection for her would not fade away. It is an inevitable event that a daughter will sooner or later leave her natal household to marry, bear children for another clan, and cease to be the daily concern of her father.

The Chinese Civil Code recognizes the daughter, even after marriage, as being as much a descendant of her parents, as were her brothers (Article 967). The married daughter still remains attached to her natural parents by visiting them and exchanging gifts with them. The underlying reason is that though she is incorporated in the new husband's family through marriage, she is still estranged in the new family. Tseng-Tzu, one of Confucius's disciples, said that if a woman died before she was presented to the ancestors of her husband in the ancestral temple, that is, before she gave birth to a male child, the body was returned to be interred in the cemetery of her own kindred, which indicated that she had not yet become a wife in the full sense.[46]

In short, the strength of the father–daughter relationship is cemented by complete obedience to the father and his obligations to provide for his daughter's support until her marriage.

Mother and son relationship

Confucian ethics inculcates two principles in respect of the roles of the father and the mother: that of esteem and that of affection respectively.[47] The *Li Chi* presents the difference of the roles of father and mother:[48]

> Here now is the affection of a father for his sons; he loves the worthy among them and places on a lower level those who do not show ability; but that of a mother for them is such, that while she loves the worthy, she pities those who do not show ability; the mother deals with them on the ground of affection and not of showing them honour; the father, on the ground of showing them honour and not of affection.

The heavy responsibility the father bears is to discipline and provide for the education of his children, while the mother is concerned with providing loving care and in fostering. It is out of tune with the mother's role to punish her sons, except to warn the obstinate one that 'if you don't listen to me and misbehave yourself, I am going to report you to your father'. Because the father is in a commanding position, and in charge of disciplining his children, the greatest difficulties arise when he dies prematurely.

As a son approaches adulthood and becomes to a greater extent absorbed in the activities and interests of family affairs, he relies less on his mother. This does not imply a weakening of his affection for her; rather, he turns to his mother for warmth and security in the patrilineal system. Since the mother does not enforce discipline, she is able to gratify her son with a minimum of frustration and repression. Although Confucius did not elaborate on the mother–son relationship, the mother undoubtedly occupies a central position in her son's interest, for he responds naturally to his mother's love and shows her respect.

However, the emotional relationship of mother and son is threatened when he marries. It often occurs that the mother becomes jealous of the young wife because the latter takes away the attachment of the son; it is jealousy that gives rise to difficulties between mother and daughter-in-law. There is a common saying: 'A son is lost when he is married'. An understanding mother who likes to see her son and daughter-in-law happy will make whatever effort she can to maintain the original relationship between herself and her married son. During the first years of marriage the son no doubt indulges in romantic enjoyment and hence he estranges himself from his mother, but generally he becomes more appreciative again of his mother's effort and sacrifice on behalf of the household, and thus restores the previous close relationship and intimacy with his mother. A reasonable daughter-in-law is pleased to see the renewed intimacy between mother and son, and instead of thinking ill of her mother-in-law, she does her best to cement the bond between herself and her mother-in-law. When the son and his wife are middle-aged and have their own children, the mother–son relationship is renewed with the son's family. The grandmother will love her younger grandchildren and play with them, while the mother is occupied with domestic chores.

With regard to the status and function of the mother, she is the one who is brought up in a different family and social environment. She is incorporated into her husband's family by marriage; her function as a wife is to perpetuate the family name by bearing male children. Unless this goal is attained, her position in the family is precarious, irrespective of what virtue she may possess, for barrenness is one of the seven grounds leading to her repudiation.

The son is the head of the household after his father is dead, and the mother is under the son's authority. When a piece of land or a house is sold, the decision rests in the hands of the first son, though the mother is consulted to vouch for it. These relations are seldom observed by the people in everyday life, except when controversies arise as regards family property and its inheritance and the continuity of family life. But when the division of family property is inevitable in consequence of the father's death, permission must be obtained from the mother unless the last will of the deceased can be proved. Once the family has been dissolved, it is usual for the mother to live with one of the sons, usually the eldest; this son is entitled to receive an extra portion of land for the care and support of the mother.

In brief, in her relations with her son, a mother finds solace, comfort, and happiness. There are indications that an intimate and affectionate relationship between mother and son threatens to create strains in the family on the part of the daughter-in-law, but such cases are unlikely. The mother acts as a buffer in the father–son relationship. It is unthinkable for the mother, bound as she is to the family happiness, to support her son in defiance of his father. On the other hand, the father is not disposed to show jealousy of his son's affectionate relationship with his mother, since a father's relations with her can be enhanced by an affectionate mother–son relationship.

Mother and daughter relationship

In feudal times a boy occupied a higher social status than a girl.[49] If a boy was born, a bow was placed on the left of the door; and if a girl, a handkerchief on the right of it.[50] After three days elapsed, some archery was practised for a boy, but not for a girl. At the end of the third month of birth, a suitable day was chosen[51] for shaving off the hair of the child – a horn-like tuft for a boy and a circlet on the crown of a girl.[52] When the girl grew up, she would not receive any literary training. Even late in the T'ang, Yuan, Ming and Ch'ing dynasties, the value of male children over female was upheld because the former were needed to preserve the family lines. A girl was not given as much education as a boy since she was debarred from public life, and education for education's sake would be regarded as a waste of time and money by all except very wealthy parents.

There is no tension between mother and daughter. While a mother may have loved her son more than her daughter, she has much more intimate and frequent contact with her daughter than with her son. The daughter stays with her mother most of the time, assisting her with arduous domestic tasks, helping her mother to clean the house, to wash clothes, to cook, to grind millet and to look after the younger children. When the mother is busy, her daughter sews for her father, mother and herself. At harvest time she collects crops in the field and stores grain in the family granary. The daughters even go to market in a group to buy household goods. When the daughter comes of age, it will be her mother who arranges the marriage and takes a proposal into serious consideration, but on no account can she betroth her daughter without the authorization and approval of her husband; the father is the legal arbiter. Apart from betrothal of a daughter in childhood, which does not, of course, require her consent, the daughter is expected to express her consent. The bonds of affection between the mother and her married daughter remain as strong as before the marriage and are kept alive by frequent visits and exchanges of gifts. The mother tries to learn whether her daughter has been warmly received by her husband and kindly treated by the members of the new household. If the marriage is happy, the daughter will appear happy when she pays her mother her first visit; but if the marriage is disappointing, the daughter will cry at her mother's feet and her mother will deplore her daughter's ominous fate.

The roles played by a son and a daughter are different. A son is the bearer of the family name, legal heir of the property and responsible for the family reputation and heritage. A daughter, on the other hand, is reared to marriage outside the family; and she is not considered to be a permanent member of her own lineage. The daughter's share in paternal property is determined by her marriage. If her father dies without a male heir, the property is divided between her and the other daughters; she must, however, bring what she has previously possessed into the common fund before she can have a share of the whole. Where there are male heirs, unmarried daughters are entitled to a legacy of half the son's share[53] before the family property is divided among the brothers. After the family partition, it is usual for her to take her marriage portion and live with one of her brothers, usually the eldest. Married daughters, regarded as members of their husband's family, are excluded from inheritance.[54]

Husband and wife relationship

In feudal times a special system of morals was formed in which the wife was subject to her husband in marriage but the mother developed a power which assumed to a certain degree the attributes appropriate to paternal authority. The wife, by her marriage, was given a status which corresponded to that of her husband in his own family. The authority established from olden times laid the foundation of the discipline of the harem, which contained the value of a statutory order. Thence the ritualists postulated that polygyny[55] with sisters had been justified as a good institution. Throughout Chinese history the sororate has been practised, but, as a result of infant betrothal, its occurrence has been rather sporadic. Where the institution of the sororate was prevalent, it coincided with marriage with the wife's brother's daughter because, in the absence of a marriageable sister, her brother's daughter was considered a seemly substitute. *Kung Yang Chuan* says 'When a feudal lord married, his bride was accompanied by eight bridesmaids called "ying", who were his future concubines'.[56] The institution of 'ying' served to warrant a large number of descendants for succession in the feudal lord's office.[57]

The polygynic institution was disrupted when, under the impact of the agnatic law which sought to bind successive generations together, it ceased to be strictly sisterly. In other words, solidarity in the group of brides was less cohesive than the group mingled with nieces. Among the nieces, (the daughters of an eldest brother and the younger sister) quarrels over precedence arose and rivalry was inevitable. The brides contrived to make their influence predominate. The order of rank within the harem would depend upon the tact of the husband, who could be led astray by the skilful beguiling and the jealous altercations, which were illustrated in what the *Shih Ching* (*The Book of Odes*) accounted for in terms of threatening incantations.[58]

If the first wife or principal wife died, a 'ying' was substituted and acted for her in the ceremonial capacity, but she was not entitled to be the principal wife. In the light of historical evidence, the 'ying' custom was categorized as 'legalized incest', whereby the emperor and feudal lords might be assured of an heir. In spite of some evidence, such a custom could not have been universal, even among the nobility. The reason would be not simply a limited supply of women, but a contradiction of the generation principle of the period, which more than once disintegrated the family system. For instance, a feudal lord was required to marry outside his own state. The rationale was that if the lord had been married to any women within the confines of his own state, her parent-in-law would automatically be a generation higher than he, and could not continue to be his subject.

Maternal authority and rights were derived from the rights of the parents-in-law and the husband. Thus the husband was empowered to repudiate his wife by order of the parent-in-law. For one of the seven grounds upon which a husband might divorce his wife was disobedience to her mother-in-law. The repudiation resulted in the rupture of the ties between the repudiated mother and her child. The *Li Chi* says: 'She who was my wife was also my son's mother; when she ceased to be my wife, she ceased to be the mother of my son.'[59] This notion suggested that the ties of parentage would depend upon the bond between the father and son. The mother should treat her husband with deference as a lord; she must be submissive[60] and adept at women's chores, but she was the equal of her husband, placed in the same rank at the ceremonies of the ancestral temple.[61]

The foregoing description portrays the husband and wife relationship in the feudal period. Now we enter into the description of the husband and wife relationship in China's traditional family after the feudal period.

Marriage in China is somewhat more than simply obtaining a wife for a husband. It is a contract between two parties. The kin of the woman agree to marry their daughter to the man, and his kinsmen pledge that the terms of agreement will be executed. Furthermore, new social relations are created by the marriage not only between the husband and the wife, but also between the wife's relatives, or two family groups. In terms of its function, we conceive of marriage as an event that, on the one hand, does honour to the ancestors in the temple, and, on the other, creates new generations. In Western societies marriage should be a union mainly based on personal choice. In traditional China marriage was considered rather as an alliance between two families; therefore personal adjustment and love between a man and a women did not constitute a nodal factor in the choice of a spouse. This neglect gave rise to the problem of adjustment for the newly married couple. Although the couple often developed a genuine affection for each other after a short period, they were reproved for demonstrating love and affection in public. If a young husband continued to be a filial son, he was expected to preserve closer relations with his family than with his wife. The inhibited affection between husband and wife was motivated on account of pressure from the former's mother; naturally she was loath to see her son divert his feelings to his wife, and thus a spite between mother-in-law and daughter-in-law arose as a matter of course. Should the wife find it difficult to get along with the family, her husband regardless of his feeling, was obliged to maintain the family integrity at the expense of his wife.

One way of avoiding this conflict was a cross-cousin marriage. These were between a married woman's son and her brother's daughter, but not vice versa.[62] In theory, cross-cousin marriage was discountenanced from the beginning of the first century AD.[63] Later, in the Ch'ing Code such marriages were allowed. The general Code of Laws of the Ch'ing dynasty reads: 'In the interest of the people it is permitted to marry with the children of a paternal aunt or of a maternal uncle or aunt.'[64] Cross-cousin marriage was desirable and advantageous in that identity of family background of the mother-in-law and daughter-in-law would knot the family bond more closely, on the one hand, and, on the other, lead to an easy and mutual understanding; any disagreement that might occur could be resolved by the intervention of the parent of the daughter-in-law.

A young husband, must neither mention his wife often nor praise her in family gatherings, and a young wife must similarly be restrained from showing her love for her husband. It is considered most seemly for the wife to love her husband within bounds so that her love will not spoil his career or induce him to neglect his duty to his family. A good wife is willing to perform the household duties with her mother-in-law or sisters-in-law during the day; at night she ought not to go to her room in company with her husband until all the family has retired. At social gatherings a well-bred wife does not sit with her husband and should keep herself aloof from him.

A young wife inevitably feels lonely because she has been brought up in a different family and in a different environment. A wife can never cease to be a stranger in her husband's family until the birth of children; the arrival of a child will entitle the mother to be embodied in her husband's clan. She becomes the wife of a husband whom she may have never seen before marriage and affiliates herself to a new family. Unlike the situation in an elementary family where the wife is subject only to her husband, now after marriage her affiliation with his lineage weighs much more than her simple status of a spouse. On this account it is incumbent upon her to comply with the established traditions and mores of the new family. Again, the long face of her mother-in-law and the simulated dignity of the father-in-law will make her feel that she is entirely at the mercy of these strange people. The only person who can succour her is her husband. Since her husband has never experienced romantic affairs before, he can now express his romantic ideas and reveal his love for his wife.

The young couple must endeavour to make the most of the marriage, since divorce is ruled out. The husband will not beat his wife unless he is under strong pressure from his parents; on all issues the wife is the loser. It is not difficult to see whether the marriage is a happy one or not. A loved wife is enlivened, high-spirited and active in her work, while an unhappy one is listless and dismal. In an unhappy marriage the husband goes to bed with a great sigh, whereas his wife can only weep in secrecy for her unfortunate lot. That they live together and have children may lead one to think that their marriage is successful, but it may not be a happy one. However, if an unhappy marriage survives at all, the relationship between husband and wife will improve with time. In their old age when they see their children grow up, their feelings towards each other become mellow. Early marital constraint being removed, the old couple can be at ease to walk in public and joke with each other in the presence of other people. In their conversation, instead of using the pronoun 'he' and 'she' they address each other as 'child's father' or 'child's mother'.

In their bedroom the wife tells her husband about the trivial round of the household chores and her views on problems connected with the house. The husband, on the other hand, talks about irrigation, the field crops, the need for more hired labourers and about their work. Needless to say, although he is not supposed to listen to, or believe, his wife's complaints about the household, he often agrees with her ideas and secretly acts under her influence in other matters. As for the husband's authority over his wife, in traditional China a wife could never act alone: a woman depends upon her father before she is of age. She depends upon her husband at marriage, and she depends upon her son after her husband's death.

At the age of fifty, or sixty, the wife commonly becomes the dominant person in the household as a result of having one, two, or even three daughters-in-law. She may be the grandmother of a long line of grandchildren. Psychologically the middle-aged sons feel more attached to their mother than to their father. Now that the father has retired, his authority on the farm diminishes, and he is unable to discharge the duty of taking the farm products to the market and doing business with the dealers. Likewise, in relation to the neighbours his importance is dwindling because he has been deprived of his real authority; within the family his status as the family head is more nominal than real although all the household still treat him with deference and respect. The duty of the wife now is to see that her husband is well fed and well attended to.

The rites that are performed in the ancestral hall are conducted by, and in the presence of, men; their daughters and wives are not entitled to participate in the rites. Nevertheless, whatever inferiority women have in ancestor worship, they occupy a central position in 'home cult'; they are assigned the duty of lighting incense in the domestic shrine and of keeping the ancestors' death dates and praying to them in need. But when the sacrifices are made to the domestic shrines by the joint family head, the wife attends them because her welfare is bound up with that of her husband and children. Yet women address themselves to their husband's ancestors, not their own; the domestic shrines will house in due course her own memorial tablet along with her husband's, to which sacrifices will be given by their own sons and daughters-in-law.

Sibling relationship

The reference name	hsiung (older brother)	ti (younger brother)
The vocative or addressing name	ko or ko ko[65]	younger brother's name

The division of the fraternal relationship is based on age, which accounts for the kinship term. An older brother calls his brothers by the term 'ti ti' which means younger brother, and they call him by the term 'ko ko', which designates him as older brother. All boys at the time of their birth are given the name of their generation, to which is added their proper name. For example, in Lin Yü-tang's book *Moment in Peking*, three brothers in the Tsang family are called, Po-ya, Sun-ya, Hsian-ya, 'ya' being the name of their generation.

Ego addresses his older brother as ko ko. In case there are several brothers, they are numbered according to their ages. For instance, ego calls his eldest brother ta ko (first) and the second oldest erh ko (second) and so forth. Ego calls his younger brother by his milk name if he is under twenty and unmarried; if he is older and married, he should be called by his proper name. Again, ego can call his younger brothers by number alone. If ego is the eldest, he calls his next younger brother lao erh (the second younger brother), lao san (the third younger brother) and so on.

Brothers growing up together in their natal family develop a mutual attachment and identity of interests on the basis of common upbringing. The common background and surroundings of brothers are manifested in their playgroups. Brothers of the same joint family between whom there is not a wide age gap play together and learn from one another practical knowledge of life. Thus the common body of experience moulds their social personalities and orientates their interests and ideals towards culturally established goals and values.

There is no doubt that a conflict arises among brothers in both traditional and contemporary China. The tragedy of the Yüan Wu Gate[66] (AD 624-6) throws light on the 'power' struggle among the siblings. During the reign of Kao Tsu, the first emperor of the T'ang dynasty, Shih Ming, later the second emperor of the T'ang dynasty and the second son of the emperor Kao Tsu, gained popularity with the court, and the people at large turned his brothers, Chien Chang and Yuan Chi into enemies. They tried to poison Shih Ming, but they failed as the dose was not large enough to cause his death; then they conspired to assassinate him. Shih Ming, having been informed of this intrigue, had the entrance to his father's palace guarded by his own soldiers. When the two brothers came as usual in the morning to pay respect to their father, the Emperor Kao Tsu, Shih Ming shot Chien Chang with an arrow and caused his instant death, while Wei Ch'ih-kung, a staff officer of Shih Ming, shot Yuan Chi and sent him to his fate. Owing to the grief caused by this tragedy, Kao Tsu abdicated and enthroned Shih Ming who became Emperor T'ai Tsung.

The ties of mutual attachment, association and solidarity in social matters that unite brothers vary according to their genealogical propinquity. They are far closer for full brothers than half-brothers, and progressively less close for those who are parallel with collateral cousins. Brothers are devoted to one another and always, as far as my personal experience goes, loyal and helpful to one another in relation to other people. Older brothers are seen to carry their baby brothers, though they appear to be impatient when caring for the baby for a long time. Therefore, if one happens to see an infant embraced by a boy from nine to fifteen years old one can almost be certain that they are full brothers.

During boyhood, brothers are playmates and are on equal terms. Quarrels are commonplace, but are not frowned upon. Rather, between brothers near to each other in age, squabbles betoken their equality and familiarity. Afterwards, the older brother should be friendly to his younger brother, while the younger one is expected to respect the elder. Age is an index of their orientation towards life, since with age arises their tendency to seek outside friendship, and it increases with the approach of adolescence. From the age of about fifteen to twenty boys are inclined to marry. Before they marry, even when only the eldest brother has married, they get along well with each other. They work shoulder to shoulder in their farming or in the home, under their father's guidance. In spite of rivalry and occasional clashes, there is in general co-operation and mutual help. But after marriage their relationships change. At first they endeavour to maintain the original friendliness and affection, but their wives, strangers as they come from different lineages, sow the seeds of competition and jealousy that undermines the solidarity of the brothers. When an individual wife fights, she fights on behalf of her husband and their children as well as on her own account. It ensues that the conflict between brothers rests mainly on the conflict between wives. Brothers are disrupted from each other on account of their being married to different women, the latter being also different by having different mothers. This leads one to think that the differences introduced by women into the household are due to their being diverse or heterogeneous in their local and kinship origins.

A further factor accelerating the household towards its fission is a brother's inordinate closeness to his own wife which invariably alienates other brothers. This can happen in the absence of a strong father. Again, if the family head is a strong father and lives to an old age, the partition of the family can be averted and no independent elementary family will emerge; this is the mechanism for the continuance of the joint family. However, the death of the family head presages the division of the family and the establishment of new families.

When the partition occurs, all brothers have equal rights to inheritance and an equal share in the family property. Owing to the disappearance of primogeniture, the eldest brother has a pre-eminence among equals rather than predomination over his younger brothers; senior status by age weighs less than senior status by generation.

The relationship between a woman and her husband's elder brother is distant but is marked by respect. The elder brother is tabooed from entering the bedroom of his married younger brother, or, when it is absolutely necessary, the younger brother's wife should be informed in advance so that she may leave her room. Joking between an older brother-in-law and his younger brother's wives is permissible in family gatherings or in the old parents' room where the family members gather. The formality decreases in proportion as all the brothers and their wives reach middle age. Obviously sexual relations between a man and his brother's wife are strictly forbidden, but are far less reprehensible than incest with the father-in-law, which destroys a father's authority over his son and his daughter-in-law. It happens now and again that a love affair between a woman and her husband's younger brother develops. A love affair with a person related in the third degree is regarded as incest and one of the ten offences. During the T'ang and Sung dynasties the punishment for incest with a brother's wife was banishment for both parties to a distance of two thousand li (about 700 miles). According to Yüan law, the offender of incest with a brother's wife, who lived under the same roof, was given 107 strokes. In Ming and Ch'ing laws the punishment for such incest was strangling for both the man and the woman.

Brother and sister relationship

Reference name:	hsiung (older brother) ti (younger brother)	tzu (older sister) mei (younger sister)
Addressing or vocative name:	ko ko (older brother's name) ti ti (younger brother's name)	chieh chieh (older sister) mei mei (younger sister's name)

Both sex and age factors exercise considerable influence on the relations of brothers and sisters. In the early years a girl is dominated by her brother, due to the male superiority in the Chinese family; yet this does not obstruct emotional attachment between brothers and sisters. An older sister takes care of her little sisters and brothers on the one hand, and, on the other, when a boy is older and reaches twelve to fifteen years of age, he begins to feel responsible and dutiful towards his sister, even if she is older than he. It is the brother at this age towards whom his younger sister can turn in troubles. Before twelve to fifteen years of age, a girl can associate with any boy, but after this age a girl will be permitted to associate only with her own brother. To the extent that the girl is strongly tempted to have male company as she grows older, she is anxious to accept her brother's company and protection. The affection between unmarried brothers and sisters is very striking. When the boy is interested in a particular girl, he asks his sister time and again to act as a go-between and arrange a rendezvous. The sister may help her brother in serious courtship and reveal his ambitions to their mother. On the sister's side, although she may long for a certain young boy, she is rather shy to reveal her feelings to her brother; she may confide her heart to her mother. Sometimes her pretending to be sick suggests that she suffers from love-sickness. A brother may have a yearning for courtship, but he would often be callous to the same hankering in his sister. On the contrary, he resents any boy's approach to his sister and is loath to regard any young man as his sister's future husband.

There was a story of a girl student, Fei Ho, who disguised herself as a boy so that she could be associated with two male students. She fell in love with one of them called Tsun Ch'ing. To dissemble her feelings towards the boy she proposed her sister to him. The beauty and charm of the student brought home to the boy that his/her sister must also be dainty and attractive. He then entreated the student's sister to marry him. The student promised to do his/her utmost to make the proposal a reality. At length, when the boy discovered that the male student was a girl, he wooed her indefatigably and asked for this girl's hand. This story describes how sisters and brothers have endeavoured to help one another in regard to marriage.[67]

In China, convention requires a rigid inhibition in the relationship between post-adolescent boys and girls. When they come of age, they are forbidden to have any relationship at all. As girls are bashful in marriage affairs, it is the parents who make an effort to find a suitable partner for their daughters.

The divergence of interests and companionship in the years following

a brother's marriage will disturb the personal intimacy and attachment of a brother and sister. The bonds of affection between a married
brother and his sister remain less strong than before the former's
marriage. The brother now has a wife, who is closer to him than his
sister ever was. The brother's new wife will widen the gap between
brother and sister if the latter is jealous of their relationship. Again, the
wife may be hostile to her young sister-in-law as a retaliation upon her
mother-in-law, for most daughters-in-law suffer from their mother-in-
law's domination and maltreatment. The mother undoubtedly stands in
favour of her daughter in any open clash with the young couple; this is
the reason for the mother apprehending that her daughter will be
married before she dies. A harmonious and amicable adjustment of
their relationship can usually be wrought when they reach an advanced
age.

Sister and sister relationship

The sororal relationship is mostly affectionate, though it is not of long
duration as it comes to an end at marriage. After marriage the sisters
may meet on their visits home, but seeing that such visits need the
approval of their parents-in-law, they are not recurrent and regular. The
relationship between married sisters is not so clearly defined as that
between brothers, nor is it so vital to the family. There are no taboos
between sisters before they are of age. Younger sisters are disciplined,
protected by older ones, and are also taught how to sew, cook, serve
parents, and perform their duties as members of the family.

The warmth of the sororal relationship is apt to create certain
problems of adjustment for the women. First, there are the strains
which arise from the disruption of this relationship at the time of marriage. According to the *Li Chi*, in the family of the girl who has been
given in marriage, the lamp is not extinguished for three days; parents
spend the time awake, thinking of the imminent separations.[68] Second,
the past comfortable environment and affectionate companionship will
make the girl's position in her husband's family more unbearable, since
she is married into a strange lineage in which she can never be free to do
whatever she wishes.

When a married sister has children and returns home for a visit, her
unmarried sisters like to look after her children and help to sew dresses
for the sister's children. Since full sisters feel extremely close to each

other, the children of married sisters always feel attached to their 'yi yi', a term used by the children to address their mother's sisters. On this account a joking relationship exists between children and their 'yi yi'. If the children are naughty towards their maternal aunts, they will not be restrained by the latter, but corrected by their mother.

Since unmarried daughters are loved by their mother, they can ask her to give material help to their married sisters, especially when the latter have many children. This is one reason why married daughters are not welcome home by their brother's wife. In addition, because of the closeness of full sisters, the married sister's husband has a joking relationship[69] with his wife's sisters, regardless of who is older. From my personal observation, I have never seen 'chieh fu', a married sister's husband lose his temper with his wife's unmarried sisters, however boorish the joking relationship may be. Many a time chieh fu said to his sister-in-law: 'I have found a charming young man for you, and you should be married soon'. Or 'Your sister whom I married is not so pretty as you are; so I would like to marry you'. Also the married sister's husband is always eager to visit his wife's parents, since he has usually been accepted with generous hospitality, and the parent-in-law, if he cares about reputation, would feel that he had lost his dignity if he did not treat his son-in-law generously.

Grandparents and grandchildren relationship

Grandparents and grandchildren constitute a part of the kinship organization and are united by kinship. They are separated both by age and by the participation in the social life of the kinship system, which gradually push the grandparents into retirement. However, in contrast with the many constraints between parents and children, grandparents and grandchildren usually enjoy a relationship of simple friendliness relatively free from restraints. Their joking relationship indicates ignorance of 'age'; such relationships are expressed with tenderness resembling that between mother and child. Having grandchildren is the goal of most couples, and embracing them gives the latter great pleasure. Since the grandparents take precedence over the parents in the context of generation, they are in a position to enforce their will. The grandparents seldom bring pressure to bear upon the parents unless absolutely necessary, but it occasionally occurs that a grandmother of strong character attempts time and again to interfere in parental authority.

The grandfather rarely exercises authority and control over the grand-child, but he indulges him and serves as a mediator between father and son, when the former is cross with the latter. The grandson has no specific obligations towards his grandparents as long as his father is living and performs filial piety.

The attitude towards a grandfather differs from that towards a father. Although the child owes his grandparents obedience and respect, their relations are undoubtedly based on amicability and intimacy rather than avoidance and aloofness. In relation to the grandfather and grandmother, the children of both sexes seem more afraid of their grandfather than their grandmother, loving the latter more. The greater majority of grandparents have no preference between boys and girls, but those who do almost always prefer boys, due perhaps to the status of a male child as a legal heir. The grandfather, sometimes, though seldom, shows a certain reserve which will cause his grandchildren to keep out of his way and to respect him.

A grandfather is in a better position than a father: as no direct responsibility for a child's training and care falls on a grandfather, a warmth and fondness which may be absent between a father and his son are likely to develop between a grandfather and grandson. A son will often use his relationship with his grandfather to ease the tension in his relationship with his father. This complication can well be illustrated by the story in *The Dream of the Red Chamber*.[70]

Chia Huan, the brother of Po Yu, reported that his brother Po Yu, attempted to seduce Golden Bracelet, a maid in his mother's room. The maid resisted and was tortured; then she committed suicide. Chia Cheng, Po Yu's father, was angered and shouted to his servants: 'Seize Po Yu and bring him here'. The attendants, trembling in fear, seized Po Yu and tied him to a bench. Then at the Chia Cheng's command they began to beat him with a heavy bamboo rod. Unsatisfied with their attack, Chia grasped the rod himself and beat his son more than ten strokes with all his might. Suddenly Lao tai tai (old madam), the mother of Chia Cheng came along. Before her appearance on the scene her coarse voice was heard: 'Kill me first and then you can kill him'. Chia Cheng hurried out to meet his mother and said: 'I, your son, am trying to discipline my son that he may save the honour of the family and the traditions of the ancestors at heart'. The matriarch said: 'How could you expect Po Yu to bear your cruel beating . . . ? You can beat your son if you want to, since he is your son. I suppose you are getting tired of us. It would be better had we left you alone'. Chia Cheng knelt and kowtowed saying: 'Mother, your words leave your son with no ground to place his feet!' The matriarch said: 'Of course a son should be disciplined when he misbehaves himself, but you should know where to stop'.

This episode describes a conflict between generations within the family which is typical both among the gentry and among peasants. I have observed the same conflict in my village. Such a clash inevitably brings about strains in the relationship between the parents and the grandparents. Further, it occurs that in the antagonism of mother-in-law and daughter-in-law an intervention in their conflict on the part of grandparents only worsens their relationships within the family. As has previously been mentioned, the warmth and affection between grandparents and grandchildren provide a source of gratification, but are a threat to the solidarity of other family relationships.

Since the grandparents are treated with less respect than parents, there exists a joking relationship between grandparents and grandchildren, in which no offence is taken. The essence of the joke is the pretence at ignoring the difference of age and status between the grandparent and the grandchild. Again, at a meal the grandchildren may disregard all formal etiquette and share their grandparents' dish at ease; such behaviour is unthinkable when the father is present. In terms of social function the joking serves to provide the social conjunction of friendliness and distance.

The relationship between maternal grandparents and their daughter's children are friendly and even affectionate. But maternal grandparents regard those children as belonging to an outside lineage. The writer's grandfather used to say that those children were not in our descent group. Of course, the kinder the maternal grandparents are towards their married daughter's children, the happier their parents. However, for fear maternal grandparents should make their own sons and daughters-in-law unhappy, they are restrained from doing their married daughter's children a good turn materially. For example, the daughter's children are not welcome for long visits to their maternal grandparents. The writer's paternal grandfather used to tell his married daughter jokingly to return to her husband's home. One of the reasons was that a long visit to maternal parents would arouse the parents-in-law's suspicions about the happiness of the married daughter with her marriage.

Maternal grandparents do not see their daughter's children as frequently as paternal grandparents their son's children. Yet in the first years after marriage, married daughters frequently visit their parents, especially after their children are born. Sometimes four- or five-year-old children are left in the care of their maternal grandparents for two weeks on end. This gives great pleasure to both the maternal grandparents and the child, though it sometimes happens that the child is not eager to stay with them because he is homesick. When one of the children is sick, his maternal grandparents or their son pay a visit to their married daughter's home. As the maternal grandparents are on a par with the child's paternal grandparents, they have to be received with respect and courtesy. At their meeting they address each other as 'ch'in chia', relatives. This visit is very short, that is to say, maternal grandparents do not customarily stay overnight unless they have come a great distance.

Naturally the death of a grandchild is a great source of grief for grandparents of both lines. But maternal grandparents do not wear mourning for him as parents do, since the child belongs to a different lineage. Again, the maternal grandparents do not attend the child's funeral. After the loss of a child, his mother pays a visit to her mother's house. When the married daughter and her mother meet, both of them weep together and the daughter remains for a few days with her mother. This is due to their bereavement. Likewise, a married woman's parents do not attend her funeral personally if they survive her, but other members of her natal family, usually her brother and brother's sons are present at her funeral.

The foregoing description and account of the relationship between grandparents and grandchildren provides a general pattern for both upper-class and peasant families. There is a variation in local customs in different parts of China.

In some, the adjustments between the members of a large family are delicate and indispensable, and it is only when friction can be reduced to a minimum that a large household can remain undissolved. Jealousy, division and antagonism between certain members of the family will throw the organization into disequilibrium; unless an effective and immediate remedy is sought for the situation, the household may be disrupted. Stern parental authority is the mechanism of maintaining a stable family system. Since conjunctive and disjunctive components of inter-family relationships are maintained and combined, heavy responsibilities are imposed on the head of the household to keep the relationships functioning and running smoothly. The tact and the managerial ability of the family head would not be successful if traditions, rituals, and social sanctions were not used as controls within the family system.

Chapter 3

Filial piety and kinship

> That parents, when alive, should be served according to propriety;
> that, when dead, they should be buried according to propriety; and
> that they should be sacrificed to according to propriety.
>
> *Lun Yü* (*The Analects of Confucius*)

We have previously seen that the father-son relationship is the kernel of
the family system. In spite of tension and discord between them,
parental and filial duty and devotion towards each other is conspicuous.
The parents take great interest in the children throughout their lives,
and their children, imbued with the doctrine of filial piety, are constantly reminded of their bounden filial duty towards their parents. The
following stanzas seem apt to express parental affection towards the
child:

1 Parents, showing love to their dear child,
   Would do with grace all forms of self denial.[1]

2 Tender mother holding thread and pin
   Sews the coat of her departing son.
   Stitches after stitches she puts in
   Lest his return may be a tardy one.[2]

The last two lines seem to mean that, for a mother, separation from
her child always seems so long as to be unbearable, and that her anxiety
and longing are vividly expressed in the sewing with which she hopes to
make the garment durable, for she fears that the garment will not out-
last the child's absence.

71

One may readily pose the questions: What is piety? What is the function of piety in the Chinese family?

The expression of piety for one's ancestors is found in all forms of society, and there are as many varieties of expression as there are cultures. Religious veneration of the dead and of the head of the family are interrelated, so that piety depends upon natural feeling rather than upon distinct ceremonial duty. In Egypt, however, there is a widespread tradition of veneration for the dead which is quite distinct from the family habits of respect and obedience towards parents.[3] In India the main purpose of marriage is to bring up a male child who will be able some day to perform sacrifices to the names of the father. Among the Romans filial piety accorded to the *pater familias* had a legal basis. Apart from the legal character, a sentimental element was also included; so in 603 BC a temple was erected in honour of the *pietas* of a daughter who preserved her father's life with milk from her breast, when he was sentenced to death by starvation. In Greece the father in his old age laid claim to the support of his son. The worship of gods and the obligations towards the dead and fatherhood were considered the highest duties. Piety towards the father, in terms of obedience, was held in higher esteem than affection for the mother. Among Semitic peoples piety towards parents is correlated with religion; obedience is believed to win God's blessing, and disobedience incurs his wrath. In Islam, the Qur'an prescribes a submissive love for father and mother and demands that they shall be looked after in their old age. In Judaism, filial piety is a control on the pattern of life, disobedience incurring the curse of Jehovah, and in Christianity the new relation between God and man resembles that between father and son. However, in Christianity it is clear that the demands of religion take precedence over family obligations: 'If any man cometh unto me, and hateth not his own father and mother and wife and children and brothers and sisters, yea, and his own life also, he cannot be my disciple'.[4]

The character 'hsiao', filial piety, (see the Glossary) is composed of two parts.[5] The top part stands for 'old' and the lower part represents 'tzŭ' son or child. 'Hsiao' means what the children 'tzŭ' owe to the aged 'lao', the old in general, and to their parents in particular. Related to 'hsiao', filial piety, is the character 'lao', old venerable or septuagenarian: a man whose hair and beard 'mao' have become white. Note the strange modern contraction of 'jen', man, and 'mao', hair, that is originally an old man.

Thus the word 'filial piety' refers in general to punctiliousness in the performance of duties naturally owed to parents and relatives. Confucians conceived of piety as devotion towards the spirits of ancestors or dead parents. In the *Book of Songs*, 'piety' (hsiao) means, precisely, piety towards the dead. Out of twelve instances, nine have this sense, while the other three are more ambiguous.[6] Also in the *Analects* piety is applied to filial conduct or comportment towards living parents. Dr Hsu described filial piety as the foundation of social organization and emphasized it more significantly in the patrifilial nexus in the family system; the son has to respect and support his parents in their life and sacrifice to them after their death. This is an elaborate, moral doctrine based on Confucian tenets.[7] Again, Confucius said that:[8]

> to remember the ancestors, to perform the same rites, and the same music which they performed when living, to reverence what they reverenced, to love what they loved, to serve them after death as they were served during their life, and to serve them though they have disappeared as if they still existed, that is perfect filial piety.

Selected doctrines of Confucius on filial piety

To understand better the meaning of filial piety, it is necessary to expound at length selected doctrines of Confucius on this point.

1 The Confucian *Analects* say that:[9]

> a youth at home should observe the doctrine of filial piety, that is, fulfil his duties in the best manner possible to his parents; and, when away from home, should observe the doctrine of fraternal deference, i.e. to fulfil his duties in the best manner to his elders. He should abound in love to all and be attached to the virtuous. When he has leisure, he should employ it in cultural studies.

2 Filial love is inherent in the doctrine of filial piety, which constitutes not only the nodal element of the Chinese family, but lays the corner-stone of Chinese civilization. Confucius asserted that 'civilization commences with filial piety, the root of virtue.'[10] This statement will hold invariably true if one thinks that men are innately capable of loving their neighbours (a sentiment of which beasts are devoid) and of lending support of their nearest relatives. Confucius taught that piety is the basis of all happiness in the life of people.[11]

There is a possibility that filial piety is an obstructive instrument of paternal control, used when the younger generation impedes social progress in some way. Also, it is sometimes gathered that the traditional observances of filial duty are made solely out of a combination of cowardice and hypocritical self-interest. Confucius, however, thought of piety as a quality inherent in human nature, free from self-interest and fear.[12] Confucius's followers undertook to endow the parent–child relationship with more than the mechanical, compulsory pattern pre-dominant in upper-class families, where a father's relation to his son resembled, in many of its aspects, that of a feudal lord to his vassal. On the contrary, Confucian ethics demand that the practice of filial piety should not be thought of as fulfilling a cold formality, but should be carried out as a natural and spontaneous product of filial affection. The *Li Chi* says that 'the pious son and his wife shall care for parents with an appearance of pleasure to make their parents feel at ease'. Thus the Confucian concept of filial piety differs not only from Chinese feudal ideas, but also from the Protestant notions of respect and fear. The Chinese sage would entirely disagree with what Luther once said: 'To respect one's parents is better than to love them'.[13]

3 Chinese virtues have been grounded upon the concept of filial piety, which is the root of the virtue 'jen', universal love.[14] The doctrine of universal love connotes equality and is the doctrine of the Confucian school which preaches that men should, from their youth, learn to 'abound in love to all'.[15] It is this equal love that led Mo Tzŭ to criticize Confucian doctrine. Mo argued that it would run counter to man's nature to love another man's father just as one's own and that 'bond-man who serves his parents does not merely serve men', thus implying a distinction.[16] Since universal love should be cultivated within the family, filial piety has exerted influence upon social and political life.[17] In fact, common people show little interest in political affairs simply because, under the influence of filial piety, they are submissive to the village self-government preached by elders.[18] Again, filial piety affirms the value of the temporal life and differs from Indian Buddhism, which glorifies life after death. It is also the most potent force for cementing and consolidating all human beings in universal brotherhood.

4 In discussing filial piety, Mencius embraced the teaching of Confucius, thinking that this virtue can supersede a religion. He said: 'Do not seek far, do not attempt anything arduous; that which you ought to do is quite near and easy. Piety towards parents, respect towards superiors'.[19] For the people, filial piety is in fact 'propriety' - 'li', which, starting in the family, can even be applied to the state. The

sovereign issues orders and ministers carry them out; fathers are tender
and sons are obedient; elder brothers are affectionate and younger
brothers are respectful; husbands and wives are in harmony; mothers-in-
law are tender and daughters-in-law dutiful; these constitute the idea
'li'.[20] 'Tao' in Taoism, 'thusness' in Buddhism, and 'li' in Confucianism
amount to reason, law and principle respectively.[21] Human nature is
bound up with 'li', while 'li' is identical with Heaven. However, to
interpret 'li' or Heaven as a mere abstract principle does not do it justice.
The completion of 'jen' or goodness is a moral principle. It creates and
recreates and thus it is the greatest of virtues, arousing in us positive
emotions.[22] Again Fung says: 'Investigation of things will lead to the
realization of "li," which in turn will lead to the full realization of one's
nature and thus serve Heaven.'[23]

We note that from this philosophy, 'all is one and one is all', two
questions may arise. The first is whether such a philosophy is reminiscent of atheism. Hu Shih, a Chinese philosopher, has indicated that
Chinese religious thought tends towards rationalism and comes to the
conclusion that the original Chinese religion consists of a worship of
ancestors, certain spirits and Heaven. Thus, according to Hu, the
religious idea is simplified by the naturalism of Lao Tzŭ and the humanism of Confucius. Moreover, Confucianists of the Han dynasty (206 BC–
AD 220) attempted to simplify it further so as to make it a religion of
filial piety. Another aspect is an elaborate and fanatical Buddhism,
which temporarily overwhelmed the Chinese, but their rationalistic
mentality gradually reasserted itself and revolted against Buddhism.[24]
Neo-Confucianism in the eleventh and twelfth centuries made the
Buddhist element – 'meditation and insight' – a philosophy of individual
perfection through intellectual training.

It happens that despite the father's tenderness, sons show filial impiety; younger brothers can be disrespectful, while elder brothers can
lack affection. For example, in the days of the emperor Yung Lo (AD
1403-25) there lived in the Shun T'ien district a Prefect whose name
was Ni Shou-lien. At the age of seventy-nine he met a girl named Mei
shih, seventeen years old, and married her. His elder son, Shan chi, bore
his father a grudge. He said that the old man had done a foolish thing;
he was an old bundle of years and resembled a lighted candle in a
draught; he knew that he had but five or six years to live and yet he had
acted as stupidly as this. He linked himself to this young flower of a
girl, who would in all probability be unable to endure being a wife in
name only. Many similar cases showed that having been united with an

old man, young brides were found to run wild. The father, Ni, insisted on everyone calling his young wife 'little mother' or 'madam'. In defiance of his father's command Shan chi refused to address his step-mother as 'mother'. He even said: 'We cannot tolerate such a state of affairs and must not be too polite to her lest she should think too highly of herself'. The elder son and his wife grumbled together and all day long they murmured at their father's stupidity. Prefect Ni was fully aware of the feelings of his son and daughter-in-law and though he was displeased with them he disguised his displeasure in his heart. Then a boy was born and was given a personal name, Shan shu, in common with the first character of his brother's 'shan' and thus the elder son and younger one were half-brothers. When Shan chi learned that his younger brother was named Shan shu and would have equal footing, he became angry with his father. At the age of fourteen Shan shu was intelligent. One day Shan shu came to ask his elder brother Shan chi for a piece of silk to make a coat. The latter retorted: 'You little bastard, how dare you talk to me so boldly! I warn you not to make me lose my temper.' 'We are both our father's son,' replied Shan shu, 'how can you call me bastard? Do you think you can do my mother and me mischief and then take the whole of the estate for yourself?' 'You vile little wretch!' shouted Shan chi. Then, seizing his young brother's arm, Shan chi beat him on the head with his clenched fist a dozen times until he had bruised him severely.[25]

The commentator appraised this story: 'A brother's love quickly disappears; on one tree there grew two branches: one was full of sap, the other rotten through and through'.

This story no doubt describes the filial impiety of the elder son against his father in view of his alliance with his wife and the antagonism between the elder son and his step-mother. What underlay the impious attitude was the son's fear that on the coming of age of the half-brother the step-mother would stake out a claim to the family property. Moreover, the father was afraid to show his displeasure at his son's impiety and punish it. On the one hand, the father's authority was diminished on account of his age, and on the other his marrying such a young girl caused suspicion of a blot on his character. As regards the conduct of the elder son, he obviously acted against the code of filial piety. According to Confucian ethic, the love of parents ought to exceed all others, even of wife or children, throughout life until death. To prefer one's wife or children to one's parents is a grave sin. Pao divorced his wife because she insulted her father-in-law by calling him a dog. The love of parents beyond measure can be illustrated by one of the twenty-four stories of filial devotion, in which the mother was saved from starvation at the cost of a child:

Kuo Chu, living in the Han dynasty, was very poor. His son of three years must share a portion of his grandmother's food. One day Kuo said to his wife: 'We are so poor that we cannot provide for our mother and let our child share her food. Why do we not get rid of this son? We can have another son, but not another mother'. Kuo's wife did not dare to object to this strange proposal. Kuo then began to dig a grave. When he had reached a depth of three feet, suddenly he saw a vessel filled with gold ingots, on which were inscribed these words: 'Heaven grants Kuo Chu this gold because he was ready to sacrifice his son for his mother's sake. This treasure is the reward for his filial devotion. Let no official deprive him of it, and no other person take it!' At the same time the life of the child was saved in a manner similar to the story of Abraham and Isaac.

At another time, a person resigned his high office to make it possible for him to live with his aged parents during their remaining years. The famous scholar, Li Mi of the Chin dynasty (AD 265–420) made a petition to the emperor to release himself from his office so that he might fulfil his filial duty to his parents. His petition was phrased as follows:

> Your humble minister could not be what he is without his grand-mother,[26] nor can she live her remaining years happily without him.[27] I have suffered from misfortunes and experienced early sadness and grief. When I was just six months old, I lost my loving father. At the age of four, my uncle forced my widowed mother to re-marry. Then, filled with pity for my loneliness and weakness, my grandmother brought me up. At the age of nine, I could not walk on account of illness. Now I am forty-four years old, and my grand-mother is eighty. I could serve you for many more years, but my grandmother has only a short time to live. Having a sentiment similar to that of a crow that nurses its own old crow I entreat your majesty to grant me leave to fulfil my filial duty to my grandmother, so that she will enjoy a happy and tranquil life for her remaining years. Then I should devote my life to your majesty and, after death, knit straws.[28]

This episode sounds peculiar to modern thinking in that it was not a problem, for the problem could be easily solved. In view of the long

distance, perhaps a thousand li (Chinese miles) between the court where
the Minister Li served and the province in which his grandmother lived,
his ministerial function and the fulfilment of his filial devotion seemed
incompatible. In traditional China to decline a diplomatic post abroad
in pursuance of filial duty was not uncommon. We should keep in mind
that the refusal to take an official post on account of old parents is in
no way called for by the doctrine of filial piety; it is simply a matter of
individual concern. Furthermore, notwithstanding the Confucian saying:
'Do not seek far, do not attempt anything arduous,' filial piety does not
oblige children to stay with the parents. On the contrary, when children
grow up, the parents expect them to be well established and achieve
success and distinction in life. This is in conformity with the notion of
filial piety understood in the classics:

> Filial piety is of three grades: the highest is to honour the parents by
> achievements, the lesser is not to disgrace oneself, thus casting
> reflections on the parents, and the least is to be able to support the
> parents ... lack of self-respect is want of filial piety; disloyalty in
> serving the sovereign is want of filial piety; negligence in the
> administration of office is want of filial piety; insincerity to friends is
> want of filial piety ; and lack of bravery in battle is want of filial
> piety .... Trees should be cut and animals should be killed according
> to season .... Filial piety consists in exerting oneself for the parents;
> mediocre filial piety consists in practising benevolence and righteous-
> ness; great filial piety consists in conferring extensive benefits on
> mankind.[29]

> Filial piety begins with love of parents, matures in service to the
> sovereign, and ends in establishing oneself according to truth and
> righteousness.[30]

One may pose the question: What is the relevance of filial piety to
loyalty to the state, to conduct towards friends, and service to society
and cutting of trees or killing of animals? It is naturally the parents'
wish that their children resign themselves to do duty for the state, so
that any conduct complying with parental wishes is filial piety, and
conversely any act contrary to them is stigmatized as filial impiety.[31]
With respect to the chopping of trees or killing of animals not according
to season, this is considered to be cruel, and any form of cruelty is
opposed to virtue of which filial piety is the root. This shows that filial
devotion, apart from the love of parents, serves the state. Such a

Confucian idea is in accord with modern thought, which conceives of filial piety as 'fides', faith, which pertains to the extra-familial, i.e. political life among the Romans. Likewise, Lewis and Short subscribe to the notion of piety (*pietas*) as dutiful conduct towards the gods, one's parents, relatives, benefactors and country.[32]

5 Filial piety plays the role of religion. *Hsiao Ching* (*The Classic of Filial Piety*), a compilation of conversations between Confucius and his disciple, Tseng tsan contains religious elements, but becomes popular. The *Li Chi* (*The Record of Rites*), a compendium of forty-six short works, claims to contain Confucius's own words and is said to have been compiled in the first century BC. Both these books attest to the religious content of filial piety in Confucianism. This religious factor has its rituals, its moral code and all the paraphernalia of religion, save one distinctive feature, that is, a body of ordained priests. Yet in every family, the head, or the older generation, enjoys the status and plays the role of a priest. Regarded as 'the son of Heaven,' in literal terms, the emperor is the high priest, ordained by Heaven. To reduce common people to obedience and tractability the emperor resorts to filial piety, which is believed to be the most holy obligation which it is man's life-long duty to discharge.

We must bear in mind that though filial piety is connected with ancestor worship, it is clearly distinguished from the latter. First, filial piety dispels the complex of religious fear or awe of the dead which is characteristic of most worship of the dead and supplants it by the higher religious motive of gratitude. Second, filial piety provides common peoples with a religion which the poorest of them can profess as effectively as the Son of Heaven or any official. The following words of Confucius may well form the essential basis of filial piety:[33]

> Filial piety is the root of moral power in man. His trunk and limbs, his hair and skin are received from his father and mother, and the beginning of filial piety consists in his not daring to injure them. To establish his moral character, to walk in the right way and to extend his good name to later generations, thereby satisfying his father and mother, this is the final accomplishment of filial piety.

The idea of life-long gratitude is contained in the *Li Chi* (*The Record of Rites*) and throws into relief the stories of famous filial sons and devoted daughters-in-law. When the mother-in-law was pining for fish to eat in the depth of winter, her daughter-in-law, a young woman, lay down on the ice of a pond, baring her breast to melt the ice in the hope of catching the fish which might accidentally swim up to the hole. Her hope was met with reward. This story shows that Nature smiles on those who entreat it with sometimes miraculous results, and those who persevere in filial love, self-imposed sacrifice and devotion.

In connection with the religious nature of filial piety, Confucius attached a prime importance to the three years of mourning for parents, whereas he insisted on an unfailing vital need for filial duty to parents while they are alive. He said:[34]

> Filial piety urges that, during the life of parents, one should not go
> far away, or at least that the place one goes to should be known to
> the parents and that one should only be there with their consent. As
> long as one has one's parents, one must ask their advice before any
> undertaking is attempted, and only act with their approval. A pious
> son should always have retained in his memory his parents' exact
> date of birth in order to rejoice at their longevity and anticipate
> their death with becoming grief.

This explains a son's love for his parents. During their lifetime, the parents must be served as the rites decree, and after their death they must be buried, and then posthumous offerings must continue to be made to them as the rites decree.[35]

Uneducated Chinese think that the dead are dependent on the living for sustenance and support. It is thus essential that men and women leave behind them offspring, borne or adopted, to make sacrifice to them. With regard to ancestor worship, just as the lineage is not the family writ large, the worship is performed in the home by people who are related to the dead whom they have known in life. At all levels of lineage, the sentiments required by the kinship system are expressed in the course of religious acts.

In fact, Confucius did not form a religion and, as a result, indicates, rather, a way of life, his immediate followers were agnostic. However, he embodied quasi-religious ideas in three aspects of filial piety. (1) One is taught not to move one step without thinking of one's parents. (2) The memory of parents replaces the reverence for a deity seen in other religions; conduct is to be guided by a sense of pleasing ancestors. (3) Morality is derived and diffused from the sense of reverence and love for one's parents. He who loves his parents hates no man; he who reveres his parents is discourteous to no man. It is in this tenet that the religion of Confucianism lies. The religious beliefs of ancient China, that is, Heaven and gods of mountains and rivers, are instilled into this new religion. As Judaism survives, through the Old Testament, in Christianity and co-exists with it, so the old religious ideas and practices of ancient China were perpetuated through the ancient pre-Confucian classics and taught by the Confucian school.[36] When emperor Wu Ti of the Han dynasty (140–87 BC) elevated Confucianism to the status of the national religion of the empire, it had embodied the traditional beliefs and superstitions of ancient China, which Confucius and his adherents attempted to eradicate or to purify.

6 Filial piety never implies a blind obedience to one's parents, nor serves them as a pretext for perpetrating unrighteousness.[37] Confucius said: 'A father has a critical son'. This suggests that one may and ought to reason with one's parents when their orders conflict with righteousness, such as orders to commit crimes or tell lies. In such circumstances a blind obedience would be deleterious to parents and run counter to the true spirit of filial piety. Having stressed the nature of filial piety, Confucius added: 'In serving his parents, a son may remonstrate with them but gently; when they do not incline to follow his advice, he shows an increased degree of reverence, but does not abandon his purpose'.[38]

Chu Hsi made comments on the passage and said that when the son sees his parents' faults, he is under an obligation to expostulate with them gently and humbly. But the parental refusal to acquiesce in the son's advice does not allow sons freedom from filial devotion. Later, when an opportunity occurs, that is, when the parents are more favourably disposed, the sons are obliged to give their parents advice again, even at the risk of arousing the parents' anger and of being well beaten. In this lies true respect and piety. Hsiao Ching says: 'If a father has a son who dares to admonish him, the son would not act against principles'.[39]

In view of the intensity of filial piety and the keen parental interest in their children, one is likely to raise the question: 'Is there any conflict between the state and the family in terms of loyalty and allegiance?' The duke of Yeh said to Confucius: 'People think it right that if his father steals a sheep, the son will testify against him.' Confucius replied: 'Among us the upright act quite differently. The son shields the father, and the father shields the son; we see this as upright.'[40] Confucius subscribed to this idea that the mutual protection on the part of parents and sons is consonant with human nature and thus has the upright inherent in it. When Shun's blind father killed a person, Shun carried the body away and retired to a hiding-place by the sea; his love for his father prevailed over justice. To keep an act secret is different from telling lies. *The Analects of Confucius* say: 'The father conceals the misconduct of the son'. The word 'yin' in this context means 'concealment' and implies no lies, but a retreat from the public office. Chu Hsi, however, criticized this point and said that though filial piety was emphasized, rectitude must not be abandoned. According to the account in *Tso Chuan*, Chou Yu of Wei State murdered his ruler, Hwan. The people of Wei put Chou Yu to death in Puh. Shih Hou, the son of Shih Tseuh was involved in this conspiracy. Shih Tseuh, the minister of Wei, said: 'These two men, Chou Yu and Shih Hou, are the real murderers of my prince, and I venture to ask that you, the people of Ch'en, will instantly take the proper measure.' The people of Ch'en made them prisoners and requested Wei to manage the rest. In the ninth month, the people of Wei sent Chou, the superintendent of the Right who put Chou Yu to death at Puh, and Shih Tseuh sent his steward, Nou Yang Chien who put his son, Shih Hou, to death in the capital of Ch'en. A superior man may say: 'Shih Tseuh was a minister without blemish. Shih hated Chou Yu with whom his son was art and part, and did not he thus illustrate that great righteousness prevails over affection?'[41]

Confucius did not believe that the interests of the family and the state were basically opposed. It was in the family, Confucius held, that the individual learned those attitudes of obedience and co-operation, and gained the experience in socialized activity, which make it possible for him to be a useful citizen or official.

In like manner, the bounden duty of the son towards his parents gives way to loyalty to the state. In the T'ang dynasty, during the reign of Tien Pao (AD 713-42),[42] An Lu-shan rose to the emperor's good graces and was a commander in the repression of the raids of the Tartars. An was so successful that he was ennobled as a duke. This no doubt led him to rebel against the emperor and usurp his throne. While the emperor was compelled to flee to the Szechuan province, An boldly proclaimed himself to be the first emperor of a new dynasty. The rebellion, however, was short-lived and soon crushed, and An was assassinated by his own son. This story bears out that loyalty to the emperor and the state outweighs filial devotion.

It can be further urged that since filial piety is the root of virtue,[43] it is also the root of morality. The essence of morality is expressed in the word 'ought'. That is to say, morality is what is prescribed as due from an individual to society as a whole or a state as well as to the members of the family. It is within the family, one of the social sub-systems, that children are bound to afford obedience and help to their parents, from whom they receive comfort, loving care, protection, security, teaching and food. The word 'ought' reflects what is felt as a natural obligation on both sides, parents and children, dictated by nature and verified by experience. Bad parents are as entitled to filial piety as good parents.[44]

Piety involves reciprocal relationships compounded of reciprocal sentiments[45] and thus constitutes the mandate of morality, which embodies traditional rules of conduct. Morality, in this sense, is understood in its objective aspect, while its subjective aspect is a sense of 'ought' fostered by observance of these rules. The obligation is not only limited to piety in the family; it also imposes due loyalty and service on the family members towards the state. *Shu Ching* says: 'It is you who are possessed of excellent virtue, filial and respectful. Being filial, and friendly with your brethren, you can display those qualities in the exercise of government'.[46]

The above description of stories and the classical texts shed light on the relationship between the family and the state in the context of filial piety. There is no conflict between these two systems. In the case, however, of conflict, people are expected to attach greater importance to the state than the family. This conflict appears in a common saying: 'It is difficult to realize loyalty and piety simultaneously'. There are voluminous classical texts pertaining to the question under consideration, but as they are beyond the scope of our investigations we have left them out of account.

7   Regarding filial piety and the doctrine 'tzǔ', the word 'tzu' means 'tender', 'kind', 'gentle' and applies especially to parental tenderness. This notion of tenderness or lack of it is applicable to one's children and grandchildren as well. It is the Confucian ethic that between parents and children there should be mutual affection, that is, parental love or affection for the children is proportional to filial piety. One of the Confucian axioms states: 'a kind father makes a filial son'. Hence filial sons are bound to avoid situations which are liable to forfeit the parents' reputation for kindness. On the ground of such an ethic Confucius reproached his disciple Tseng tzǔ for his imprudence. On one occasion, Tseng tzǔ had allowed himself to be beaten unconscious by his father. The Master told his disciples that Tseng tzǔ was wrong not to escape from his father's violence. For had he allowed himself to be killed, he would have been guilty of gross filial impiety in forfeiting his father's righteousness; and, what is still more serious, his father would have been held responsible for killing a subject of the emperor. Even though Tseng tzǔ did obedience to his father, whenever he risked his

life, he would find it difficult to explain away his temerity. It seems that the Confucian reprimand of Tseng tzǔ contradicts what he said elsewhere that should a parent punish his son or beat him until blood flows, he is not supposed to murmur. In practice, this is not enforceable. There is a conflict of opinion here.

The social relations of father and son and mother and son are a compromise between paternal discipline and filial respect, and maternal tenderness and filial affection. This idea has been touched on previously. In the Chinese family system, children cherish their mother and respect their father. Loving attention and fondness are the distinguishing qualities of the mother in contrast to the austerity of the father. In conventional terms the word 'tzu', 'the tender or gentle one' refers to the mother, while the word 'yen', 'the grave or severe one', refers to the father. However, this must not be taken too literally to imply that the father is invariably unkind and stern. Chinese parents have the reputation of over-indulging their children. The father is popularly spoken of as the 'severe one', which, however, does justice to the Confucian ethic 'should the father spare the rod, he would spoil the child.' The mother, on the other hand, is felt as a centre of tender-heartedness, one to whom children can always come in sickness, hunger, or trouble of any sort. We do not deny that some Chinese parents were held in disgrace in the past for their female infanticide. It arose from penury rather than from their abhorrence of female children. Parents might have felt that it would be better to destroy female babies than to see them suffer torture from starvation. Nevertheless, the laws of the Ming and Ch'ing dynasties forbade female infanticide and, as a result, bear witness to the decrease of this infamy.

The relation between parents and children is considered important and sacred in every society, yet the degree of the sacredness varies with different societies. The following story, compiled from the romance of *Three Kingdoms*[47] (about AD 200) is intended to illustrate the predominance of parental and filial ties over political intrigue. It is narrated in Chapter 54 of the first volume under the title 'The Dowager Marchioness Sees Her Son-in-Law Liu at the Temple, who took a Worthy Consort.'

Sun Chuan, the leader of Wu State (about AD 200) contrived to eliminate Liu Pei, his rival for the empire. Sun plotted to lure Liu to Wu by means of a feigned proposal of marriage to his younger sister. The machination was that after Liu Pei, a recent widower, arrived in Wu, he should be confronted with the demand for the return of the city,

Chingchow, and, on his refusal, be taken prisoner and killed. However, to the surprise of Sun Chuan, the news of a possible royal wedding reached the royal mother, the Dowager of Sun. She at once summoned her son, Sun Chuan, and sent her servants out into the town to see what was going on. Having been informed that the whole town knew of the coming wedding, the Dowager was terribly shocked, so that when Sun arrived, he found his mother beating her breast and weeping bitterly.

'What disturbs you so much, mother?' asked Sun Chuan.

'You have treated me as a nonentity,' said the Dowager.

'Please speak out plainly, mother,' said he, 'What is this great sorrow?'

'When a son is growing,' she said, 'he takes a wife, and when a girl is old enough, she goes to her husband; that is right and proper. But I am the mother and you ought to have told me that your sister (my daughter) is to become the wife of Liu Pei. Why did you keep me in the dark? It is my right to promise her in marriage.'

'There is no such marriage', said Sun. 'It is just one of the ruses of Chou Yü to get hold of the city of Chingchow. He has resorted to this means to inveigle Liu Pei to hold him captive until Chingchow is restored to us'.

'You feeble strategists,' she said. 'You cannot retake the city Chingchow save by using such a disgraceful and shameful strategem!'

'Arrange that I may look at Liu Pei', she continued. 'If he displeases me, you may work your will on him. But if he satisfies me, I shall simply let the girl marry him.'

Sun Chuan was above all things pious and at once agreed to what his mother said. When the Dowager saw Liu, she was so well satisfied with him that she gave the girl consent to marry him. Faced with such an unexpected predicament, Sun Chuan was struck dumb with shock because he could not, and would not, do anything that might agitate his mother's feelings.

The story in the *Three Kingdoms* throws light on political intrigue rather than filial piety. Nevertheless, in describing the way the plot of Sun Chuan was foiled, the author must have instinctively sensed that the parental relationship was so sacred and inviolable that it must be respected even at the cost of the political purpose. To be otherwise or to act against the wish of the Dowager would be regarded as flouting filial piety.

In *Shui Hu Chuan – All Men are Brothers*[48] – (a thirteenth-century novel) the kind of filial devotion that Confucius demanded towards one's loving mother was dramatically depicted. The keen anxiety of the noble robbers was about their parents. When the foes of the robber chieftain, Sung Kung-ming, plotted to lure him out of the fortress, they forged a letter informing him of his father's death. Sung immediately left for the funeral.[49] Another robber experienced many perils to make his visit to his mother possible. When the victim of the robber attempted to arouse his compassion, he spoke of his old mother rather than of his children and wife, and the robber, thinking of his own mother, was moved and showed mercy to the victim.[50] Both tales emphasize the deep 'mother–son' relationship.

The term 'filial piety' often connotes the idea 'ti', which conveys the behaviour of a dutiful younger brother. The Confucian doctrine requires that a youth should do his best to fulfil, at home, his filial duties to his parents (hsiao), and, abroad, his brotherly duties to his elders (ti). Such an ethic is considered not only as requisite for the function of a refined personality, but also as contributory to good government. *The Book of History* points out: 'You fulfil your filial and brotherly duties and render your service to the government'.[51] Likewise, Mencius has spoken most emphatically about the subject as follows: 'The path of duty is near, but some people seek what is remote;'[52] the fulfilment of duty is easy, but some people seek what is difficult. 'If every person would love his parents, and respect his elders and superiors, the whole world would be peaceful.'[53] The text is made more intelligible in the following paraphrase: The path of duty is, in fact, near, but some people are inclined to neglect the duties that are immediate to seek what is remote. The fulfilment of duty is, in fact, easy, but some people are inclined to neglect the duties that are plain to seek what is difficult. If every person loved his parents and respected his elders and superiors to whom respect is due, the whole world would be peaceful. Chu Hsi said that love for parents and respect for elders and superiors are the easiest duties; and it is in these two duties that the nature of man lies. Nevertheless, some people, forgoing the easy duties, seek the difficult ones.

The above two passages convey the same ideas. A political organization or a community is composed of multiple constituent units, that is, individuals. If every person plays his part in serving the community, it will function well. Yet the necessity of playing one's part requires that one must first of all attend to one's immediate duties. This being neglected, it would be meaningless to talk about the fulfilment of others that are of a more unresolvable nature.

One may ask: Does the word 'ti' refer also to sisters? If there are brotherly duties, are there also sisterly duties? Arthur Smith levelled criticism at the Confucian doctrine, which has omitted to mention daughters, weighted everything in favour of the sons, and degraded the wife to an inferior plane. The absence in Confucian doctrine of an account of the duties of wives to husbands and vice versa is also criticized.[54]

It is difficult to agree with Smith's opinion. In teaching the fulfilment of filial duties the Confucian doctrine makes no discrimination in sex. Filial piety, being a virtue to be practised by one's children, sets up no sex limitation. The Confucian teaching 'Honour thy father and thy mother' is equally applied to sons and daughters. More clearly still would the need of performing filial duty be imposed on daughters when sons are not available.

It is said that Hua Mu-lan lived during the fifth century AD under the Liang dynasty which ruled in the South, with its capital Nanking; others claim that she was a subject of the Wei dynasty in the North, which ruled from AD 387–557. The story is that Mu-lan was living with her family, which consisted of father, mother, a young sister, Mu-nan and a little brother. She set an impressive example of filial piety. As a substitute for her conscripted father, who was old and ill, she left home disguised as a man, and fought for twelve years in the army. Of her companions, none suspected her sex, and her chastity was preserved. When the fighting was over, she came to see the emperor. He asked her what reward she would like to receive. 'My ardent desire is', she said, 'to return home'. At home, she threw off the armour and once more wore a skirt. The Mu-lan poem is sung as follows:[55]

The Mu-lan Poem

chih chih, once more chih chih
Mu-lan at doorway weaves.

Do not hear sound of shuttle loom,
Hear only maiden's sighs, moans.

Ask maiden: 'Of what do you think?'
Ask maiden: 'What do you now recall?'

Maiden does not dare to think,
Says: 'Nothing do I now recall.

'Saw last night army list,
The Ko Han widely conscripts men.

'Army list ten and two rolls,
Each roll, each roll, bears father's name.

87

Filial piety and kinship

'Honourable father has no grown son,
Mu-lan has no elder brother.

'Am willing to prepare, offer price, for saddle-horse,
Will, in place of honoured father, march'.

. . . .

Sunrise leave Yellow River, start;
Sunset reach Black Mountains Peak.

No longer hear honoured father, loved mother calling-daughter sound;
Hear only, on Swallow Hills Barbarian horsemen ride: thud, thud.

Pace ten thousand li with weapons-of-war machine,
Cross hill of Frontier Pass as if on wings.

Breath of Dark North clings to gold broadaxe,
Light of Han Country reflects from Linked-iron clothes.

Great generals in one hundred battles die,
Strong soldiers in ten years return home.

Returned-home come before Heaven's Son.
In Audience Hall sits Heaven's Son.

For ten and two years statagems, loyal efforts, have continued,
Above One bestows one hundred, one thousand fiefs.

Ko Han asks what I desire?

Mu-lan cannot use official rank,
Would borrow bright courser to go one thousand li.

'They send me, "a youth", home to old village.

'Honoured father, loved mother, hear daughter has come:
Go out from walled village to meet and escort.

'Younger sister hears elder sister has come;
Within door rearranged make-up and rouge.

'Little brother hears elder sister has come;
Grinds knife rhr, rhr, hurries towards pig and sheep.

'Open my door in Eastern Pavilion
Sit on my bed in Western Room.

'Take off my fighting days clothes,
Put on my olden days skirt.

'Within door arrange a cloud head-dress,
Before mirror stick yellow flowers in hair.

'Go outdoors, meet my "fire companions";
Fire companions hesitate, startled.

'Together we marched for ten and two years,
Never knew Mu-lan was a woman young person.

'Foot of male hare pads to Dark North,
Eyes of female hare dart hither, thither.

'Two hares run in near-by field,
How know which is male, which is female?'

The apparent misunderstanding of the Confucian doctrine may arise from equivocal pronouns in the Chinese language. The word 'son', as was previously stated, seems to mean only a 'male' child. In effect, however, a thorough examination unmistakably bears out that the same word refers to 'daughter' as well, i.e. sibling of both sexes, because it originally denotes 'descendant' or a 'child' without any modifier.[56] Similarly the word 'brother' sometimes means equally 'sister'. A passage in the Confucian *Analects* lends support to the argument. The Master says: 'Kung Yeh chang can be given a wife. Although he was put in bonds [in prison] he had not been guilty of any crime.'[57] Again Confucius allowed his son tze (literally it means 'son' a male child), that is, his daughter, to be married to Kung Yeh chang.[58] Elsewhere, Confucius gave Nan Yung, the daughter of his own elder brother (called Meng Lang), as a wife. Here again, the word 'tzǔ' (male) means the daughter, not the son.[59] With regard to the word 'brother', referring to the female, the following example is found in Mencius: 'The wife of Mi Tzǔ and the wife of Tzǔ Lu are brothers [hsiung ti].'[60] Thus the criticism raised by Smith is devoid of foundation. For if he holds that a female child is just one member of the family among others, and that the family system does not only embrace male children, he brings no convincing argument to rule out the role of a female member in filial duty. Here again, if social scientists were to inquire into the social function of the female, they would discover that she is obliged to perform the same filial duties as a male child. Just as Anglo-Saxons recognize the existence of women in spite of their using 'mankind' to describe the human race, the use of the pronoun 'he' by the Chinese should not lead one to think that only the male sex is meant.

8 Regarding filial piety in the relation of husband and wife, the critique made by Smith that the doctrine of filial piety relegates the wife to an inferior status is misleading. For her status as 'daughter-in-law' is simply assimilated to that of her husband; this assimilation involves no inferiority. It is the custom that, on the marriage of their son, the parents, in recognition of the bride as a successor to the mother's position in the family, concede the new couple their best room, as the father's parents once did, when he was married. The wife living with her husband's parents should be subservient to her parents-in-law and respect their wishes in the same way as her husband does. Mencius supports this obligation and says:[61]

> At the capping of a young man his father admonishes him. At the marrying away of a young woman, her mother admonishes her, accompanying her to the door on leaving, and cautioning her with these words: 'You are going to your home; you must be respectful; you must be careful. Do not disobey your husband'.

The rule for women is to be in compliance with their husband.

If the husband is compelled to earn his living away from home, the wife would, if the distances were not too great, visit her husband's parents as often as possible, especially when the latter have reached an advanced age and have no younger children to have recourse to. Thus the criticism that Confucius omitted the duties of wives to husbands and vice versa is unsound. *The Book of Odes* reads: 'Harmony with wife and children is as sweet as the music of the lute or the harp. When concord prevails among brothers, life is delightful; conduct thus thy family and be happy with thy wife and children'.[62] In praising this ode Confucius said: 'This will make the parents happy'.[63] The *Li Chi* says:[64]

> The ancient enlightened kings made it a rule of government to set an example of respect, i.e. showing affection to their wives and children. There are good reasons for this because the wife forms the principal link of parental relation, whereas the children form the succeeding links of it.

Elsewhere Confucius said:[65]

> The constant duties of all humans in social relations are five, and the requisite virtues for their fulfilment are three. These five duties are those between sovereign and subject, between parent and child,

between husband and wife, between elder brother and younger brothers, and between friends.

The philosophy of these human relations is benevolence, i.e. sympathetic conception of those duties, and courage, i.e. vigorous application of one's mind towards these duties, while the sole means of attaining these virtues is to be true to one's soul.[66] Mencius has dwelt on this subject as follows:[67]

Between parent and child, there should be affection; between sovereign and subject, there should be righteousness; between husband and wife, there should be respective mutual duties; between elder and younger brothers, there should be fraternal kindness and respect; between friends, there should be sincere fidelity.

The idea of mutual devotion between husband and wife is expounded in one of the passages in *The Book of Rites*. This passage runs: 'A woman when young or unmarried, follows the father, and in widowhood, follows her son'.[68] We must note that the last part of the passage has often been mistaken for the 'manus' which keeps the woman under perpetual guardianship. What is really meant is that a woman who seeks advice should turn to her father and, on his death, to her elder brother, then to her husband and last to her son.

We, of course, concede that the Chinese husband always leads the wife according to a common saying: 'The husband sings, the wife follows'. This is reminiscent of the command of the Bible: 'Thy [woman's] desire shall be to thy husband, and he shall rule over thee.'[69] As a result of this common saying, whatever the duty, for example, filial piety, the husband discharges, the wife has no alternative but to follow suit. More than in ordinary filial obedience, the husband must show filial piety in case of conflict between his parents and his wife, in which he must side with his parents, much to his wife's chagrin.

The duty of filial piety is not in any way attenuated by Christian principles, which require a man when he marries to leave his father and mother and cleave to his wife. Chinese people would think that to cleave to the wife need not entail parting company from the parents, nor would attachment to the parents inevitably diminish their affection for the wife. Here again, the injunction which aims at separation from parents rather than keeping them company is not incompatible with the notion of filial piety. The verse 'shall a man leave father and mother, and cleave to his wife' appears only once in the Bible, whilst the words 'honour thy father and thy mother' are reiterated five times.[70] Further, to say that Confucianism obliges man to cleave to his father and mother and to compel his wife to do the same is a misunderstanding. Since the husband and wife are but one person, the wife follows her husband as a matter of fact. The above Confucian teaching obviously conforms to the following Christian doctrine: 'Husband and wife are one person, or they are no more twain, but one flesh'. It is interesting to contrast the Confucian doctrine of filial piety with that in Christianity, but this is out of the focus of our discussion. There seems to be a conflict, in terms of filial piety between husband and wife, since the husband must show filial piety to his parents at the expense of his wife. But in fact, in view of the 'oneness' or indivisibility of husband and wife, the latter is under the moral obligation to show the very same filial duty to her parents-in-law that her husband does. This reflects Confucian ethics. *The Book of Rites* (*Li Chi*) says: 'Day and night do not disobey the commands'.[71] What is the duty of the wife is clear from these passages. It is the superiority of man over woman that underlies the relations between a man and a woman in traditional China. The wife takes her low position for granted and accordingly she does not feel she is mistreated when she sees that her husband takes sides with his parents. In this context, tensions and conflict between husband and wife do not seem to develop. Furthermore, to serve her husband's parents is the unshakable duty of the wife. Failure to do so often results in severance of the relationship between parents-in-law and daughters-in-law and in divorce as well. *Li Chi* states that: 'When a daughter-in-law is disobedient and unfilial, her parents-in-laws should instruct her; when she is obstinate, her husband should divorce her.'[72] We learn from the book *The Table Talk of Confucius* that Tseng Shen divorced his wife because she failed to cook a pear well for his parents.[73] In the first century AD, that is, the Han dynasty, Chiang Shih divorced his wife because she was too slow to fetch water from the river to satisfy her mother-in-law's thirst.[74] Liu Huan, in the Han dynasty, repudiated his wife because some dirt from a pair of shoes hung on the wall dropped on her mother-in-law's bed.[75] To press home this similar point, the *Li Chi* says that a son should divorce his wife, in spite of his fondness for her, if she incurs his parents' displeasure.[76] Lan Chih, in the early third century AD, and the wife of Lu Yü were very much loved by their husbands, but they were compelled to leave them because of their falling into disgrace with their mothers-in-law.[77] The right to divorce a wife merely on the grounds that she is disliked by her parents-in-law is upheld by the greatest scholars. The filial duty the husband is obliged to perform to the satisfaction of his parents is a moral principle or 'propriety', the stringency of which is reinforced by some passages from the Chinese classics. Those who evade this duty infringe a moral principle. In contrast, the Mosaic Law (Deut.24:1) prescribed that a husband should give his wife a 'bill of divorce' if he discovers in her some uncleanliness (apparently some sexual irregularities). This injunction shows that the individual rights of the husband are more important in the religion of Judaism than those of the wife, so that when they are violated, as in the case of his wife's adultery, she will be repudiated. In Chinese society, however, with its emphasis on filial piety, the satisfaction or dissatisfaction of the parents-in-law with their daughters-in-law will determine the fate of the latter.

In the New Testament the acceptance of the Gospel might cause the break-up of a home. A beloved husband or wife might have to be given up, and evidence of this can be derived from St Paul's permission to the new Christians to re-marry when his or her former partner refuses to acquiesce in the change; this is referred to as the so-called 'Pauline Privilege.'[78] The Christian social outlook resulting from the new attitude towards individual freedom might create a serious challenge to the Pauline Privilege. Even St Paul himself said that everyone should lead the life which the Lord has assigned to him and to which God has called him.

Filial piety is rooted in human nature in the view of Confucius, whereas with Christians it is more the result of their belief in God. Hence, while a new convert to Christianity is allowed to re-marry to safeguard his faith if his or her partner refuses to adopt the same faith a Chinese husband is justified in divorcing his wife when she displeases her parents-in-law. This illustrates the polarity between Christianity, a supernatural religion, and Chinese humanism: the former is established by a divine order and holds its followers accountable to God for their conduct, but the latter which originated from Confucian teaching, teaches men to follow the dictates of nature so that whoever deviates from them is liable to be ostracized and condemned by law because filial impiety is a serious, indictable offence.

It is true that in traditional Chinese society the father and mother are given more respect and consideration than the wife in the family as well as in society. This is for three reasons. First, the wife with her youth and charm attracts, as a matter of course, her husband more than his aged parents. Mencius said:[79]

When a man is young, he turns his thoughts to his father and mother.

When he begins to feel impressed by beauty, he turns his thoughts to a young and beautiful girl; when he is married and has children, he turns his thoughts to his wife and children; a man of great filial piety turns his thoughts to his father and mother for life.

These passages imply that a man naturally cleaves to his wife, while the parents, as they advance in age, are in danger of being neglected, unless there should be doctrines to maintain family equilibrium or stability; besides, a man's married life is long, whereas his life with his parents may be short. Second, it is only a matter of time before the wife herself attains motherhood. The temporary identification of her filial duty with that of her husband towards his parents only paves the way for the future; the doctrine of filial piety seems to work against her, but it is operating in her favour. Third, the doctrine of filial piety aims at protecting the aged parents and making them happy. As a result, an aged Chinese father or mother would seldom feel, to quote Goldsmith, 'remote', because their children always cleave to them; 'unfriendly', because he or she is constantly shown attention by children; 'melancholy', because he or she is not to live alone; and 'slow', because he or she is not shunned by the young in spite of his or her age and infirmity.[80]

There is a contradiction in Confucian doctrine which arises when the parents enjoin the son to repudiate his wife in spite of his love for her. At the end of the Han dynasty, in the middle of the Chien An period (during the reign of emperor Hsien Ti, AD 196–219), Chiao Chung-ch'ing of Lu Chiang hamlet, a petty clerk in the prefecture, had a wife of the Liu clan. Although she was obsequious to her mother-in-law, she was repudiated at the latter's instigation. In the hope that she would be reunited with her husband, she took an oath not to remarry. Unfortunately, when she returned to her natal home, her brother compelled her to be betrothed in order to shirk his responsibility of supporting her. To keep her word not to remarry, she drowned herself. When her husband, Chung-ch'ing, heard that his wife whom he held very dear had died with hatred, he plunged into grief and hanged himself from a tree in the courtyard. In pity for the sorrowful lot of the couple the people of the time told the story in the following ballad. Here I am presenting only a few verses:[81]

The Wife of Chiao Chung-ch'ing

BALLAD

A peacock flies East of South
Flies five li, flutters back and forth.

The young wife speaks to her husband:

'Ten and three could weave silk threads;
Ten and four learned to cut out clothes;
Ten and six hummed lines of Classics: Poems, Writings;
Ten and seven became wife of my Lord.
Now, in heart's centre, is often bitter grief.
My Lord had become Prefect's Clerk,
Preserving chastity, my passion never alters,
Lowly wife remains in empty bridal chamber.
We see each other, indeed, but rarely,
You come, can never bear to go , bear to go,
At cock-crow I enter loom to weave,
Nightly, nightly, do not attain to rest,
In three days cut off five rolls of silk.
Nor because my weaving is slow, but
Because they dislike me, Husband's Honoured
    Parents reprimanded.
In my Lord's household 'tis difficult to be a wife.
Unworthy One cannot endure being ordered, driven
    like a beast;
'Tis vain to stay: – useless!
Pray tell Honoured Father, Venerable Mother,
Time has come, I should be sent away, returned to
    father's household'.

Prefect's Clerk, on hearing this,
Ascends Guest Hall to tell the Mother:

'Son assists with salary that is but poor,
Yet has good fortune in possessing such a wife.
She knotted hair, came to my pillow, sleeping-mat;
Until descent to Yellow Springs, we shall join hands
    in companionship.
Three or two years she has lived with, served us,
From life's beginning, to its end, is a long time,

Wife has acted without deceit, disloyalty.
What are your wishes? Why is affection not deep?'

The Mother answers Prefect's Clerk:

'Why so much chatter, chatter?
This wife has no knowledge of Rites or honourable
    behaviour,
Herself takes initiative, assumes to discriminate.
My ideas have long been treasured in my bosom,
    heart is divided in hate.
You! do you have your own way?
In household to East is a virtuous maiden
Calls herself Lo-fu from Land of Ch'in.
Her body is admired, unequalled!

I, The Mother, will beg her for you.
Then can quickly send away this one;
Send her away, let her go, be cautious, do not
    keep her'.

Prefect's Clerk kneels a long time; speaks:

'I lie prostrate in order to inform my mother:
If this wife be sent away,
To end of old age, will not take another'.

The Mother, hearing these words,
In rage, pounds bed with her fist:

'Is miserable son without veneration?
How dare he utter aid-wife words?
Already, toward me, you fail in gratitude,
    rule of right conduct.
You will not follow me! . . . indeed?'

. . . .

The young wife says to Prefect's Clerk:

'What is the meaning coming from these words?
Both of us have suffered urging, forcing,
As my Lord acts, so Unworthy One will act.
At Yellow Springs, below, we will see each other.'

. . . .

This day oxen low, horses neigh.
Soon after yellow dusk, young wife enters
    bright green rent
At margin of stream, at margin of stream.
Silent, silent, all people are at rest.

    'My life is this day cut short,
    'Soul goes, body long remains'.

Grasps skirt, slips off silk shoes,
Raising body walks into clear green pool.

Prefect's Clerk hears of this happening;
Heart knows separation, division has come.
Turns his head, walks back and forth beneath
    a tree;
Hangs himself from the southeast branch.

Two households beg they be buried together,
Buried, together on Flower Mountain slope.
East, West, plant pine and cypress trees,
Left, right, sow seed of 'wu tunt' trees.
Branches, branches, join in canopy,
Leaves, leaves, interlock each other.
In the centre, fly a pair of birds,
Their names 'yuan yang' – birds of love –
Lifting its head, each to the other calls.
Nightly, nightly when Fifth Watch is reached,
Passers-by halt their tread, listen . . . .
Widowed wife rises, talks, is irresolute,
    doubts where to go.

This ballad couches the inexorable rules of the feudal system, which rules that a mother-in-law or father-in-law, be he or she right or wrong, must be pleased by his or her son and his wife. The Chinese would be in sympathy with the young couple and condemn the harshness and cruelty of the mother-in-law, but would think that the young woman, in failing to gain the affection of the mother-in-law, had broken the doctrine of filial piety. There is nothing in the poem to suggest that a revolt against filial piety would have solved the problem; the poem merely reflects an unresolvable conflict within the family in ancient China.

9 Herbert Spencer declared a religious system of some sort to be a necessary constituent of every society which has made any progress in civilization. Like secular religions formed by Saint-Simon and Comte, filial piety has been elevated to the status of a secular religion. This substitute religion is to be based upon a code of conduct suitable to make the family stable, a basis strengthened by natural emotional ties and by the supernatural concept of Heaven. As has already been indicated, the ideals of filial piety are present in many systems of morals and ethics. It is particularly instructive to compare the Chinese conception with its counterpart in Christian doctrine.

(a) Li Chih-tsao and Hsú Kuang-ch'i were leading converts of Mattheo Ricci, the pioneer Jesuit missionary. Li attempted to equate God with the Confucian concept of Heaven as head of the moral order, and he emphasized the convergence of the Confucian moral ideal with the Christian doctrine of self-perfection. In speaking of self-cultivation, Confucius said that one should endeavour first to serve one's parents and, through this medium, to know Heaven. Mencius emphasized the doctrine of self-cultivation and service to Heaven. Serving Heaven and serving parents are one and the same thing. In speaking of Heaven, the *Book of Changes* (*I-Ching*) says that the primal power which governs Heaven was the king and father of all.[82]

Further, the Buddhists abandon their homes and desert their parents and, in defiance of Heaven, hold the Lord (Di) in contempt, respecting themselves alone. In his book *The True Meaning of God*, Li Chih-tsao said that:

> 'Men perform the duty of serving their parents, but lack the knowledge that the Lord (Di) of Heaven is the parent of all; similarly, men are aware that a nation must have a rightful ruler, but are blind to the fact that "Di", who alone governs Heaven, is the supreme ruler'.

A man who does not serve his parents cannot be a true son. Filial impiety transgresses Confucian ethics and accordingly is judged as an offence and liable to criminal prosecution, whereas the negligence and defiance of parents violates the fourth commandment and is therefore a sin. By the commandment men are bound in their conscience, while the Confucian tenet imposes injunctions on people to avoid filial impiety. It is enjoined in the *Great Learning*: 'Whoever wishes to cultivate his person must bring a change of heart. Whoever wishes to rectify his heart first seeks to be sincere in his thought.'[83] This passage unmistakably makes the Confucian doctrine a mandate binding conscience, but it appears to be concerned only with the duties to parents and rulers. In Christianity, however, whoever infringes the commandments is a delinquent accountable for his breach with God. The Old Testament warns that crows would scratch the eyes of those who quarrel with their parents. Again the book *The True Meaning of God* pays particular attention to the question of good and evil, and of retribution in the form of blessings and calamities. The social virtue of filial piety has been highly esteemed by all the Chinese, and its observance has been inculcated into youth and children by examples. The twenty-four stories of filial devotion have been written to dramatize the good effects of obedience and respect and the bad consequences of their opposite.

(b) Christianity makes the relationship between God and man analogous to that between parent and child. The term 'fatherhood' is altered in proportion as the emphasis is laid, not upon the child's dependent and subordinate position, but upon his unconstrained affection. This shift of emphasis is accompanied by a change from fear to reverence in the interest shown in the child's attitude. In Confucian teachings on filial piety there is nothing greater than the reverential awe of one's father, the highest form of which equates the father with Heaven;[84] from the natural emotions of awe and affection, the philosophers have abstracted the concepts of reverence and love.[85]

Sin against filial devotion is conceived of by the Confucianists as an infraction of one of the general laws of nature. In the States of Ch'u a man reported to an official that his father had stolen a goat. The official, Ying, executed the son on the grounds that, while he was loyal to his ruler, he defied his father.[86] This view was held by Confucius, who attached greater importance to filial duty to a father than to loyalty to the state, and considered filial impiety a sin against nature. Dr Hsu reported a case where sin was against nature, that is, a father committed incest with his daughter-in-law. The son uttered the most abusive language against his father, while his wife bore a grudge against him. The father's will weakened noticeably and a serious conflict between the father and his son developed. It is said that incest was a religious offence against the ancestors of the sinner as well as against some other gods. This incestuous union caused irreparable disharmony in the household because the daughter-in-law had a jealous spouse, and so did the father. This sin exposes the existence of psychological disruptive force, i.e. jealousy.

Filial piety as described by Hsu is the corner-stone of Chinese social organization and is given the same meaning expatiated upon in the *Analects of Confucius* and other classics. It is also the measuring stick of all behaviour of the individual within the family and is held for the cult of ancestors. Filial piety, as interpreted by Confucians, means that children must please, obey and support their parents while alive, mourn and ritually serve them after their death. It is incumbent upon the male child, in the light of filial piety, to see that the ancestors' souls will be attended to from generation to generation.

Filial piety is associated with loyalty to the household, clan and affined relations, and the community; but the basic point of cohesion is the individual family and requires the clever device of division under the same roof to hold the joint household together. Nevertheless, what is more to the point is the patrifilial nexus in the Chinese family and descent system. 'The basis of kinship is patriliny', says Hsu, 'and the most important relationship is that between father and son'. The father has authority over his son, while the son has to respect and support his parents under all circumstances. Mourning and worship after the death of the parents constitute integral parts of the son's duties and responsibility. Moreover, in China the first-born son occupies a special position in the sequence of the generations; in former times, the eldest son was the direct propagator of his father's line and had the sole right to make sacrifice to deceased parents. This was also associated with the pre-eminent rights of the eldest son with regard to inheritance and the ancestor cult.

Chapter 4

Ancestral rituals and kinship

> The cult group in this (Greek and Roman) religion consists solely of persons related to one another by descent in one line from the same ancestor or ancestors.
>
> A. R. Radcliffe-Brown.[1]

Given the nature of filial piety in Chinese society, we shall consider the religious phenomena of ancestor worship in which filial piety plays a leading role. Kinship and the ancestor cult are prominent in the household and the economic organization among the Chinese. Parenthood and kinship are supposed to underlie the worship of their ancestors. It is the ancestral cult of the Chinese which has imposed agnatic kinship. Fustel de Coulanges said that the source of kinship was not the material fact of birth; it was a religious cult. He went on to demonstrate how succession and inheritance are interlaced with the domestic ancestor cult. However, before embarking on an exposition of ancestral worship, it would be appropriate to clarify the concept of the soul as it is conceived of in China.

Here three questions arise about the nature of the soul in Chinese thought. What is the Chinese conception of the dissolution or disintegration of the person at death, and how do they regard those who have departed? On what principles is the fate of the soul determined? I shall discuss these subjects and furnish illustrations but I should say at the outset that the Chinese are neither clear nor very explicit about the matter, and even Confucius himself evaded the question.

As I have said, Confucius avoided as far as possible speaking of the fate of the soul and the life after death. When he was urged to do so, he answered that this question was beyond the reach of human intelligence.

101

His reticence fits in with his total lack of eschatology. For Confucian religion is worldly, a religion of nature and harmony of life. He neither pretended to know nor did he care what would happen to the soul after death. But Chinese classics put forward two main concepts of the soul.

1 The dualism of the soul

The *Li Chi - The Record of Rites* teaches that the universe comprises two souls or breaths, called 'yin' and 'yang', or earth and heaven respectively, which are worshipped together. The 'yang' symbolizes light, warmth, productivity and life, and also the heaven from which all these good things emanate, while the 'yin' is associated with darkness, cold, death and the earth.[2] The 'yang' is subdivided into an infinite number of good souls or spirits, called 'shen', the 'yin' into evil spirits, called 'kuei' or spectres. It is these 'shen' and 'kuei' that animate every being and every thing. Equally, it is they that constitute the soul of man. *The Record of Rites* reads as follows: 'It is that man consists of the beneficial substance that composes the heaven and the earth of the co-operation of the "yin" and the "yang" and of the union of a "kuei" and "shen"'. Likewise, according to *Shuo Wen*, man comes into being through the union of the spirit with matter. When the vital spirit leaves the matter, each of the components returns to its source. Thence it comes that the 'kuei' is called 'return', while 'shen' (spirit) called 'hun', is immaterial, ethereal, or heaven itself from which it emanates, and it forms man's intellect and the finer parts of his character and virtues: 'kuei' or 'p'o', on the other hand, is thought to represent his less refined qualities, man's passions and vices derived from material earth. In birth these souls are infused and in death they are dispersed, the 'shen' returning to the 'yang' or heaven and the 'kuei' to the 'yin' or earth.[3] At death the body was laid on the ground to facilitate the return of the 'yin' element, while the 'yang' element was searching in the favourite haunts of the deceased, but especially on the house-top as the most elevated place.[4]

The character 'kuei' (ghost) is a symbol (return) of the vaporous silhouette of the deceased. The character 'kuei' has two meanings. First, etymologically, it imports the entry of a young woman into the family of her husband, the family to which she will belong, on which she will hereafter depend for her support and for which she will bear children. It is in this sense that the orthodox or non-sectarian interprets the character 'kuei'. Therefore, after death the deceased is dependent on his former family for maintenance of his afterlife, by offerings. Second, the character 'kuei' (return) means 'manes', the returned ones, returned for a time into peace, 'reality'. This is the great Taoist thesis. Again, the term 'kuei' is Taoist. In fact, the 'kuei', the deceased, are dependent on their posterity for the offerings and libations for which they long. The offerings and services are performed in two aspects: those intended to appease the 'yin' element of 'kuei', and those intended to propitiate the 'yang' element or 'shen' (spirit).[5]

2 The belief of the Chinese in the soul

It is difficult to point out what all the Chinese from the Chou dynasty until contemporary China really believe and teach as to the future existence and the fate of the soul. No consistent theory has been developed and enunciated by Chinese writers on the subject.

Confucius himself gave a very indefinite answer to the question as to the future destiny of the soul. Explaining the composition of man to his disciple Ts'ai O, Confucius said: 'Man is composed of two parts, one of which the substance is aerial, the other is the spermatic substance. Everyone dies. Then the corpse and the inferior soul go into the earth, and decompose there. The aerial soul, however, rises and is glorified for its merit'. The character 'ch'i', to breathe, employed to describe the substance of the superior aerial soul, indicates etymologically the 'vapour' which steams from hot boiled rice. In his study of the soul among the Lodagaba, Dr Goody has put forward the same point. The Lodagaba hold that a human being consists of two elements, the body (skin) and the soul or double (sie) for which the body acts as a home. To live literally means 'to breathe'.[6]

Tzŭ Kung, one of the disciples of Confucius, asked him: 'Are the dead endowed with knowledge, or are they destitute of it?' Having evaded further question, Confucius said:[7]

if I say that they are endowed with knowledge, filial sons will kill themselves in order to join their deceased parents. If I say they are devoid of knowledge, unfilial sons will not trouble to bury their deceased parents in propriety. Let us leave the matter alone; it is not of prime importance; after death you will know it.

The statement of Confucius: 'reverence the spirits as if they were

103

present'[8] evades its issue. For 'as if' does not mean that they are. He shared, in his attitude towards the state of the dead, the common conviction of provisional survival and extinction at some unknown date. He thus held that the obsequies of the recently dead should be properly performed, their survival being almost certain. Those long dead, he held, should not be deprived of offerings, supposing they were not perhaps yet extinct. He said:[9]

> To treat the dead as if they ceased to be our concern, and to let
> them sink into oblivion, would be inhuman. But to treat them as
> living would be irrational because they are not like the living any
> longer. Hence offerings of eatables are made to them in vessels of a
> disused, obsolete form; these vessels are themselves sacrosanct
> because they are peculiar to the glorious 'shen' spirit.

There is an early story (300 BC) which is relevant to Confucius's attitude to the supernatural. The widow queen of an emperor of the Ch'in dynasty (Ch'in Hsuan), ordered when she fell seriously ill, that, if she were to die, her lover, Wei Ch'ow-fu, should be buried alive with her. Being much disturbed by this honour, Wei asked one of the Ch'in officers, named Yung Nei, to reason with her, saying:[10]

> Either the dead maintain knowledge, or they are deprived of it. If
> they are deprived of it, what use would it be for your lover to be
> buried with you? If they still retain knowledge, the deceased king,
> your husband, must already be furious with you at your debauchery;
> do not run the risk of confronting your lover with him.

What underlies Confucius's indifference towards the spirits and his reluctance to offer them prayers, is his persistent emphasis on the aspect of human affairs and problems. Lu Hsin defends this apparent indifference by suggesting that spirits were so much a part of the culture in which he lived that Confucius would never have felt prompted to question them. But although he confessed their existence, he refused to speak of them, which marks the shift from deism to atheism in his thinking.[11] Also the writings of the philosophers of the Sung dynasty seem to cast much doubt on the subject, reminding us of the doubts of the Greek philosophers concerning the immortality of the soul.

The sentence written in the Sacred Records: 'when a man dies, the "hun" ascends and the "p'o" descends', implies that when this transformation has occurred, the soul becomes 'non-existent'.[12] In refuting Confucianism on the subject of the soul and ghosts, Moism argued that

Confucius upheld sacrifices and valued ancestor worship despite his doubts about the existence of the soul and ghosts or spirits. Confucius's statements are contradictory: in one place he said 'reverence the spirits as if they were present', whereas in another place he says 'the presence of the spirits is imperceptible, but real; although invisible, they are present'.[13] With regard to the 'manes' Confucius said:

> How powerful is the action of the manes, who have become 'genii?' One neither sees nor hears them but they are on a neighbourly footing with the living, and do not leave them. It is for them that men purify and clothe themselves, perform ceremonies and make ritual offerings. They are everywhere, above, to the right and to the left.

With reference to the Confucian view on the nature of the soul, Doolittle holds that the Chinese think that man has three souls, or spirits. One goes to his grave, another is established in the tablet by the soul-dotting rite, and the third passes into the underworld to undergo judgment, punishment, and usually rebirth. This seems to be in line with the Buddhist doctrine. The soul in the grave is attended during the yearly or twice-yearly visits to the tombs. It is served with food and drink of which the living partake so as to establish a communion between the dead and the living. The soul in the tablet remains in the household shrine until it is transferred to a new tablet in an ancestral hall. The soul which passes into the underworld needs the aid of the living in the form of material comforts and of intercession for its rebirth.[14] A passage from the *Li Chi* reads as follows: 'The spirit tablet was supposed to be a resting place for the spirit at the religious services in the temple. The deceased king was treated as a heavenly spirit and was deified'.[15] The spirits of dead ancestors which are thought to adhere to the tablet of the domestic temple or shrine include those of the recently deceased, but not those which have been dead for four generations. Addison holds that after the third or sometimes the fifth generation the tablets of the ancestor's soul or spirit are burned, or removed to ancestral halls belonging to clans.[16] At the domestic level the rites performed to the spirit of ancestors symbolize the rites of kinship solidarity in which ancestors are projected as agnatic foci, and the rites of 'memorialism' in which ancestors are attended to simply as forbears, independent of their status as agnatic ancestors of the worshippers. This point will be developed below.

We subscribe to the opinion of Dr Yang that the Chinese do not worship their ancestors in the way in which gods are worshipped because after death the soul is decomposed into 'kuei' and 'shen' (spirit), the latter having been reduced to its source - the 'yang' power. There are two levels of belief in ancestor worship belonging to the intellectuals and the mass illiterate population respectively. The opinion of Dr Yang represents the intellectual level of belief. The belief that the ancestors, if deprived of money and food, will become demons and afflict the living with illness does not appeal to Chinese intellectuals. Similarly, Addison has indicated that according to the theories of the highly sophisticated students of the classics the only proper attitude towards ancestor worship is an expression of complete devotion, gratitude and obedience to the memory of the ancestor; the actual existence of the ancestor has been denied. At the other extreme are the masses of peasants who believe in occasional retribution for neglect; they stress that a man who has died is not entirely finished.[17] Greeks and Romans honoured the memory of the dead by periodical sacrifices at the graves. The Jews also have a yearly visit to the grave, the so-called 'Jahrzeit'.[18] Their service in memory of the dead is part of their synagogical liturgy. On All Souls Day in the Catholic Church the supplications which are made to the souls of the faithful departed have the same symbolism and the same significance.

It should be noted, with regard to the above opinion of Dr Yang, that this issue is more complex than it may appear. For the illiterate Chinese worship their ancestors as gods and think that living they are men, when dead they are gods. This kind of ancestor worship gave rise to an unyielding controversy between the emperor K'ang Hsi and the Pope.

The oldest Chinese documents speak unequivocally of an Elysium where disembodied souls enjoy every satisfaction, but are reticent on the subject of purgatory and enduring punishment. The elaborate eschatology of Buddhism provides a vivid description of Amithaba's Happy Land of the West. Also the Chinese derive the concepts of purgatory and hell from the Buddhist doctrine of fictitious sufferings in endless reincarnations.

A belief in transmigration, which is one of the main tenets of Buddhism, has been held by a great many Chinese. Yet in respect of the ancestral cult the Buddhist doctrine has not been accepted without modification. The Buddhist denial of the existence of the soul in the transmigration complicates the question of posthumous reward or punishment.[19]

Taoism adopted Buddhist notions and developed its scheme of life and death, amplifying its description of renewed lives, which are understood to succeed death itself.[20] In the third and fourth centuries BC Taoism, under the auspices of which such inquiries concerning life and its connotations, the nature, motives and mysteries of existence had arisen, changed to a large extent to a system of idolatrous rites.[21] Licius, in the fourth century BC said: 'The living and the dead know nothing of each other's state'.[22] Chuang Tzǔ, in the third and fourth centuries BC asked: 'what should the dead know of the living and the living know of the dead? You and I may be in a dream from which we have not yet awaked'.[23] One of the aims of Taoism is the prolongation of life, or the transformation of life into a higher existence, which is to be attained by quietism, by regulation of one's breath and by using medicines.[24] Lao Tzǔ says that 'to a perfect man life and death are but as night and day, and cannot destroy his peace'. Again, Chuang Tzǔ states that: 'for the sage life means death to the life of seeming or reputation, of doing or action, of being or individual selfhood'.[25]

Wang Chung, a philosopher of the Sung dynasty (AD 960–1278), held a position mid-way between Confucianism and Taoism, and subscribed to the opinion that 'the dead do not become ghosts but are unconscious, and that sleep, a trance, and death are essentially the same'. He said that 'human death is like the extinction of fire. To assert that a person after death is still conscious is like saying that an extinguished light shines again. The soul of a dead man cannot become a body again'.[26]

However, Taylor argued that the worship of ancestors among the Chinese which begins during their life is not interrupted but intensified when death makes them deities. Manes-worship is not a rite of mere affection; the living need the help of the ancestral spirits, who reward virtue and punish vice.[27] Where Taylor's explanation falls short is that he does not attach importance to the affectionate aspect of the relationship between the dead and the living in the Chinese religious system. One must recognize, in the fate of the soul, a sensible relation which is explicable by reference to the condition in which the soul of the dead manifests itself to the living and some social circumstances; more explicitly, there is the 'retribution' connection between the social circumstances from the past behaviour of the dead, whose soul is now active, and the social circumstances drawn from the behaviour of other living persons.

Hsu holds that there are three classes of spirits:[28] (1) ancestral spirits;

(2) spirits of persons unrelated by kinship or marriage; (3) spirit officials in the world of spirits. The attitude of West Towners varies with these spirits. The first group of spirits is considered friendly. They help their own descendants as far as possible; their behaviour in life, as well as in the world of the dead, exerts influence on the fate of their descendants. The relations of the living with the dead are patterned upon that of the living with the living. More still, by glorifying the spirit of the dead, they set the standard for kinship relationships. This pattern determines the worldly attitude of all spirits and the wordly orientation of the majority of West Towners.

The second group of spirits, spirits of unrelated persons, may be indifferent or dangerous if they are offended. West Towners find it necessary to avoid offending these spirits. Ritual offerings to them must be made at the prescribed time, lest they may be annoyed and take it amiss. However, if ritual offerings are overlooked, retribution does not inevitably overtake the culprit, since special propitiatory rites may serve to pacify the angry spirits by showing submission to, and invoking, still higher deities than those offended. In Hsu's account, a cholera epidemic causing, a heavy death toll in the early part of 1942, is said to have been caused by the wrath of certain deities as a response to man's loose behaviour. This is in common with many Christian ideas. In averting the calamity, deities were invoked each day at a prayer meeting when rich offerings were made.

The spirits of officials, including those of ancestors and vagrants, are ranked in hierarchy in the manner of the official hierarchy in the world of the living. These spirits may be benign, malicious or helpful. The spirits of another culture are irrelevant. If a person died a violent death or drowned, or is no longer worshipped at the family altar or clan temple, his spirit will become a ghost and haunt the site of his death to fetch a living man as a substitute.[29] Suicide ghosts are particularly malignant.[30]

Graham is of the opinion that deceased ancestors, if they are deprived of money and food, will be relegated to the status of ghosts or demons and will molest the living.[31] Kulp points out that spirits can control human affairs according to their pleasure. If their descendants do not supply the necessities of life, the spirits will become angry and take vengeance upon the living by sending misfortune.[32] This concept may be well expounded by mortuary rites and popular stories. In the past as well as in contemporary China the people not only performed the ceremony of closing the period of mourning and cleansing the home but also sent the dead man away and cut him off formally from living. For he is dispatched by these rites and is abjured to turn away from the living.[33]

For Fei, the living must carefully perform those rites of ancestral cult. Misfortunes and sickness result sometimes from doing damage to the coffin shelter by selling land or houses.[34] Addison accepts the common belief among the Chinese that neglect of ancestors would inevitably bring disaster upon the descendants. However, he speaks of the retribution being called down by 'heaven' – by the spirit powers other than the ancestors.[35] Freedman states that there have been numerous reports of actual cases of misfortune being attributed to the vast pantheon of local gods upon whom the immediate vicissitudes of the family often depend.[36]

I give some instances of these kinds of circumstances as illustrations.

In 535 BC in the earldom of Cheng, the deceased Po-Yu, appeared several times to announce that on such and such a day he would kill such and such a person. The person thus designated died on that day. The celebrated politician and philosopher, Tzŭ Ch'an, having considered the case, advised the son of Po-Yu to make abundant offerings to his father's manes. The apparitions and assassinations stopped at once. According to Tzŭ Ch'an, when a soul has providers, it calms down and causes no harm; but if it starves, it plunders of necessity. Owing to its ruin, the family of Po-Yu ceased to make the offerings which reduced his soul to brigandage for survival. From the time that Po-Yu's son resumed the ritual offerings, its plunderings ceased.[37]

A ghost of a murdered person or of a suicide is believed to be particularly dangerous and revenging. The duke Ch'i was infatuated with an alluring woman, Wen Chiang, his half-sister, who was married to the duke Lu, and committed incest with her. Knowing that this crime was revealed, duke Ch'i commanded his son, Pong Sheng, to murder duke Lu for fear that he should seek revenge. The State of Lu lodged a strong protest demanding capital punishment for the murderer. To exonerate himself from this nefarious scandal duke Ch'i pronounced a verdict on the innocent Pong Sheng and ordered him to be executed. At the moment of his execution Pong Sheng inveighed against duke Ch'i, declaring that he would become an aggrieved ghost and seek vengeance upon him after death.[38] One day when duke Ch'i was hunting with his officers, he suddenly saw a pig-like animal, similar to a cow without horns. He was so terrified by such a monster that he went out of his mind and fell from his chariot. The animal took away one of his shoes.

Later when one of his officers rebelled against him, duke Ch'i hid himself under the bed. But the missing shoe betrayed his hiding place, and he was killed by the rebel.[39]

Another case is that of a woman's ghost haunting her kinsman after her suicide. In Chekiang province, Mukisin, the police constable, accumulated a considerable sum of money and obtained a post for his son, Ma Hoantchang, by bribery. Mukisin took a young concubine whom he loved very much, and, as he was dying, he spoke to his son of his will to make his concubine his heir. No sooner had Mukisin died than his son Hoantchang desired to exploit the young concubine. Hoantchang handed her money immediately, saying 'Depart without delay and don't come back.'

After the concubine returned to her own parents she refused to re-marry. Her little savings were quickly used. On 12 July she bought incense and other necessary objects for offerings as was customary on that day, and returned to Hoantchang's house to lament with the family. However, his wife gave the concubine a very cold reception and said rudely: 'Are you not ashamed to return after your expulsion?' In the morning when Hoantchang and his wife wanted to expel her, they found her hanged. Hoantchang hastened to put her body in a coffin and send it to her parents. Having been persuaded that suicide would bode ill for the house, Hoantchang sold it to a Mr Chang.

One night this woman appeared to Chang in the form of a ghost and wailed loudly. She spoke bitterly of Hoantchang and was indignant at his vile misconduct. Chang answered humbly: 'I bought this house from Hoantchang, having no intention of wronging you. Hoantchang and the perfect Wu must be responsible for their wickedness.' Hoantchang had been taken ill. On the same afternoon he died. The prefect Wu also died suddenly a few days later. The two families of Hoantchang and Wu were entirely destroyed. Thus the ghost of the suicide took revenge for injustice on Hoantchang and the prefect Wu.[40]

As to whether the ancestors are of a benevolent or a malicious nature, and whether they intervene in the interests of their descendants, Singapore Chinese assume that ancestors are thought to be interested in the family affairs of the living descendants.[41] If they can exercise the necessary influence on their supernatural world, they would intercede with a supernatural power on behalf of the descendants for blessings. Freedman's view appears to agree with what Hsu has found in West Town in terms of the nature of ancestors. He says that ancestors do not bring disaster to their descendants; on the contrary, they help the living.[42]

110

In Hangchow, Che Kiang province, Cheng Ling-shen woke up one morning, dressed and went out. After some time he came back and having locked himself in his room he appeared to be talking to some invisible person. Then he left home again. His family felt disquieted by the strange event. Suddenly a cooper brought him in unconscious. When he recovered consciousness, he told them what had happened. 'This morning', he said, 'while walking I met a man dressed in black. He said to me: "Go home and fetch what is necessary: I will take you to see some female water-spirits". On the shore of Hsi-Hu (West Lake) I saw far away, on the surface of the lake, azure palaces and beautiful girls singing and dancing. The man asked me which is more pleasurable, to enjoy the girls or to study for a degree. "Of course", I said, "to enjoy the girls". Then the man told me: "Jump into the water and you shall enjoy them". At the very moment I was attempting it, I heard a voice call out loudly: "Mind the step: It is an evil demon tempting you. Don't do it, don't do it". Looking round I saw it was my dead father in the water. Then the man in black jumped in and struggled with him. After a time, both of them disappeared'. Then a voice was heard from an invisible being: 'Isn't it written in the classics that a good man tries to edify others and a sage undertakes to make others intelligent? We who are drowned try to drown others and we who are hanged tempt others to hang themselves.'[43]

The following explanations can be gathered from the account I have given of the ancestors' interest in their living descendants. The good nature of ancestors arises from the adjustment between generations. This does not mean that conflicts, though of mild nature, do not exist within the family. (1) No open conflict is seen between the role of the father and that of his son in the family and in the wider society, except that there is a great deal of tension and strain because of the great power and authority of the father over his son. In a wealthy family the adult son inherits property and sometimes a title and in return he is expected to pay tribute to his father; poor sons, however, owe their parents their life and sustenance, and, in return for these benefits, support them in their advanced age; (2) there is a lack of strong matrilineal ties which could give the son outside connections and support him in opposition to the father as in many African societies; (3) there is infrequent polygamy in China, as opposed to most African societies where the possibility of tension between father and son results over conflict between co-wives. Concubinage among the wealthy is common in China, but since the concubine is of inferior status, the danger of tension referred to above is unlikely to take place.[44] (4) the Chinese know well that any external sign of hostility between parents and sons indicates a lack of family solidarity, and they are obliged to make their relationships better and live on good terms. There is no need for ancestors to be a coercive force to control their disobedient descendants.

That the neglect of ancestors will bring supernatural retribution means that the neglect of rites and norms of solidarity will cause moral decay and the eventual disintegration of the family. Ancestor worship serves as a uniting force of stability both within and beyond the family group and overlaps with social relationships. Also, it is on ancestral worship that the greater 'corporate' or 'we' feeling between ancestors and descendants largely depends. In making sacrifice to their ancestors, the illiterate Chinese believe that their ancestral spirits live in a world very similar to theirs, and are partially dependent on the contribution of their descendants. This contribution takes the form of periodically burning paper money and making offerings of food and drink.

The ancestral tablet

Our next discussion will be concerned with the ancestor cult or worship in the context of the location where the cult is performed and the paraphernalia of ancestral rites and the established forms of ancestral cult.

The ancestral ceremonies are performed in the family, in ancestral halls and at the tombs.[45] The ceremony was held during the four seasons[46] of the year in the temple or the hall of kneeling down and making obeisance to the wooden tablets on which the names of their ancestors are inscribed. As to its origin, it is said that Ting Lan who lived during the Han dynasty (about AD 25) was assumed to be the originator. While he was working in the field, his mother brought him some refreshments. Having tripped by accident against the root of a fir tree, she fell to the ground and died, whereupon Ting Lan took the same root from the tree and carved on it the images of his parents. If what Ting did was the origin of the ancestral tablet, apparently he did it unintentionally. Nevertheless, it is to him that the custom of worshipping deceased parents and ancestors under some visible symbol has been commonly attributed.

At the sacrifice, it is to the tablet that the filial son can attach his feelings of affection for the deceased. The 'Hsia' dynasty used a tablet made of pine so as to stimulate themselves; the 'Yin' dynasty used a tablet of the wood cypress (po) so as to urge themselves (po-ts'u); the

惠 山 祠 堂 圖

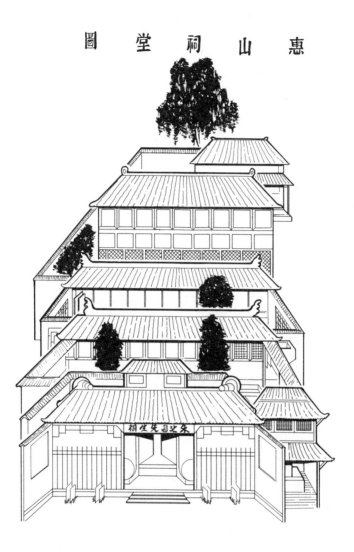

Figure 4.1 The main ancestral hall of the *tsu* of Chu in Kiangsu named after the first ancestor Lo-fu-king. From: Chu shih Tsung-p'u, ch. 2, 'Pictures of the Ancestral Halls', p. 1a.

Source: Hu Hsien-chin, *The Common Descent Group in China and Its Functions,* New York, Viking Fund Publications in Anthropology, no. 10, 1948.

113

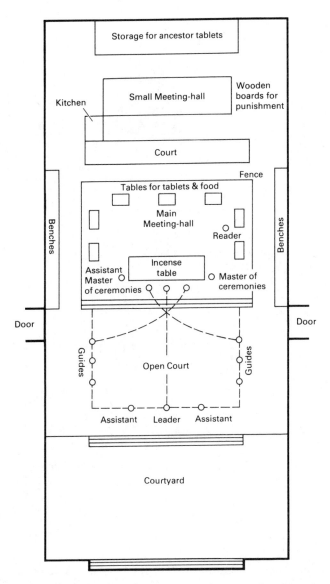

Figure 4.2 *Ancestral hall of the* Tsu *of Ch'u during the annual ritual*

Source: Hu Hsien-chin, *The Common Descent Group in China and Its Functions*, New York, Viking Fund Publications in Anthropology, no. 10, 1948.

'Chou' dynasty used a tablet of the wood chestnut (li) so as to inspire themselves with 'awe' (chan-li).[47] The tablet is of wood to resemble man in his growth and decay.

The ancestral tablet is simply a piece of wood, chestnut being the most orthodox; it varies in its size. It is twelve ts'un (inches) in height representing the twelve months, four ts'un (inches) in width denoting four seasons, and one inch and a half in thickness, standing for the twelve hours.[48] The best sort is made of fragrant wood, parts of which are elaborately carved. Some of the tablets cost a few pounds apiece. There are three pieces of wood, one being a pedestal, and the other two upright pieces.[49] The top is ranked like heaven, whereas the bottom is flat like earth. In a family temple the tablets are arranged on the shelves in chronological order, the number gradually increasing downwards, beginning with the founder of the family down to the last generations. On each tablet is inscribed the name of one or both heads of a family, with the number of the generation, and commonly the dynasty under which the individuals live.

Among the tablets of the dead, those of living persons who are advanced in age and of note in the family are set in their place, but they are distinguished by the use of red paper. The inscription is made with black ink, and the strip on which the characters are written is painted or varnished. The inscription is exemplified as follows:[50]

Mother's Tablet		Father's Tablet	
Hwang	(of the) Imperial	Hwang	(of the) Imperial
Ch'ing	Ch'ing (dynasty)	Ch'ing	Ch'ing (dynasty)
hsien	this illustrious	hsien	this illustrious
pi	consort	k'ao	completer of probation
li	expecting	shih	
		tso	sub-magistracy
		lang	
tsiang	to receive	wei	
jü	title of lady	ching	named complete virtue
jin		teh	
		shih	shrined
		Yung	eternal progress
		fah	
Hwang	Hwang	Hwang	Hwang
mu	mother		
Chen	Chen		
T'ai	noble	kung	Lord
Chün	family	fu	family
chi		chi	
shen	spirit's tablet	shen	spirit's tablet
chu	lord	chu	lord

The father's is thus: 'The tablet of Mr Hwang Yung-fah (late Ching-teh), the head of the family, who finished his probation with honour during the imperial Ch'ing dynasty, reaching a sub-magistracy'.

The mother's reads: 'The tablet of Madam Hwang, originally of the noble family Chen, who would have received the titled lady, and in the imperial Ch'ing dynasty became the illustrious consort of her husband'.

The spirit tablets are of different sizes for the domestic shrine and the ancestral hall. The tablets in the central hall are at least two or three times larger than those used in domestic shrines. They are placed in a niche, which is divided into shelves so that they are not all on the same level. The tablet, being called 'shen-wei', that is, the spirit's abode, is preferable to 'shen-chu', or divine lord. The meaning and purpose of the ancestral tablet is that when the decendants look on the tablet while offering sacrifices they might see their ancestors embodied in it. If they entertain such ideas, they would be considered pious in their sacrifices.

Ancestor worshippers have attached importance to the tablet in two ways. The first is that at a man's death, his bodily form can no longer be seen, but his descendants have a longing for him. For the satisfaction of this longing some visible objects must be used, which, being ever before their eyes, will keep the departed one in constant and vivid remembrance.[51] Tseng Tzǔ, the disciple of Confucius, said: 'Let there be careful attention paid to the performance of funeral rites to parents, and let these be followed, until long after their death, with the ceremonies of sacrifice'. Second, for fear of their departed ancestors being deprived of any settled place of abode, the descendants set up tablets in which their spirits may rest. Being aware that a mere piece of wood, as such, may not serve as the abode of the spirit, when the tablet is set up, some important personage is invited to dot, with red ink on a brush, the character 'wang' which then becomes 'chu', meaning the dwelling places of the spirits. By means of a living person or a personificator, the departed soul is called back. Before the dotting, the writer breathes upon the brush, using the following form:[52]

> The spirit rests in this wooden tablet
>> And the wooden tablet is spiritualized by its resting.
> The spirit and the wood together dwell
>> In ages of unending spring!

The breathing upon the brush conveys the idea of communion; the custom of dotting the tablet with the blood of the sons of the descended prevails in some parts as in the capital of the province of Kwangsi

(South-West China). It sets forth the notion of fellowship in a common life, and of a continuity which death itself is not capable of destroying.

The Chinese in all parts of the country see a close connection between the attending of ancestors and filial piety. They feel it their duty, in return for the gift of life and sustenance, to pay the seniors respect and support them during life. Such a duty does not come to an end with the death of the elders. They must carry on succouring their ancestors by tending their tablets and providing them with the necessities of the afterlife. Among the majority the dead have been thought to be dependent somehow on the living for sustenance and support. If the descendants fail to make offerings to the satisfaction of the ancestor's needs, the latter become hungry ghosts wandering in the world in search of food, and molest both other souls and the living. The controversy over whether the ancestors are malicious or benign has been discussed previously.

Prayer to the dead

I have dwelt upon the concept the Chinese have of the soul, the ideas and affections they have for it, and some of the actions which, they think, bring about the intervention of the spirit or ghost in human affairs. A brief consideration of some prayers addressed to ancestral spirits will be given now because they are used by Chinese only when they make sacrifice to ancestors.

For obvious reasons one expects that at ancestral sacrifices most of the prayers to the dead ancestors would be petitionary, and presumably the books of ritual provide well-formulated prayers for these occasions. However, there seems to be no set form of prayers. Like the North American Indians, the intellectual Greeks, war-like Romans and priest-ridden Egyptians, the ceremonious Chinese are punctilious in rendering religious homages to their departed relatives, and do what they can to pacify, to gratify and to honour their manes in the world of spirits.

The Confucianists live a prayerless life, whether with regard to God or to the spirits. However, Confucius confessed that he prayed for a long time. When he was very ill, Tzŭ Lu one of his disciples, requested permission to pray for him. Confucius asked: 'Is there such a thing as praying?' Tzŭ Lu replied: 'There is. Prayers have been offered for thee to the spirits of Heaven and Earth'. The master said: 'I have prayed for a long time'. Wang Chung, however, nearly two thousand years ago (in the early Han dynasty) was rather sceptical about sacrifice, and about the result - blessings or calamity - if sacrifice was neglected. He assumed this to be merely a superstition. Nevertheless, it is a common belief that when sacrifices are duly offered according to a prescribed ceremonial, the blessings and protection of the ancestors will be bestowed upon the family. The Reverend J. Jackson provides us with two or three examples of prayers addressed to the ancestors at the time of family sacrifice. He maintains that the prayers have not been derived from books, but supplied to him by scholars who consider the prayers to be fairly representative of those in general use.[53]

First Offering

The first sacrificial rite is performed,
The sacrifice is spread and presented;
Come in peace and partake -
Great are our Ancestors!

Second Offering

The second sacrificial rite is performed,
Again the sacrifice is offered at the gate of
    the ancestral hall.
O! our forefathers,
Send down blessings without limit!

Third Offering

The third sacrificial rite is performed.
The ceremonies are completed.
Your filial descendants have felicity,
They shall be blessed for ever.

In the *Ancestral Worship* Jackson has presented well-formulated prayers offered at the Spring Sacrifice at the graves at the time of the New Year and Spring Festivals.

Prayer Offered at the Spring Sacrifice

Today is the Festival of Spring, and we come for the purpose of offering worship and sacrifice to our ancestors. May they in the world of gloom be free from suffering the penalty of sin! May your souls for ever exist to protect your descendants and give them sons and official rank, and so your protection shall not be in vain! We think upon you our ancestors when you were alive as possessing ability. Your souls will certainly not be dissipated now that you are dead, but you will protect your descendants and grant them posterity, riches and honour.[54]

Prayers Offered at the Graves at the Time of the New Year and Spring Festivals

At this time we descendants come with offerings of incense and wine to sacrifice at the graves of our ancestors. Your bodies have returned to the earth, and so may be at rest, but your spirits should return to your former home to protect your descendants. Now at the New Year's season all men have grateful memories of the departed. At the Spring Festival all families burn paper and sweep the graves with a sincere mind. Although your descendants are foolish, yet may your vital energy not waste away in the grave, but invisibly protect your posterity, and give them happiness and wealth for ever. May the spirits of our ancestors effectually come and enjoy the offerings![55]

Prayer Offered at the Tomb

The spring dews are now distilling their fertility, and my grief cannot be forgotten. I improve the time to examine and sweep the grave and visit the fir hall [the tomb]. Prostrate I pray your protection to surround and assist your descendants, that they may be powerful and honoured; let every son and grandson in the house receive a happy sign, and become conspicuous over all, their fame rivalling the lustre of their ancestors. Looking up, we pray you to descend and accept our sacrifice.[56]

These prayers shed light on the significance of the relationships between the living and the dead. The glory of one party reflects on the other. Like the Nuer who emphasize by their public prayer that, in relation to God, all are members of one another, the Chinese, in their prayers to their ancestors, asking to be elevated to an official status and granted riches and honours, seek to form the total unity of which they are individual members. Distinguished ancestors are established in the ancestral hall and their honours reflect on their descendants, while the celebrity of the living correspondingly enhances the status of their ancestors. Equally, the sins of the living blot their ancestors' escutcheon.

119

In the graveyard, entombment is laid out according to generation, age and sex; seniors in generation and age must be entombed on the upper terraces. On the same terrace, a senior should be entombed at the left of a junior. A man and his wife should be interred side by side, the man on the left of the woman. The left-hand side is thought to be the side of honour. These are general principles of burial, though they are not always observed. In many graveyards, not only are the tombs arranged in disregard of a certain order of generation, age and sex, but husbands and wives are buried apart from each other. There are several factors which have a bearing on the disregard of the basic principles of burial, such as generation, age and sex. First is a limitation of space. The size of many family graveyards is limited, due to the cost of land.[57] Even though families own more than one or two terraces, tombs will be accumulated throughout many generations, to such an extent that no burial ground will be available. There is still a more important factor that when members of a family have received high honours, they bring glory and honour to the graveyard in which they are laid; their descendants find it proper to entomb them in an honourable terrace. Individual achievements deserve special consideration and may outweigh all other principles of rank in the arrangement of tombs. The third factor is that graveyards are arranged according to geomancy. Geomancy (Feng-shui – the Art of Winds and Waters) is the art of adapting the residence of the living and the dead so as to co-operate and harmonize with the local currents of the cosmic breath. It is applied to houses of the living and tombs of the dead. If they are not properly adjusted, evil effects will injure the inhabitants of the houses and the descendants of those whose bodies lay in the tombs, while good siting will bring about their wealth, happiness and prosperity.

The dead of the prosperous do not lie compactly ordered in graveyards, but the poor may be interred in the burial grounds provided for them, although when their family rises in fortune, their descendants will transfer them to more propitious surroundings.[58] The rise in fortune from generation to generation and the constant search for geomantic fortune has encouraged people to disperse their dead. A Chinese aphorism speaks of the scattering of graves: 'In the southern mountains to bury the father, and in the northern mountains to bury the mother'.[59] In fact, good geomancy requires that graveyards must be above or below one another. If in the family cemetery the higher terraces stand for a better or senior or more prosperous position, the family graveyard which lies directly above another has taken the lucky wind out of the other family graveyard's soil. In geomantic thinking, the better the tomb of the family is situated, the better their immediate descendants will succeed in their worldly undertakings.[60]

Ancestor worship as ritual and religion

Some aspects of this topic have already been discussed in the context of filial piety. In the present discussion, I approach it from a different point of view.

In the ancestor cult conducted in the ancestral halls the lineage leadership is able to show that ritual is performed. When a domestic ancestral tablet is removed as far as four generations from the living head of the household, it will be replaced by a different kind of tablet to be deposited in the ancestral hall. If all the tablets of remote ancestors are placed in the hall, they are arranged in accordance with generation and seniority; and the shrine will represent genealogy and thus it takes no account of any hierarchy other than that of kinship principle, that is, genealogical principles of arrangement are taken into account by the social status of the dead and their living descendants. Dr Hu said that in many cases the ancestors are worshipped on an equal footing, but that in other cases tablets are arranged by their social status rather than by their position in the kinship hierarchy. A lineage in Wusih divides its tablets into three groups: the tablets of the first ancestor and the founders of the five sub-lineages; those of men who have achieved a scholastic or official status through outstanding virtue;[61] and those of ordinary members of the lineage who have died without a blemish on their characters.[62]

In China there is not an established church with well-formulated dogma; yet in Confucianism there is a body of religio-philosophical beliefs which express the point of view of man in society and of society in nature. In fact, these beliefs constitute the official religion, which has been practised in ancestor worship in ancestral halls or family temples. Although the official religion is 'Ju Chiao' or the teachings of Confucius, it has not been entirely free from other religious elements. Taoism and Buddhism have contributed to the ideas of the soul and the emergence of clergy, as has been seen.

In the light of historical evidence, ancestor worship has been regarded as falling into the category of a low type of religion and as marking the stage developed from earlier nature worship and animism. In the Roman

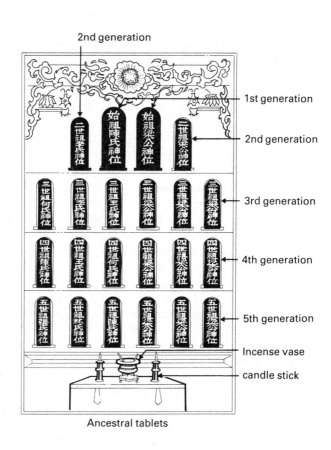

Figure 4.3 *Ancestral tablets*

Source: J. Macintyre, 'Jottings from the *Book of Rites*,' part 1, 'Ancestor worship,' *China Review*, vol. VII, July 1978–June 1879, p. 296.

empire, man-worship, in the deification, for instance, and worship of emperors, is regarded as a great falling off from the simpler faith of the earlier times. Augustus, the son of the deified Julius, was venerated as a god; even his name conveys the ideas 'consecrated, venerable, majestic, awe-inspiring'. An inscription in a stone discovered in Asia Minor is read as follows: 'He [Augustus] is the paternal Zeus and the saviour of the whole race of man, who fulfils all prayers, even more than we ask. For land and sea enjoy peace; cities flourish; everywhere are harmony and prosperity and happiness'.[63]

Ancestor worship existed in China long before Confucius, but he exhibited his sagacity in adapting his teaching to filial feelings of human nature and attempting to introduce a few simple observances and adopt bloodless ritual. That is to say, when ancestor worship is practised, it can be regarded as a form of religion as well as a body of moral rules. Like the Jewish Talmud, Mohammedan Koran and Christian Gospel, the religious tenets of 'Ju Chiao', Confucian religion or teachings, are formulated in the ancient writings and in the records of the past. With this in view, Confucius compiled digests of what seemed to him most valuable in the sayings of earlier thinkers and in the events of his own and earlier times.[64] It is therefore natural that he did not take metaphysical notions into account and warned his followers against any kind of abstract thought.

Worship, a form of religion, may be regarded as a body of moral rules ('li'), and is supported by law. Here is the relationship between 'li' and 'law'. The teachings of the Confucian school have always attached much importance to 'li', the propriety of conduct. The word 'li' is best expressed as approved patterns of behaviour between individuals standing in a definite social relationship.[65] According to *The Analects of Confucius*.[66]

> if the people be led by laws, and uniformity sought to be given them by punishments, the people will try to avoid punishments, but have no sense of shame. If they be led by virtue, and uniformity is given them by the rules of propriety 'li', they will have the sense of shame and, moreover, will become good.

In the view of Chen, this statement represents the attitude of the Confucian school in opposition to the application of a rigid code of laws, because it applies sanctions against a crime only after its perpetration. On the other hand, 'li' is applied to prevent crime before its inception.[67]

123

Confucianism exerted great influence on the formulation of law codes and the administration of justice. Furthermore, judicial judgments based on Confucian ethics often go beyond the articles of a code. For example, I Kuan always applied the ancient classical doctrines in judging law cases.[68] In the later Han dynasty, in the second century AD, Ying Shao wrote a book *Chun Chiu Chüe Yü*[69] in which judging cases was advocated on the basis of the *Chun Chiu* (*The Annals of Autumn and Spring*). After the Han dynasty, Confucians in official posts seized upon the opportunity to incorporate Confucian teachings, 'li', into the law codes. The *Chin Shu* mentions the abrogation of the law which decreed that the father and sons were to live apart in order to put an end to their possessing separate properties.

The Confucians laid emphasis upon family relationships and urged the proper relationships in the kinship system, for example, the mourning system and juridical rights and obligations. All these relationships presuppose a law which will impose the appropriate degree of punishment on offenders. As I have previously explained, filial piety is strongly emphasized by the Confucians: 'li' urges children to serve and support their parents. Thus 'not supporting the parents' makes children liable to punishment. According to 'li', children should not have separate private property. Having private property is legally punishable. Again, Confucius taught that the father and the son should conceal each other's crime. Such concealment is, therefore, in the light of 'li', permissible, though the law has not made it imperative that children should bear witness against their parents or bring accusations against them. In the State of Ch'u, as previously stated, a man who reported to an official that his father had stolen a goat was sentenced to death. What justified the capital punishment of the son was, as Confucius interpreted it, that while he was loyal to his ruler he was remiss in filial piety to his father.[70] Confucius himself maintained a similar attitude in another case of a goat-stealing father.[71] It follows that what is approved by 'li' is also approved by law, and vice versa. In the Han dynasty Chen Ch'ung, the Minister of Justice, said: 'What is left by "li" is covered by punishment. To transgress "li" amounts to infringing the law. The two are two sides of the same thing'.[72]

It may be concluded that 'li' is originally enforced by social sanction and later by legal sanction. A prescribed pattern of behaviour enforced by social sanction is 'li'; the same pattern of behaviour is law when legal sanction is applied.

In terms of social function, ancestor worship is thought to be the bond holding the family members together, and the main support of morality and decency in family life. Filial piety ('hsiao') and its complement, ancestor cult, form the core of the Chinese religion. There are no priests. The emperor, who is the Son of Heaven and therefore himself divine, acts as mediator between Heaven and earth and, as a part of his duties, performs public rites and offers sacrifice for the welfare of his subjects. Nevertheless, those rites which are connected with ancestor worship are conducted by the head of each family. The objects of worship and sacrifice are the spirits of the dead who are still regarded as members of the family to which they belonged.

The word 'sacrifice' in Chinese does not have the same sense as the English word. We must not read into it the fullness of meaning which Old and New Testament usage has conveyed to us. Etymologically, the character is formed by the combination of the ideas in its three parts, symbolizing a piece of flesh – the sacrificial object, a hand, and spiritual beings or heaven. The meaning of this character is that sacrifice is a gift offered to supernatural beings and to the spirits of ancestors with whom the worshippers need to ingratiate themselves. They intend to ensure that objects reach the spiritual beings by sacrificial rites. Sacrifice is conceived of as an offering to spiritual beings, whereby communication with them is effected. This is the meaning given in *Kang Hsi Dictionary*.

Sacrifices are offered as gifts to ensure favour and blessing for the descendants of the ancestors so honoured. Hsu points out that the needs of ancestors in the afterlife must be met by the living for fear they should turn into spiritual vagabonds and call down misfortune on the living. This is one of the basic assumptions of Chinese ancestor worship, though it is held with suspicion by intellectuals. Here we must make a distinction between ancestor worship among the masses and among the enlightened, the former worshipping, called 'pai', and the latter sacrificing, 'chi'.[73] To the educated Chinese, offerings are not connected with any idea of propitiation or of supplication, but are tributes of duty and gratitude.[74]

Communion with the dead has always been a chief feature in sacrificial cult not only among the Chinese, but also among many other peoples. Among the Semitic and Greek people a communion feast is connected with sacrifice. The Zebah Shelamin is a communion sacrifice.[75] Robertson Smith sees the communion in the practices of the totemic cult, the origin of sacrifice. In fact, in totemism the totem or the god and its devotees or sacrificers of the same flesh and blood; the purpose of the sacrifice is to maintain the communion of life that animates them and the association that binds them together. The communion meal is the simplest means of obtaining this result. In the view of Robertson Smith, it is the 'communion meal' in which the devotees participate and, by eating the totem, they assimilate it to themselves, are assimilated to it, and become allied with each other or with it.[76] Nagas Aborigines of North America have also this custom.

The continued existence of 'hun' (soul) is the *raison d'être* of Chinese ancestor worship. The sacrificial offerings at this worship are simply the materials of a feast, at which the living and the dead are supposed to meet together. According to Legge, the Chinese hold that ancestor worship is not merely commemorative, but a pretended real intercourse with the world spirit, supposing that the happiness of the dead depends on the sacrifice by their descendants.[77] Moreover, death, far from having cut off the relationship of the dead to the living, has merely changed the relationship; it is maintained through ritual. Some rites are performed to provide comfort for the dead, whereas still other rites are conducted to invoke the dead to sanction marriage and family division and act as disciplinarian for the young generations. It is Confucian thinking that at the time of great offerings every deceased person ought to have his 'shih', representative. The sons, no longer seeing their deceased father, are distressed; therefore the 'representative' is dressed in such a way as to make him the living image of the vanished reality. 'Shih', is a representative or impersonator of the worthy who is sacrificed to. The dead, existing now in their state 'shen' or spirit-state, are, of course, not visible, and one of the sacrificer's relatives is selected to be taken possession of, for the time being by the represented, so that we read in the *Li Chi*: '"shih" to mean "shen hsiang"; the "she" is the visible image of the spirit'. The person thus selected for this part, according to certain rules of kinship in the *Li Chi*, is necessarily inferior in rank to the principal sacrificer, but for the time being he is superior to him in that he personifies this departed ancestor. As soon as the impersonator 'shih' appears in the temple, the sacrificer has been instructed by the director of the ceremonies to ask him to be seated and to eat, thereby preparing himself to receive the homage given to the dead. This gesture is expressed by 'yu' and 'chüan', which mean to urge someone to eat and drink.[78] In one ode the response of the ancestors through their impersonator 'shih' is thus given:[79]

The offerings in your dishes or vessels of bamboo and wood are
clean and fine.
Your friends assisting at the service,
Have done their part with reverent demeanour.

Your reverent demeanour was altogether what the occasion required,
And not yours only, but that also of your filial son.
For such filial piety, without ceasing,
There will ever be conferred blessing on you.

What will the blessings be?
That along the passages of your palace
You shall move for ten thousand years;
And there will be granted to you for ever dignity and posterity.

Similarly the *Li Chi* describes the passionate longing of the sons for
the deceased father and says:[80]

> No visual shade of some one lost
>> But he, the spirit himself may come,
> Where all the nerve of sense is numb;
>> Spirit to spirit, ghost to ghost.
>
> Descend, and touch, and enter; here
>> The wish too strong for words to name;
> That in this blindness of the frame,
>> My ghost may feel that thine is near.

Elsewhere the *Li Chi* puts it: 'Sacrifice is not something coming from
outside but is issued from one's heart'. The heart of sacrifice means that
externally all things attain their utmost, and internally the will attains
its utmost.[81] When Hsun Tzu read this passage, he said that:[82]

> sacrificial rites are the expression of a man's will, emotion, remem-
> brance and love. They represent the height of loyalty, faithfulness,
> love and respect. With sorrow and reverence one serves the dead, he
> serves the living and departed as he serves living in the presence.
> What is served has neither appearance nor shadow, and yet the social
> order is completed in this way.

In the context of the social structure sacrifice serves to fulfil human
relations. Honouring ancestors is a way to fulfil these relationships,
which have been interrupted but not terminated by death. In the past,
the educated performed ceremonies and made offerings before ancestral

altars, not to entreat for blessings or to provide deceased parents with material needs, but to demonstrate their affectionate feelings of filial piety and respect.[83] However, after the importation of Buddhism to China the form and meaning of sacrifice were adulterated. But the central conviction that human relations need to be continued despite death remained unaltered. Here again, Confucius thought highly of sacrifice because it helps one to remember one's origin. The *Li Chi* says: 'All things originate from heaven and all men originate from their ancestors . . . . The sacrifice is to express gratitude towards the originators and recall our beginnings'.[84] Also, Hsün Tzǔ wrote that rites are rooted in three things: Heaven and Earth as the origin of life; ancestors as the origin of human beings; rulers and teachers as the origin of ordered government. Hence the rites are used to serve Heaven above and Earth below, honour our ancestors, and make eminent our rulers and teachers.[85] Kinship lies behind the ancestral cult of the Chinese; nor can their kinship system be entirely accounted for without rituals. To trace genealogical relationship it is indispensable to recollect human ancestors; if they have religious values, ritual performance to a common ancestor forms an intrinsic basis of kinship bonds and its most potent sanction. Kinship relations are necessary to the individual and serve the social well-being of the society as a whole; they are embedded in all social activities.

The meaning of these rites corresponds to that of the rites which have been described by Dr Goody.[86] Durkheim regarded religious rites as mechanisms for expressing and reinforcing the sentiments most essential to the integration of society. Tseng Tzǔ said: 'If people are careful about funeral rites and remember their ancestors in sacrifices, the morals of the people will resume their proper excellence'.[87]

The term 'religion' (Chiao) has two meanings for the Chinese, that is, 'a religious system' and 'teach'. This is the meaning of the ancient saying that the ancient sages established teaching on the way of the gods. The Confucian school does not believe in the existence of supernatural beings, but stresses the performance of sacrifice in order to give emotional satisfaction:[88] Hu Shih seizes the same idea that teaching a moral life is the essential thing, and worship of the gods and religious observance merely provides one of the possible means of sanctioning the teaching. That is in substance the Chinese concept of religion.[89]

Ancestor worship thus understood in the Chinese religion bears a resemblance to the Comtist religion which was a secular church with himself as the high priest. In the ceremony of ancestor cult, the father plays the role of priest. George Eliot has brought to light famous lines about the choir invisible of those immortal spirits who are immortal as they live on in 'humanity'[90] and live in those whose lives are made better by their presence and influence.[91] This idea accords with Chinese ancestor worship. J. Jackson wrote: 'The virtues of our ancestors live on in us, one blood circulates in them and us, we all partake of the same vital breath. Our care should be to live worthily of them, and all through our lives we should be careful only not to disgrace them.'[92]

In Chinese ancestor worship we can see clearly its social function to assert, renew and strengthen those sentiments on which the social order and stability lie. As we said previously, the cult group consists of persons related to one another by descent in one line from the same ancestor, and then only the members of the group can participate in the cult. In other words, ancestor worship consists of rites performed by the members of a larger and smaller lineage related to the deceased members of the lineage. When the members of a lineage multiply over several generations, the kinship group grows large and contact between the members becomes sporadic; nevertheless, the gathering in the ancestral cult will serve to remind the kin group of the common origin and keep alive the social duties between the members. The principal duties due to the one lineage are those to the members of the still living, and to those who have died and to those who are not yet born.

In fact, kinship relations imply moral obligations which import rights, duties, virtue, respect and support. In carrying out those duties the object on which the individual's sentiments are expressed is the lineage itself, past, present and future. Likewise, the pitch of the Chinese kinship system rests in its function as a mechanism through which the basic morality is translated into the concrete activities. Again, in ancestor worship the Chinese feels that he depends on his ancestors for his life and livelihood that are his inestimable treasure. If he fails to put his ancestors' expectations or wishes into practice, his negligence will invoke their ire and he will be punished. The ancestors are thought to be not only fellow members of the corporate group, but also authority figures who sustain the norms of social action and call down evil upon their descendants if the norms are infringed. The existence of these ancestral supports purports that the traditional norms of society are transmitted from on high, just as God handed down to Moses the two tablets of stone. Here social control is exercised beyond the vagaries of human action and its validity is established by sanctions so that no human agent can on any account defy. Furthermore, it is the idea of memorialism that participants in ancestor worship are prepared to show their gratitude towards their ancestors for whatever has been lavished on them, and their dependence upon them. The ancestors are worshipped simply as forbears regardless of their status as ancestors of the agnates of the worshippers. The sense of dependence has two aspects. On the one hand, Chinese people can bear the tribulations bravely when they know that there are powers and forces of ancestors who succour their descendants; on the other hand, they ought to abide by the rules of society which have been handed down. Within the descent group the idea of family continuity and the thought of what is due to one's ancestors has undoubtedly brought about some lingering influence for good upon those who cherish such ideas. Ancestor worship, as Jackson put it, is conceived of as the bond which gives rise to group cohesion and collective consciousness.

Conclusion

Confucius is thought to be a religous man because he attempted to establish moral principles which may connote religious ideas. We are told that he did not talk about spirits and his opinion was that, though spirits should be given respect, they should be avoided. He seems to have regarded spirits and demons as undesirable subjects. In this respect there seems no doubt that Confucius may be regarded as a purifier of the polydemonistic times in which he lived. In one passage he said: 'To sacrifice to a spirit not of one's own, i.e. outside one's family, is sycophancy'. The formal worship of Heaven and earth and of the powers of nature is practised only by the emperor and, at infrequent intervals, by the high officers of state. The political system of China includes the worship of the greatest sage, and the social system derived from his writings requires homage to be paid to the family lares. That the sages sacrifice to gods does not imply that such gods are thought to have existed, but simply that this paves the way for conveying instructions. This materialistic philosophy, which began in 289 BC and culminated in the eighth century AD, has contributed noticeably to the growth of ancestor worship among the people and has enabled Buddhist ideas to captivate the masses. Confucius never permitted the making of an image of Shang-Ti. The ancestral temples are kept free from idols, though pictures of the male and female who founded the clan or family are hung on sacrificial occasions.

The Chinese feel that to renounce ancestor worship as filial piety would mean a renunciation of the innate obligation expressed by the word 'hsiao'; it would mean also defiance of paternal and patriarchal authority. The institution of ancestor worship is seen as the norm of society, and the system of authority itself, projected into the supernatural plane. Among the masses the same institution seems to be a body of religious beliefs and ritual practices, correlated with rules of conduct, which serves to assert the principle of juridical authority as a sacrosanct value-principle of the social system. Juridical authority is vested in the father by virtue of kinship status and superior authority, which is supported by supernatural sanctions as the cement of social life, morality and politics.

Chapter 5

Various aspects of social life in the Chinese kinship system

> Funeral rites are for the living to send off the dead as if they were living; to render the same service to the dead as to the living.
>
> *Li Chi*

In the first chapter we have laid out, by means of a diagram, the general framework in relation to the social structure of the family and social relationship within the family, aspects which are observable in ancestor worship and filial piety in the context of inter-family relations in the orbit of village organization. Here we must bear in mind that we are dealing with these aspects in China proper, and in a period from the Chou dynasty to the beginning of the Communist government.

In a range of relationships between various members of the family up to the clan as warp and of the relationships between various different functions of these members as woof, the society is woven into a functional, organic structure. As an approach to the functional structure we may frame an abstract outline in our mind as follows: the family is the economic unit, the compound the political unit, while the lineage and clan form an all-embracing unit. Functional structures are not fixed, but can vary to suit the immediate social requirement. The ancestral hall originally had a religious function only; but later the number of its functions increased and the organization of the hall became more complex, the social structure adapting itself to changing function. Also ancestor worship in Chinese society has a wide range of social functions. If our framework is accepted, our subsequent procedure is the examination of the connection between the structural aspect of social life and the corresponding social process as both are involved in the kinship system.

The economic aspects of social life

In nearly the whole of China, agriculture forms the basis of production and livelihood. The clan which corresponds in some respects, to what has been called maximal lineage in anthropological literature is often only one section of the village, and embraces each individual family. However, in southern parts of China, such as Kwangtung and Fukien, many villages constitute a single clan. The same structure is also found in South-East Central China.[1] This existence of localized clans partly results in the maintenance of corporate property, which chiefly consists of the ownership of land and favours the development of a large clan community. There are, however, regional differences and peculiarities in terms of clan and lineage organization, and this makes it difficult to generalize about China as a whole. Nevertheless, although we acknowledge social change over a long period of Chinese history, our account of social structure is aimed at bringing out the constant features abstracted from the variable forms. To this end, we shall assume that the significant features of social structure must exhibit some measure of coherence or consistency. In fact, in view of the stagnant nature of traditional Chinese culture, radical changes cannot safely be presumed. I draw attention to this important problem before I embark on the description of various aspects of social life. To deal with this problem I shall bring forward historical material which may throw light on the cultural differences in China.

We have remarked earlier that the family is an economic unit consisting of relatives, in the paternal line, of various generations of either sex, and various orders of seniority within each generation. Again, the family is a communal group, sharing the same cooking stove, eating together, living and working together. Each family has certain holding of land. Such an economic basis allows wealth to accumulate to some degree, and individual families to raise their standard of living and social status. Furthermore, the uneven distribution of lands provides the basis for political, educational, social and ritual differentiation.

The lands of the family belong to the head. When he retires, due to his age, his adult son is bound by filial duty to till the land and to provide for his parents, in accordance with the saying of Confucius that 'the fundamental principle is filial piety and its practice consists in the support of parents'.[2] Their ethical and social teachings lead the Chinese to lay great stress on the need for the support of their parents. Mencius enumerates five things which are considered unfilial: four of them are economic. The first is laziness in the use of one's four limbs, without attending to the support of one's parents; the second is gambling and chess-playing, and a fondness for wine, without the support of one's parents; the third is being fond of material goods and money, and selfishly attached to one's wife and children, without attending to the support of one's parents; the fourth is gratifying the desires of one's ears and eyes, so as to bring one's parents into disgrace; the fifth is indulgence in bravery, fighting and quarrelling so as to endanger one's parents.[3] The first is analogous to production, the second and the fourth to consumption and the third to distribution. According to the *Ta Ch'ing Lü Li*, a son ran away from home leaving his father in the lurch and was therefore banished, on his father's initiative, to a malaria territory on the furthermost border.[4] Another son, who had stolen his father's pension grain, was banished to Kwangtung.[5]

On the basis of the Chinese kinship system, the father has a better claim to support from his son than the son's wife and children. Although the parents are reluctant to sacrifice their sons or daughters-in-law, the Chinese feel bound in honour to care for parents first. Filial piety to support parents is not waived even when the parents happen to have economic independence, but this duty is still more exigent when they become destitute. Filial piety is both the epitome of loyalty and an absolute norm of morality.

Father's rights and authority over family property

The head of the family exercises control over the administration of the family's property. The son has no private savings, and all his expenses for food, clothing and shelter are paid by the head of the family. According to the *Li Chi*, 'when the parents are alive, a son should not dare to consider his body as his own, nor to regard his wealth as his private property'.[6] Thus children may not possess property of their own. In various dynasties punishments were imposed on those who infringed the rights of the father over the family property. In the Sung dynasty no son or grandson was entitled to sell a slave, cattle, land, houses, or any other types of property while the father was alive. Even if the father or the head of the family was three hundred 'li' (three Chinese li equal 1 mile) away from home, the juniors were not justified in disposing of any property without their father's consent. Only when he was unable to communicate with his father, was the son allowed to conclude property deals or settlements, and a certificate from the local government which authorized him to do so must be obtained. Failure to present such a certificate would ensure that the property would revert to its original owner, and the buyer would not be reimbursed.[7] Similar regulations were enacted in the Yüan dynasty.[8]

Moreover, living apart from the parents' household and possessing property of one's own was regarded as a more serious breach of law than disposing of family property. Independent possession of property was disapproved of as filial impiety,[9] and punishments were accordingly more severe; three years' imprisonment in the T'ang and Sung dynasties, and one hundred strokes in Ming and Ch'ing times.[10] During the life of the father, if his son was married and engaged in any occupation, he was not entitled to establish his own individual household. Nor were the children allowed to divide during the mourning period for the parents. Recalcitrant children were prosecuted by the law and could receive one year's imprisonment in the T'ang and Sung dynasties,[11] and eighty strokes in the Ming and Ch'ing dynasties.[12]

The division of the family property

It is evident from what has been said in earlier chapters about social relationships within the family that the Chinese family law of succeeding generations is based on three fundamental principles of ancient family law: there should be attention to the separate roles between husband and wife, affection between father and son, and a proper order between old and young. The old law code of the Han ·dynasty (178-57 BC) derived nearly all its clauses from ancient laws and principles. The later Code of the T'ang dynasty (AD 618-906), that is, *T'ang Lü Li*, was derived from the laws of the Han dynasty; the code of the late Ch'ing dynasty, that is *Ta Ch'ing Lü Li*, adopted almost all the laws of the T'ang dynasty, with only a few slight amendments and additional clauses.[13] Even the Provisional Civil Code of the Chinese Republic (1912-49) embodied the spirit as well as the letter of the three fundamental principles. I have particularly stressed the relationships between the ancient family laws and the laws of succeeding dynasties to enable us to see that we are dealing with Chinese traditional culture as a homogeneous culture complex. (The problem of cultural unity in diversity makes people question the validity of studying the Chinese culture complex in such a long period. In fact, Chinese culture remains more or less the same throughout the long period of Chinese history.)

In law, all brothers, old and young have equal status, but the eldest brother, being the direct propagator of his father's line, has the sole right to offer sacrifices to deceased parents or ancestors.[14] When the family property is undivided, all the brothers live together, and none of them, not even the eldest, is entitled to dispose of any of the family's goods and chattels. If, for extraordinary reasons, any son is compelled to give away something which belongs to the family, he must first seek permission from his father.[15] The head of the family has the first right to the property, but he cannot dispossess his sons of their rights to it, nor can a father bequeath his property out of the family under any circumstances; but under very exceptional and extraordinary circumstances he can disinherit individual members of his family, for instance, a criminal son. Further, no family property may be divided by the children as long as their parents are alive. The insistence of Confucian ethics on the solidarity of the family is implemented by avoiding family partition.[16]

Family division is not simply the division of a domestic unit; it is the formal division of both cooking stove and land. The rules of inheritance allot the largest portion to the eldest son, in proportion to his contribution to the family property and his responsibilities for keeping the ancestral shrine. Once the division of the family has taken place, it will lead to the creation of legally separate households, and the relations between the brothers will gradually fade rather than undergo a drastic modification from affectional involvement to indifference.

Supposing the family has five sons, C, D, E, F, and G, its property is divided equally among them,[17] regardless of the number of children each son may have:

	Father (A)		Mother (B)	
(C)	(D)	(E)	(F)	(G)
Eldest son	Second son	Third son	Fourth son	Fifth son

(C) has sons and two daughters
(D) has three sons, H, I and J; one of them is illegitimate
(E) has two sons, K and L and one is adopted and another is
     illegitimate
(F) has none
(G) has one son and one daughter

The division of the family property is thus *per stirps* and not *per capita*. If there are 100 mows of land (three Chinese mows equal one acre) at the time of division and (D), (F) and (G) are all dead, (C) will receive one-fifth of the land, i.e. 20 mows. D's legal share, 20 mows, will go to his children (H) and (I), each receiving 8 mows, while the illegitimate son will receive only one-half of the share due to a legal heir, i.e. 4 mows. E's legal share, 20 mows, is divided equally between his 'adopted' son .and his illegitimate son. The law of Provisional Civil Code confers on an illegitimate son[18] the same rights of inheritance as on an adopted son. If (F) is survived only by his wife, her legal share is 20 mows, provided she is not remarried. The son of his father's concubine has the same rights of inheritance as any legitimate son. Since he is the only son living, he has a legal right to a share of 20 mows.

Here we may present a concrete case. Ego's (the writer's) family held land in common and kept a budget and co-operated to work on farming as a big household living together (fifteen members). Ego had four brothers and an uncle, the younger brother of his father. When ego's father was alive, the unity and cohesion of the family were striking. But when ego's father died at the age of thirty-nine, the family stability began to shake. Ego's mother suffered in her bereavement and was extremely conscious of the way she was treated by ego's grandparents and the rest of the family. She showed every now and then a desire that the family should divide so that she could be economically independent. Ego's young uncle, having only a young child, also felt inclined to divide the family. Ego's family owned 260 mows. Since ego's father and uncle were of the same generation, they had an equal share in the family property, i.e. 95 mows each. Another 30 mows went to ego's grandparents and 40 mows to his two unmarried aunts. Ego's four brothers obtained 15 mows each, and 20 mows went to ego's mother as pension. Ego's mother went to live with her younger son in the old house, since the elder son was engaged in business elsewhere.

In the Ming and Ch'ing dynasties daughters were not entitled to any share in family property. If they were already married, they left their natal family for good by joining their husband's family. But a certain sum was set apart before the division for the marriage expenses of those still unmarried. In the Provisional Law Code of the Chinese Republic, unmarried daughters may claim a certain amount for a marriage dowry from the family property before it is divided among the brothers. After the division an unmarried daughter takes her marriage portion and lives with one of her brothers. Thus the daughter's share in property is determined by her marriage; if her father dies after her marriage without male issue, the property is divided equally between her and the other daughters; in such circumstances she must bring what she has already had into the common fund before she can take her share of the whole. If there are male heirs, unmarried daughters are entitled to a dowry of one half of the son's share. This legal provision can be illustrated by the following case. Having no direct male issue, Chung-fan married his daughter by a concubine to Tien-min. On the death of Chung-fan, Tien-min, liking the property, moved in with his family and took possession of the house, presuming that Mrs Chung-fan would have no children. It is alleged that when Chung-fan was alive he allotted the wing of the house to his daughter as a dowry. However, in the absence of all documentary evidence the allegation was rejected. The plaintiff, Mrs Chung-fan, pleaded not that Tien-min's claim was utterly void, but that the case had to be adjourned for three months and that his (Tien-min) rights had to depend on whether Mrs Chung-fan, then pregnant, would give birth to a son or a daughter; if it be a son, he would take his father's property; if a daughter, the house had to be divided between two daughters, one married and the other unmarried.[19]

Married daughters who are considered to be members of their husband's family are excluded from sharing in the family property. A widow, if she is also the mother of a family, can refuse her consent to the division of the family property; if she is a widow without a son, she may keep her husband's property in trust until the nomination of a proper heir in her husband's name is established.[20] We should bear in mind that on the death of a father, the legal estate rests in the hands of the sons, but equity prohibits them from dealing with it without the permission of the mother on account of her joint legal estate with her sons. The popular convention is that a son who attempts to sell the patrimony without his mother's consent will be in disgrace.

Conclusion

Family division may result from the marriage of brothers, domestic conflict, or the death of the father, but it does not necessarily create new units, the members of which become mere neighbours. The establishment of new households, and accordingly of new independent economic units, does not preclude their continuous co-operation to some degree. In a season of harvest, divided households still like to lend services to one another. With regard to religion, they continue to participate in ancestor worship in the domestic temple and share expenses in annual festivals.

Succession and inheritance

Maine held that 'the prolongation of a man's legal existence in his heir or in a group of co-heirs amounts to succession in a corporation'. The notion that 'though the physical person of the deceased has perished, his legal personality will survive and descend unimpaired on his heir, or co-heirs; a group of persons considered in law to be a single unit may succeed as co-heirs to the inheritance'.[21] What is said by Maine has led us to make distinctions between 'succession', 'inheritance' and 'descent'. Succession is not entirely the same as inheritance, but both differ from descent. According to Dr Fortes, succession ensures that authority and right do not perish with the bodily demise of man, and descent ensures that the matrix of social relations remains more or less constant through the succeeding generations.[22]

In the feudal period in China, the appointment of the heir or successor devolves upon the ruler of the state during his life. It serves to debar ministers and sons from usurpation. The *Chun Chiu*, considers the murder of the heir a crime as grave as the murder of the ruler himself. When a ruler died and his principal wife had no son but was pregnant, the appointment of the heir had to be postponed until she delivered the child. This was to ensure the legal succession. The heir is appointed from the children of the principal wife rather than from among the other sons so as to avert strife arising from love and jealousy.[23]

Brothers do not succeed one another. When a feudal lord who succeeded to the fief had no sons, the succession would pass to his other relatives as the descendants of the same ancestors. When such a feudal lord had neither sons nor younger brothers, but only paternal uncles and elder brothers born of a secondary wife, the succession should be bestowed upon an older brother born of a secondary wife, being the next of kin. In the period of *Chun Chiu*, the principle of paternal succession coexisted with the possession of entailed estate or property. In 662 BC the *Historical Records (Shih Chi)* said that the son succeeded his deceased father and the younger brother his elder brother.[24] In 489 BC when duke Chao of the Chou dynasty was dying, he surrendered his dukedom to his several brothers, but only the youngest accepted it and then he hastened to enthrone the son of duke Chao.[25]

It should be kept in mind that an heir was often chosen or designated with official advice.[26] For example, duke Cheng wang spoke to Tzŭ Shang, the official adviser, about choosing Shang Ch'en, the direct heir, but Cheng wang was dissuaded from doing so because Shang was under age. We can see that the inheritance went to the eldest son by the mediation of a younger brother, as is written in the *Historical Records*: 'Heritage is proposed to brothers in order that they should decline it'.[27]

In the Ming dynasty it was the duty of the head of a clan to appoint an heir for a kinsman who had died without a male issue.[28] In the Ching dynasty the wishes of the father with regard to the transmission of his property after his death were legalized. Although the father may sell or mortgage his estate during his lifetime, he cannot show generosity to a stranger at the expense of his proper kindred. For he holds the property in trust for his children, since the family estate can only go to persons who are either the members of the family by birth or quasi-members of the family by adoption.[29]

In theory, filial piety, as we have previously said, is the hub of the whole social life. Hence after the father's death the descendants occupy the status of the father and see that his memory is kept alive.[30] The son or successor is invested with the legal status of his father, subject to all his liabilities and entitled to all his rights. 'A son pays his father's debts' is a maxim of universal application in China. It means that the successor, whether natural or adopted, stands in the shoes of the deceased. In the view of Maine, this transfer exactly resembles the 'universal' succession, known in the oldest Roman Law, that persons can take assignments of all a man's property provided that they pay all his debts.[31] Maine viewed this as a succession to an undivided whole, to the *'universitas juris'*.[32] This form of succession necessarily leads to another point that, while natural sons are jointly liable for the debts of the father, it does not follow that any one of the kindred, not yet adopted, can be compelled against his will to undertake an insolvent succession. By contrast, in Roman Law, the succession of an assignee in bankruptcy to all a bankrupt's property is a universal succession, though, as the assignee only pays debts to the extent of the assets, this is only a modified form of the primary notion of universal succession.[33]

As to whether a man may dispose of or squander his property during his life, we only advance the point which concerns the question we are considering. For the sale of land, the seller often claims that he does so 'in want of money'. If a son could sell his land under compulsion, the introduction of this clause would make sense. This is borne out by the fact that an adopted son (I Tzǔ) may sell the patrimony for the support of himself and of his adoptive parents; (their consent, is of course, required).

Adoption

Adoption serves to continue the stock (chieh tsung tzǔ). The adoption of agnates is called 'ch'eng chi', that is, taking over the succession. 'Kuo ssu' means going over to be heir; 'kuo ssu' is understood as going over to the 'sacra'; 'i tzǔ', 'i nü' and 'ch'i tzu' or 'chi nü' mean 'godchildren' or *filii lustrici*, 'yang tzǔ' and 'yang nü' mean rearing a child.[34] One of the earliest examples of an adopted son (chi) was the adoption of Ssu-ma Yu, who was the son of Ssu-ma Chao and was given in adoption to Ssu-ma Shih, a successor of Ssu-ma I, and predecessor of his brother as dictator of the Wei dynasty.[35]

The Chinese laws of various dynasties cast much light on the earlier forms of adoption. The law of inheritance was made up of provisions for the appointment of a legal successor to the family. Its purpose was to continue the family line, and, this being once established, the property devolved upon the successor as a matter of course. Attention should be drawn to the fact that the person to be adopted had to be one of the same blood and close in kinship. In his book *Lineage Organization in South-Eastern China* (p. 28) Dr Freedman states that 'some boys were brought in from other lineages, although they may have been related to the adopting fathers by non-agnatic ties'. He says also that 'some unwanted children found difficulty of access to a rich family for adoption unless they were of common agnatic descent'. However he has made no distinction between a son adopted from non-agnatic kin and a son adopted from the closest collateral agnatic lines.

When a person has no male child, he may adopt a son-in-law; this form of adoption is called 'tao tsai men', i.e. uxorilocal residence. This adopted son-in-law is expected to adopt the surname or clan name of his wife. Sometimes two surnames appear on the lanterns before the main entrance; this means that he has refused to change his surname. However, few men like losing their surname and so they often conspire to elope with their wives who are usually ready to acquiesce, whatever their husbands choose to do. In Kulp's study of Phoenix Village, the villagers condemn any husband thus adopted who refuses to adopt the surname of his wife.[36] It is to be noted that this 'quasi-adoption' does not entitle the son-in-law to become the heir, but gives him the right to share equally with a successor to the family property, who is chosen according to the kinship rule in the usual way. The concession of inviting a son-in-law arises from natural affection.

By the principles of ancestor worship one sacrifices only to generation

above oneself; some sacrifice to their father, but a brother never sacrifices to a brother. This makes it sensible that in the absence of a direct
heir of any line a substitute from the next generation next below and
not otherwise must be chosen. No adoption can be made if there are
male children; only one person can be adopted as a successor; but
custom allows a man to invite, by quasi-adoption, two or more who
can, by right, share the property of the family. A child under three
years of age and of different clan names, for instance, may be adopted
and take the name of his adopter, but cannot become the heir of the
family. If the head of the family neglects to adopt an heir, his widow,
in agreement with the elders of the clan, or the latter alone, may do so.
If a person who had a son had been chosen for adoption but died, he
might still be adopted posthumously as a son, and his sons would
become grandsons of the adopter. The most frequent case is the
adoption of a patrilineal nephew; he is generally a younger son, and his
son becomes the grandson of the adoptive uncle. If he happens to be
the only nephew and is duty bound to continue the line of his father,
he has to marry another wife, whose male issue is regarded as that of his
uncle; then he will mourn three years for his adoptive parents, and only
one year for his natural parents.[37] Why should there be adoption? Why
should there be such a conception of kinship as to include strangers
brought into the family by adoption? To answer this question we have
to refer to the *'patria potestas'*. The foundation of agnation does not lie
in the marriage of father and mother, but in the authority of the father.
Where the *potestas* begins, kinship begins; and hence adoptive relatives
are the kindred. Where the *potestas* ends, kinship ends; thus a son
emancipated by his father loses all rights of agnation.

Once a person is brought into the family by adoption with the con-
sensus of the head of the family concerned, the adoption is irrevocable,
and the adoptive son loses his rights in his original family. In the event
of a son being born in the family after an heir has been legally adopted,
each shall inherit half the property, but the natural-born son shall be
the successor to the family if an adopted son happens to be re-adopted
into his original family. To illustrate this statement we put forward the
following case.[38] A man adopted by his maternal uncle, changed his surname from 'K'iou' to 'Lung' and begat two sons. He then applied to
return to his original family, but was refused on the ground that certain
classes of official people, to one of which he belonged, were forbidden
by law to change their surname, or, if changed, to take it back again, or
if adopted, to return to their original families. The man having died, the

emperor allowed him to resume his original surname so that his lineage might continue and his loyal ghost be comforted. No mention was made of the names which his two sons had taken, but it was probable that, in order that his lineage might continue in the direct line, one child would bear his father's original surname and the other that (Lung) of the family into which his father was adopted. The adoptive son burned incense before the ancestral tablets of the family to which he was adopted and worshipped them; he worshipped them as representing his ancestors and thereafter called himself their descendant. The ancestors were supposed to be present and, having witnessed the transaction, to partake of the homage paid to them. In this case the son adopted from the K'iou to the Lung family could not take away any share in the family property which had accrued to him by virtue of his first adoption. For only a permanent member of the family has a claim to its property. It is a legal axiom: 'The property never goes to the heir, but the heir comes to the property'.

The following is the form of a will bequeathing property to an adopted son and is extracted from a book bearing the title of *A Collection of the Various forms of Household Etiquettes*.[39]

I, the adoptive Father A.B., hereby drew up this will and bequest of my movable and fixed property for all time to avoid strife and quarrelling. Born in an unlucky hour, I have been unable to produce descendants. My spouse and I have only produced those who play with bricks [i.e. girls as opposed to those who play with sceptres, i.e. boys]. In my dreams I have not seen the divine orchid. Therefore in the _____ year _____ month _____ day, I received C.D. 'number _____ son, named _____' to be my descendant. From that time onwards he has been obedient and attentive and has fulfilled the offices of a son and has not proved unruly nor deflected from the path of filial duty etc. Now, my years being weak and feeble, in order to avoid future troubles, I invite my elder relatives to attend at my house as witnesses. What I have inherited from my ancestors, together with what I have myself amassed, fields, gardens, houses, and whatever money, grain, notes of hand, et hoc genus omne, there may be, I hand over to my adopted son. The fields and gardens which are set aside at X. to represent for the future my entailed property, are also handed over to my adopted son. From the time of his entering these possessions he must give good heed to the trifling property which during my life I have painfully amassed. He must be unpretentious and frugal, exerting his best endeavours to preserve his property. He must nourish his adoptive father and mother while alive, and sacrifice to them when dead. Most certainly must he avoid extravagance by which he would incur the jeers of men at his want of propriety, while at the same time he must not be so penurious as to cause men to sneer at him as a miser. Hereafter should any crafty persons, seizing an opportunity for creating disturbance, seek to deprive him of his property, he must take this will and appeal to the mandarin, and as a suppliant pray him to examine and settle the affair. Now, as I desire there may be a proof, in the presence of all my relatives I have drawn up this will, which I give to my descendant to preserve for ever.

Kwong Sui _____ year _____ month _____ day,
The adoptive father A.B. has written this with his own hand.

In brief, the adoption of relatives enters into the warp and woof of all Chinese family life. It is an essential of ancestral worship that the family has a continuous existence reaching from distant ancestors through the present and looking into the future. It is also within the framework of a relationship between living descendants and ancestors that the welfare of the line depends on its continuance and on the family's possessions as the joint heritage of all the members. Even the poorest classes (in the social scale) are not remiss in adopting a male child when they have not one of their own.

The political aspects of Chinese social life

The family is not confined to the economic field alone in its functions. The economic factor is the fundamental condition of family solidarity only because common ownership of property and the sharing of a common life bind all the members of the family. But for its effective function the family also needs a political basis. Although the kinship system of the family, a sub-system in terms of political structure, is an independent functioning unit, it still needs the backing of political institutions. It is the Confucian doctrine that government, whether it is on national or local or village level is for the people and by the people. The king is generally called the Son of Heaven, as he is thought to be elected by Heaven. Heaven neither sees nor hears in a bodily form, but it sees when the people see; it hears when the people hear. The Confucian maintains that the essential principle of government is to 'win the people and the kingdom is won; lose the people and the kingdom is lost'. Mencius says that 'the people are the most important element in the state'.

A village is a local political group and composed of several families. 'Lineage village' refers to a group bound by both territorial and consanguineal principles; this type of village is prominent in South China. Again, since families are the component units of village organization, it stands to reason to consider politics from the point of view of the family. But we should note that the political aspects of family life have not, until the coming of the Communist regime, undergone a drastic change for many centuries.[40]

As there are laws in every nation or state, there are laws in every family. These rules regulate the relationships among the members of the family; etiquettes must be observed in daily life, in worship, funerals, in birth, in marriage, in education of children and in management of household. In everyday life we can observe how the members of the family, after getting up in the morning, wash their faces, shave, how they cook, how they dress, how they go to family temple and make obeisance, how they greet elders, how they set about their tasks after breakfast, how the adults go to work in farming land, how women attend babies and do their washing and needlework, how children play. Further we can give an account of how the members act towards one another and what their mutual sentiments are, whether harmonious or conflicting. In the daily life of a family we trace not only the relationships within the family, but also the social interaction with outsiders, for instance, the relationship between families, between the family and the compound, branch, sub-lineage and lineages to which the family belongs, and the intercommunication between the family and relatives and friends.[41] There is no need to describe family life in every detail. Suffice it to say that every member of the family, male or female, old and young, in the common walk of life, will find all the necessary rules, usages and conventions that he or she is required to follow.

The family has its own legislation, which is naturally compatible with, and supplementary to, the conventions of a village; it has also its own judiciary to punish members who happen to infringe family codes. Disputes or altercations between two persons may be settled by the head of the family instead of going to the local court, or to the magistrate, who is appealed to in the last resort. The wrongdoer will be dealt with either by the parents or by the elder members of the family.

Disputes within a family are matters of extreme delicacy and intractability, and it is commonly said: 'Even a clever magistrate can hardly arbitrate in family matters or affairs'. Thus the magistrate would frown over family cases if they were brought before him, and he often seeks to fulfil his judicial duties by moral persuasion rather than by passing judgment on these cases. There are two cases which show what measures the magistrate has taken in dealing with family matters.

Ch'ou Lan in the period of Hou Han, a scholar, was appointed chief of his native county and was accused by his mother of being an unfilial son. The magistrate, instead of thinking evil of the mother and son, felt that they had not seized upon the importance of filial piety by moral exhortation and condescended to pay them a visit. Then in drinking with them he explained to them the moral principle of filial piety, and gave them a volume of the *Book of Filial Piety*. The man saw his misdemeanour and turned to become a pious son.[42] Another case is that of a mother and son who accused each other and appeared before the magistrate, Wei Chi. Without reproving the misconduct of the man, Wei told him, 'I lost my parents during my youth, and I have always bitterly regretted this loss. Whenever I see filial sons caring so much for their parents and supporting them I regret that I have no such blessing and chance; you are fortunate to serve your mother. Why should you behave like this?' The magistrate wept and gave him the *Book of Filial Piety* to read. Thereupon the mother and son were deeply moved and became henceforth a good mother and a pious son.[43]

The principle which underlies the constitution of the Chinese traditional family is leadership and responsibility devolved upon the eldest,[44] and the deference paid by the young to the aged in society is merely an extension of filial piety. Cheng Han-seng has pointed out that 'clan' heads, chiefs and trustees are selected on the basis of age and generation status.[45]

If the men of real power are elected by the members of a lineage as a whole and by sub-lineages, they must be drawn from larger branches of a clan and are supposed to be 'rich' and 'reliable', 'learned' and 'rational'.[46] The village officers, ts'ung chang, are elected annually. Every head of the family is entitled to be officer of the temple and is offered an opportunity to render services for the public good and order. According to Tao and Leong, 'every officer goes round from house to house by rotation'. Thus, suppose the division of a village consists of one long street, and two officers are allotted to the division, the officer will go round in this manner: the two heads of families of the first two

houses will first be offered two offices. They will be at liberty to accept
or refuse them. If they do not accept them, the officer will go to the
other houses following in numerical order. The officer is for one year,
with only a nominal remuneration attached.[47]

Apart from these annually elected officers, there are the influential
elders and scholars or 'literati' of the village. Where there are several
distinct clan groups in a village, a separate organization may be found.
The elders are the representatives of the various groups; and their role is
accepted because of their personal influence and the popular feeling of
the village. As they are the mouthpiece of public opinion, the administrative officers, that is, those elected annually, are greatly influenced by
the elder's opinion. They (elders) are recognized by the officials of the
government as holding the sole authority of the village. The annually
elected officers, on the other hand, are not recognized as such by the
government, and the functions they perform are simply administrative.

'Literati' or titled scholars attain their position through natural
endowments and achievement, because scholarly and official prefer-
ment are social values which have long been correlated. Kulp and Lin
speak about titled scholars or literati in Phoenix village and I-hsü
respectively. Kulp writes that:[48]

> political advance has always rested upon scholastic achievement
> since early times in China. During the Chou dynasty this was the
> acknowledged basis for official appointment and promotion; the
> scholars, he says, were greatly respected because of the bureaucratic
> significance of their learning. The successful candidate is the boast
> and pride of the village.

In Lin's article on I-hsü Village we read that:[49]

> formerly under the Ch'ing dynasty when official examination was
> held, whenever any member of the lineage graduated as a 'chü-jen',
> the ancestral hall was opened for worshipping and feasting, to do
> honour to the lineage ancestors for their continuous goodness. Even
> to this day the private school is attached to the ancestral hall.
> Members of the lineage who held official rank or title were invited to
> join the ancestral association by the lineage or sub-lineage leaders.

The village viewed as a social sub-system is itself a state in miniature.
Since titled scholars are well versed in classical formulas, they thus serve
as the interpreters of customary law, and, as such, are thought of as the
village lawyers, pleaders and defenders. In brief, they are intermediaries

between the family, the village, and local government. Furthermore, these scholars are also considered to be the embodiment of village ideals and hopes. Since they reflect credit upon their village by virtue of their intellectual accomplishment, they are regarded as a form of collective representation of a definite value complex of the village.

The village temple

Within a family the ancestral hall originally served as the focus for the performance of ancestor worship. During the ceremony all the members of the lineage assembled in the hall to kneel down and make obeisance to the wooden tablets bearing the names of their ancestors and to place the offerings before them on a platter. The function of the hall appears to have been simply religious. But as time went on the functions of the hall were no longer confined to religion; it was extended to embrace many social purposes. Likewise, the village temple was originally dedicated to deified mortals such as Kuan-Ti, a distinguished general in the period of the Three Kingdoms, now a god of valour and royalty, and Lung Wang, or Dragon King, a 'rain god'. Yet the temple is more a centre of social and political life than of religious life. It bears more resemblance to the English town hall than to the parish church. It serves as social centre from which radiates the network of relations among the villagers, with other villages and the neighbouring district. Should a stranger suffer any grievance from the villagers, complaints are lodged in the village temple and redresses are sought through it.

1 The village temple has sources of income. It owns lands which are available to be let out to needy families regardless of their clan or lineage. In regard to the temple itself, poor villagers are, as a rule, hired to cultivate the garden and grow some vegetables, and, as remuneration, they are provided with food and even shelter. The market of the village located around the temple is similar to that around the church in many European towns, as in Germany, for example. As a church and its immediate surroundings is a gathering place, it naturally provides for the best opportunity of trade. Dr Yang gives an interesting description of Hsinanchen, the market town, near Taitou, Shantung province.[50]

> The business section of the town has broad streets lined with shops, restaurants and inns. The second largest temple which is Buddhist is located near the market town. Hsinanchen serves more than twenty villages and it has a considerable volume of business. The five to six

drugstores to sell, in addition to drugs, sugar, oil, spices, etc. These shops are open all week but are busiest on regular market days; their owners and clerks came originally from the villages where their families still live, and customers patronize those from their own villages. Farmers go there because their fathers and their grandfathers were patrons there. On the evening before the market opens, the professional itinerant traders begin to pour in with their wares; early in the morning come the village butchers with their dressed hogs, the country merchants with their bags of wheat flour, cans of petroleum, bales of spun cotton yarn. Then farmers begin streaming in from the surrounding villages with their loads of grains, beans, fresh vegetables, and fruits, animal feed and firewood. Very few women go to market, with the exception of some old women from poor families who carry eggs, chickens, or baskets of seafood for sale, or some of their handiwork which they hope to exchange for a little money.

This description, though it is not exhaustive, gives a general picture of village markets in North China.

Kulp has described the market town of Phoenix village in South China, which is similar to that of the Taitou village described above by Dr Yang. Kulp writes:[51]

of the twenty-one open shops in the business section only five run by merchants who are members of the Phoenix Village family group. The others are rented by people from outside, who have come in to do business with Phoenix Village and with the nearby villages. To meet the needs of people the shops provide a delivery service. It is significant that competition operates here as everywhere. There are four food shops, two meat shops, two medicine shops, three bean curd shops, two rice shops under one merchant. Over half the shops are devoted to the sale of food of some kind or other. The others comprise the paper shop, the dry-goods shop and the service shops, such as the barber, and the opium and dye shops. The successful establishment and maintenance of these shops in a village as small as this Phoenix Village correlate with the change in family economy. A number of people occasionally buy there to meet the usual needs of the family. Complete independence of family economy does not exist either for any part of the village kin group or for the village as a whole. This market provides for the exchange of goods between the local producers and the village consumers and the rural consumers of extraordinary and incidental products.

149

2 As has been said, the markets are set up around the temples, whether they are Confucian, Buddhist, or Taoist. The temple provides for the annual festival; like the temple itself, the annual festivals, such as the New Year and Autumn festivals have, in modern times, lost a great deal of their religious meaning and significance. Traditionally, the festivals are celebrated in honour of the patron of the village, for instance, Kuan-Ti, but in reality they mean a social gathering, something like an annual carnival. Operas are staged in theatres before the temple, the surrounds of which are all decorated and illuminated; an influx of village folk, young and old, men and women, come to the temple square to enjoy their annual merry-making. Again, annual festivals are a great event of enjoyment and a source of income for the temple and businessmen.

Moreover, a religious parade to honour the Dragon King is held in front of the temple when there is drought. If it rains within ten days after the parade, the villagers attribute this blessing to the Dragon King and, as a token of thanks, make a sacrifice to the god and sometimes stage an opera. If no rain comes after the parade, the villagers expose the statue of Lung wan to the hot sunshine as a punishment.

3 Another important function of the village temple is to provide for its security. It is the duty of each house to supply a man to be on guard for a certain number of days and nights in the year. In the event of no man being available in the family, a small sum of money is made over. Such contributions are used to pay those who do extra watch duties. In ordinary times the watch duty is to patrol the outskirts of the village and strike the streets and lanes with a certain number of strokes with a hollow bamboo; this reminds the sleeping villagers of the danger of fire and thieves. I remember an accident befalling my family. One night a thief set fire to a great heap of our faggots laid up in a yard where no one was living. At midnight the nightwatchman awoke my father in alarm and told him that the whole pile was ablaze and called our neighbours for help. I saw more than a hundred people carry buckets of water to fight the fire. It was due to the early warning and the prompt and voluntary help of neighbours that only half the pile was burned.

Dr Gamble gives an account of how a mutual protection programme in Chai Ch'en village of Ting Hsien district was organized. He says that:[52]

the village is divided into five districts, and a leader was chosen from each district to be responsible for the protection work. Two night-watchmen were engaged. In case of theft all the village was summoned by the ringing of the village gong. If any of the villagers were hurt or killed in attempting to catch a robber it was customary that they should be given a sum for medical expenses or their families be given a funeral present. The expenses of the mutual protection programme were to be paid by the entire village.

4 The 'pao chia' system, i.e. the self-governing body, has an ancient origin. We have seen the historical development of the 'pao chia' system in different dynasties in the first chapter. In the Warring States (220 BC) it was Kuan Chung, the Prime Minister of Ch'i state, who introduced the pao chia system, which could control the whereabouts of people, particularly prisoners, fugitives and vagrants. In the Ch'in state, this system exercised a great control over families as well as individuals. It could prosecute criminals, but could not edify people. In the Han dynasty the pao chia system operated to report seducers and hinder robbers so that its functions resembled that of police. In the T'ang dynasty the same system served to keep watch on any unlawful acts and to enforce tax returns. Such a system is very similar to the pao chia system which was organized after the Sung dynasty.

The pao chia system which was in force from the Sung dynasty until the 1940s, was first instituted in an efficient form by Wang An shih, the great reformer of the eleventh century in the Sung dynasty. It is more than likely that in China proper, particularly in North and Central China, the system survived until the coming of the Communists, though it ceased functioning and was replaced by other forms of social organization, such as 'tipao' and 'hsieng-tuan', Village Protection Organisation.[53] In 1930 Lin Yueh-hwa touched on the 'pao chia' system and said that 'lineage members, for the purpose of common defence, banded together to form a pao chia organization which raised local militia and posted sentries. All these matters were dealt with by the ancestral hall, which thus necessarily became a military headquarters and assembly point for the militia'.[54] Fei wrote also that 'the pao chia system was introduced in Fukien province, South China, in 1933, on account of the spread of Communist ideas and influences, to supersede the local self-government administration of 1929'.[55]

5 Regarding the collection of tax in a village, the heads of the lineage play the intermediary role between their village and the local district, that is, 'hsiang', in the payment of taxes. Their payment is a duty which each landowner owes to the government through the district magistrate and his collectors, but the individual landowner does not always pay his taxes directly to collectors. Liu Hsing-t'ang points out that in certain

places the collectors cannot collect taxes directly from each family. The heads of families and the head collector manage the taxes in turn. In the absence of the heads of families and the head collector, someone will take up the office on the strength of his seniority. He has the register. All government taxes are managed by lineage; but they combine many small lineages into a group to avoid being molested by government officials and their subordinates. Though this situation is peculiar to 'Chao-an' village, it is a universal fact that the lineages could defy the local government and its officials.[56]

At the beginning of every year a meeting is held to elect a 'hsian-chang', the head of a village. Those who attend are the senior members of the families. Every family may be represented by at least one member, though a number of families are not heads of families, for the heads of the upper-class families do not attend the meeting. Many farmers are uninterested in village matters, because the village will have its 'hsiang-chang' anyway.[57]

The village government, within which are the heads of the families, either old men or scholars, plays an important role, including a wide range of activities, such as defence, the maintenance of internal order and security, the payment of taxes, and the arrangement of division of families and inheritances. Because of the leading role of the heads of families, we must consider the relations between leadership springing from the genealogical structure of the lineage and that by scholars or literati.[58] In a segmentary system, the principle of seniority in line of descent was rarely manifested. Sub-lineages are often numbered in order of their seniority, great, second, third and so on, but their political status is not affected by this order. In the view of Hu Hsien-ch'ing, for the furnishing of leaders of a village on a genealogical basis all segments are normally equal.[59]

There is no denying that in the Chinese kinship system considerable power has been put in the hands of controlling groups, though theoretically the lineage is egalitarian, that is, all members have an equal opportunity of being promoted to positions of authority in accordance with the kinship principle. In practice, however, access to power is in the main ascribed to an elite in the lineage, who wields much of the power and controls the distribution of economic and ritual privileges.[60] Again, the unequal distribution of power and status can serve to demarcate the lines of segments. The component units of each lineage, though they are genealogically balanced, are often of unequal weight in terms of riches, prestige and influence. Dr Yang wrote that:[61]

152

in the Taitou Village a tsu-chang, the head of a clan, has some influence over a designated group of families. He is usually an older member but sometimes may be the person who is the head of the richest family in that particular community. for his wealth allows him to do things others cannot afford.

We now conclude our description of the political aspects of Chinese family life; but we consider it imperative to add what is the impact on the traditional village structure and kinship structure. Dr Freedman says:[62]

in societies which know no writing there need be little discrepancy between the structure of present relations and the structure cited by genealogies in the past. As the present changes, the past changes along with it. In Chinese society, however, writing enters the scene, and we may assume that literacy and records introduced into its past a rigidity which rendered it less amenable to the influence of the present.

The religious aspects of family life within the kinship system

The role of the ancestral hall in ancestor worship, and the function of the latter as a cement of Chinese family life, have been considered above.

The ancestral hall also appears to interlink with economic resources. In default of a hall and land to support it, a segment of lineage cannot possibly continue its existence. Lin Yueh-hua has described the ancestral hall in his essay on 'I-hsü' village. 'Lineages', Lin writes,[63]

sub-lineages, branches and compounds have their halls. The hall of each family, if large, is called the family hall, and, if small, a family shrine. This is not to say that all sub-lineages, branches, compounds, and families have such halls; for the establishment of a hall is closely related to economic conditions; therefore only the rich have halls for the sub-lineages, branches, compounds, and families, while the poor may have only an ancestral shrine for the lineages.

In the hall it is incumbent upon the clan (tsu) to perform the regular rites for the first ancestor (the founding ancestor) and for remote or distant ancestors of all the agnatic units as well as for the ancestors of lines of descent that have become extinct, so that no souls should sink into oblivion. Once or twice a year, in Spring and Autumn, ancestral rites were performed in honour of the ancestors. Only men participated in the rites; women played no part in the sacrifice, but were permitted to attend merely as spectators.[64] In describing the ancestor worship in Phoenix Village, Kulp says that:[65]

> all males, living or dead, are regarded as members in good standing in the religious family, i.e. the ancestral group or branch family. They may be actual members, as in the case of adults who participate in the ceremonies of ancestral worship, or potential as in the case of boys who are mere learners and future worshippers. Females, on the contrary, are not members of the religious family except by proxy. They are allowed to participate in the ceremonies of worship merely as spectators, but as such they play an important role.

For example, in the domestic shrine or temple, the wife is bound to perform the daily rites of lighting incense and preparing whatever is necessary for sacrifice; but when she dies, she becomes a member of her husband's lineage by virtue of her motherhood of sons who are worshippers.[66] Through an honourable and dutiful motherhood a woman, even a concubine, may attain a high status in her husband's lineage.

As filial piety to parents and respect to elders has always constituted the *raison d'être* of family ethics in China, ancestor worship is conducted by old men. If a clan is subdivided into sub-lineages, every sub-lineage will be presided over by its eldest member. Sub-lineage heads are selected on the basis both of generation and age. Giving priority to generation presents no problem. If it happens that the old people of the higher generation have died off, while only young people are left, a proxy, usually a village head, is appointed to assist the young head of the lineage. The choice of proxy is based on the criterion of age. Again, in the event of none of the heads being available, an ordinary male member of the lineage who is expert in ritual matters and the business of the clan can be appointed.[67] The elders not only have full control of the lineage affairs, but also responsibility for maintaining the honourable record of the lineage and for promoting the education of its young members.

Ancestor worship and the first-born son

Ancestor worship symbolizes the affirmation of rights over other individuals, and the sacrifice is always offered by the individual who holds juridical authority in the group descended from the ancestor. Only the older generation has access to the agnatic ancestors on whom the younger generations are dependent. In Chinese social organization the 'so-called "tsung"[68] is clan organization in feudal times in which the eldest brother rules the younger ones; it is also called the way of brotherhood'.[69] Only the eldest son of the first ancestor of a line (pieh tzǔ) by his legal wife can inherit his father's fief (land held from a feudal lord) and rank 'chih-pieh', be a successor to the pieh and offer the sacrifice.

The system of the 'tsung' institutes that the 'tsung tzǔ' has the right to offer sacrifice. Ho Hsün (AD 269–319) says that 'if the tsung-tzǔ offers sacrifice at a certain time, all the males and females of the tsu will meet'. The tsung tzǔ of the grand tsung, the successor to the first ancestor, is invested with the right to offer sacrifice to the pieh tzǔ and to those who are successors to the pieh tzǔ. The tsung tzǔ of father tsung has the right to offer sacrifice to his father; the tsung tzǔ of the grandfather tsung, to the grandfather. According to the *Li Chi*, 'whoever is not the head of the family is not entitled to make sacrifice to the manes either of his ancestors or his father'.[70] The first-born son is vested with the leadership, but his authority can be extended to those who are dependent upon him. In point of fact, the person who is, by right of succession or heirdom, entitled to officiate at ancestor worship, also bears a heavy responsibility to the ancestors. His faults of negligence are more likely to call down retribution if the family ethics wane.

Moreover, when a family division takes place, a domestic shrine can serve as the ritual centre for a number of agnatically related families. The uniqueness of the ancestral tablet is viewed as a device for maintaining ritual unity among closely related agnates in different households. When a younger brother moves to another locality, he will take a large board on which are written the names which are inscribed on all the tablets left behind in the shrines and kept by the senior brother.[71] The fact that the eldest brother or the first-born son keeps the original tablet in the domestic shrine accounts for his prominent status in the succeeding generations and the patrifilial nexus in the Chinese descent system.

With regard to the ancestral hall (tsu t'ang), when the clans have grown to the extent that many branches and small sub-branches ought to be formed, a number of ancestors will be honoured in several ancestral halls. De Groot has described the ramification of ancestral halls, saying that:[72]

> When a clan hall has been filled with tablets and no further tablets can be added, some members of the family will form a new temple of their own, transferring from the old hall to the new, the tablets of those ancestors who had died recently. The new hall is a branch of the older one.

For example, in the tsu 'chu' in eastern Kiangsu province all trace their descent from Lo Pu-Ching, the honorary name of Chu Po-yung, who lived around 1080. His tomb and the ancestral hall bearing his name have been set in a huge garden and they have formed today a part with pavilion and grounds with several ancestral halls set between.[73] A village in Kwangtung, with seven hundred inhabitants all of one clan, has held forty or more ancestral temples.[74]

In view of the growth of the clan in size, each member cannot lay claim to the same amount of beneficial rights from the ancestral hall. In order to have an equitable distribution of the income accrued from the ancestral property, a method must be devised. All the male members of the clan, including all widows, have a right to an equal share irrespective of their age. Leong and Tao state that 'all those who reach the age of 59 and over are entitled to a double share, a sort of old age pension; those who reach the age of 69 will have their shares trebled and those who reach 79 quadrupled and so on'.[75]

Female members who are not widows are excluded in that they are either wives whose husbands are still living, or they are duaghters. The former have no share apart from their husbands and sons, while the latter will in the end be married outside the clan, being incorporated into other clans.

Another form of assistance offered by the ancestral hall is the encouragement of education to all the children of the clan; in particular, all clans, be they prosperous or poor, endeavour to help any of their members who are attempting competitive public examinations. To glorify one's parents and ancestors is regarded as one of the most sacred duties for every Chinese, and those who cannot glorify their ancestors by acquiring public honours themselves, take a keen interest in assisting those who set their hearts on doing so. Dr Yang says that in Taitou Village:

> A young boy who had just graduated from high school in the country showed talent and interest in further study; the boy was soon recognized by the clan as a most promising member who would add to the common glory, and was helped by his clansmen to go to a college.

In another report, Yang says that:[76]

> a member of the Yang clan had a very good reputation as a student when he was in the market-town school. They all hoped that the boy would pass several government examinations and would finally get an official post. After his graduation from the primary school, the boy went to a Christian high school, and then to a Christian university. This not only disappointed his kinsmen but also the villagers, because Christian schools at that time were not known to many Chinese and they were not the 'door' through which contacts with the government could be made. This gave the kinsmen and the villagers the impression that he was not going to be a scholar or a gentleman or an official, and they became indifferent towards him.

This account shows that the interest of the clan in supporting a high education lies not so much on an interest in the development of the young man as on the prospective benefits that will accrue to the clan if he proves to be a success.

In short, ancestor worship is an extension of the authority in the juridical relations of succcessive generations. It devolves, therefore, on the ancestor's filial son to perform the ancestral service and duty of worship. Ritual services are performed and offerings are made in the family shrine or temple as well as in the ancestral hall of its clan. There the congregation serves to strengthen the continuity and solidarity of the lineage and of the wider group composed of related lineages. In addition to the religious functions of the hall, it acts as a social centre for lineage members and provides for their welfare and education. Dr Fortes points out that:[77]

> ancestor worship can be taken as a body of religious beliefs, ritual practices and rules of conduct, which serve to entrench the principle of juridical authority and legitimate right; this kind of authority and right is generated and exercised through social relations created by kinship and descent.

Other ritual aspects of social life

It is a matter of course that any religious cult normally involves certain ideas or beliefs, on the one hand, and, on the other, certain observances, positive and negative, that is, actions and abstentions, which we speak of as rites. In the view of Loisy, 'rites are in all religions the most stable and lasting element, in which we can best discover the spirit of the ancient cults'.[78] The Chinese writers do not write about religion, and it is doubtful if there is any Chinese word which can be the equivalent of the word 'religion' in the Christian sense; but they have the word 'li' to describe ceremonies, customary morality, rites, rules of good manners and propriety. As we have mentioned earlier, the character 'li' (see Glossary) is composed of two parts, of which[79] the left part refers to spirit, while the right part means a vessel used in performing sacrifices to spirit. We may therefore think of 'li' as 'ritual'. The character 'li' in Confucianism means reason, law and principle. Human nature follows 'li', which is identical with Heaven.[80]

Long before the Chou dynasty mourning grades of a simpler kind existed, but it was the Confucianists who had elaborated them.[81] Both *Erh Ya* and *I Li* mentioned the mourning system. Yet in studying these two classics we have found some divergent points. Some classical scholars have attempted to amend the *Erh Ya* and make it concordant with the *I Li* system as they have considered that the *Erh Ya* system did not meet the standard of Confucian ideals of kinship.[82] What they failed to see was that the *Erh Ya* represents an early stage of the system, while later *I Li* was worked out to conform with the mourning system.

There is no denying that the *Erh Ya* system was already to some degree modified through Confucian influence, but it is less so than the *I Li*. As a result of the Confucian ideals deeply implanted in the social structure from the second century BC onward, the mourning rites as well as the kinship system were greatly elaborated until both reached an acme during the T'ang dynasty.

The Chinese mourning system is based on the lineage structure and on the degree of relationships for the assignment of mourning grades. Hu considers the circle of mourning relatives a unit 'larger than the family but smaller than the tsu lineages'.[83] The 'wu fu' - the five mourning grades - is a category drawn up in regard to a given 'ego' as a point of reference. The agnatic 'wu fu' is defined as a mourning unit counted in a direct line of ascent to a common great-great-grandfather and a direct line of descent to the great-great-grandchildren. Hence mourning ceases at the fourth degree, i.e. fourth collateral, and at the fourth generation, both ascending and descending from ego.[84] In other words, the 'wu fu' includes ego's brothers and their agnatic descendants to the third descending generation; his father's brothers and their agnatic descendants to the level of second descending to the level of the first descending generation from ego; his father's father's father's brothers and their agnatic descendants to the level of ego's own generation; and all the sisters of the men included.[85]

Within the agnatic 'wu fu' the members of a segment or lineage have a very close relationship with patrilineal kinsmen; that is to say, close agnatic kinsmen are bound up with one another by special rights, duties and obligations which stand apart from those with men of an outside kinship category. The duties and obligations of mourning 'sang fu' worn by a man towards his agnatic 'wu fu' not only discriminate a grade of relationships between the agnates, but they do so in such a way as to indicate which are more important than others.

The five mournings vary both in the length of period and the kind of material of mourning dress; the heavier the mourning, the longer the duration and the coarser the material. The five mourning grades arranged according to the importance and closeness of kinsmen are as follows: 'Chan ts'ui', 'ch'i ts'ui', 'ta kung', 'hsiao kung', and 'ssu ma'. The *Li Chi* says: 'In counting kindred, the three closest degrees become expanded into five, these five again into nine. The mourning diminished as the degrees ascend or descend, and the collateral branches also were correspondingly less mourned for; and the mourning for kindred thus came to an end.'[86] For parties four generations removed from the same common ancestor, the mourning was reduced to that worn for three months, and this was the limit of wearing the hempen cloth. If the generations were five, the shoulders were bared and the cincture assumed; and in this way mourning within the wider family circle was gradually reduced. After the sixth generation the bond of kinship came to an end.[87] These two texts deal with generations and mournings respectively, but they define the kinship relationships in the mourning grades.

Grade 1 - 'chan ts'ui', three years,[88] but in fact the period is only twenty-seven months for sons mourning for their parents and a wife for her husband. The material of the apparel is made up of the coarsest sack of hempen cloth with a fringe, i.e. unhemmed garments.[89]

The mourning for three years for the father and mother came into force under the Yao emperor (24 centuries BC) and the mourning dress made up of hemp was in use in the Hsia dynasty (23 centuries BC), but the five mourning grades were only established in the Chou dynasty by the end of the twelfth century BC by duke Chou, the brother of king Wen. These customs were adopted by the succeeding dynasties as wisely prescribed, and they were not modified except in minor points.[90] For example, Tai Tsung (AD 627-49) increased the mourning for a great-grandfather from three months to five months.[91] According to the book *Erh Ku tu shu*, 'the kindness of the father and the filial piety flow from a natural disposition and are rooted in the "jen". The father does not consider his remembrance of his son for three years to be long; likewise the son feels three years' mourning to be proper and bound.'[92]

A staff of bamboo (chu) is used for the death of the father, while a staff of t'ung wood for that of the mother. The bamboo means 't'su', to stamp the feet, while the wood, 't'ung', stands for grief. Again, bamboo is 'yang', while 't'ung' is 'yin'. A bamboo stem is simply cut to be used as a staff, being its original natural state and thus representing the 'yang'. A branch of the 't'ung' tree has its bark removed before it is used as a staff, that is, it undergoes dressing by human skill and so it is 'yin'. The *Li Chi* says: 'The coarse staff is of bamboo, the staff without bark is of "t'ung" wood.'[93] The use of bamboo and t'ung wood convey the idea that the filial son, having lost his parents, is afflicted with such grief that during three days he could not eat for weeping; his body becomes emaciated and ill, He must carry a staff for support.[94]

Grade 2 - 'Tsu ts'ui', means one year of mourning. 'Tsu' denotes 'sewn down the edge or border and hem-line of the mourning dress'. According to the *Li Chi*, the mourning dress for the mother is three years,[95] but the mourning dress is hemmed so as to avoid an equality with the father, for whom the mourning dress is unhemmed. In later dynasties, such as the T'ang, Sung, Yuan, Ming and Ch'ing, the mourning dress for both father and mother is unhemmed. Apart from the mourning period of one year, there is also hemmed mourning dress for a period of five or three months for great-great-grand and great-grand-parents and the stepfather; these kinsmen are more remote than the parents and thus the mourning period decreases.

Grade 3 - 'ta kung' means that cloth is woven on a larger reed and it is coarser than that woven on a finer reed. 'Nine' months period symbolizes the end of all things and covers three seasons.

Grade 4 - 'hsiao kung' means a rough woven cloth on a finer reed so that its warp and weft are finer. The period of 'five' months signifies the end of 'yang' principle.

Grade 5 - 'ssu ma' indicates that the warp and weft of cloth are very fine like silk, that is, the mourning dress is made up of finer fabric. The period of 'three' months means the end of a season.

The mourning dress can be divided into four categories according to the laws of the Ch'ing dynasty. (1) The natural mourning is called 'Cheng fu', which the son wears for his father, mother, paternal uncles, siblings, and the sons of his brothers in view of affection and rights. (2) 'I fu'[96] means the conventional mourning dress which is worn for the adopted father, the maternal grandparents, the father of the wife, the father of the husband and the son of a married daughter. This obligation is founded upon rights. (3) The increased mourning dress 'Chia fu' is worn, for example, by the grandson heir who is mourning for his grandfather in place of his father. (4) The decreased mourning dress is called 'Chiang fu'; reduced mourning dress denotes a more distant degree, such as a married woman mourning for her own paternal agnates. Another mourning category is called 'Pao fu' - the mourning of 'recompense', which older generations wear for younger ones, for instance, the mourning of a father for his son or an elder brother for his younger brother. However, there is a custom that if a son dies before his father and mother, a piece of white cotton cloth about 11 feet long is placed on his coffin as symbolic mourning; the dead son must himself wear mourning for his parents before they will wear mourning for him. In addition to the categories of mourning dress there is a custom that a mourning headband called 'tan mien' or 'cha tou pu' must be worn for the agnates of collateral branch and beyond the fourth degree. This headband is made up of a cotton cloth one inch in width, and is bound round the forehead.[97]

Mourning must be worn on the day of death. If the son is absent, he must wear the mourning the day he receives news of the death. The intercalary month is not counted; if the death occurs in the intercalary month, the mourning must be worn the same day, but it is counted only from the first day of the following month.[98]

Mourning grades of a married woman for her husband's agnates

1 The wife mourns three years for her husband and her parents-in-law. Her husband wears mourning for her for one year (with the staff, if his father and mother died, and without the staff, if they are still living). The parents mourn for their daughters-in-law for one year without the staff, if their son is first-born; otherwise, for nine months.

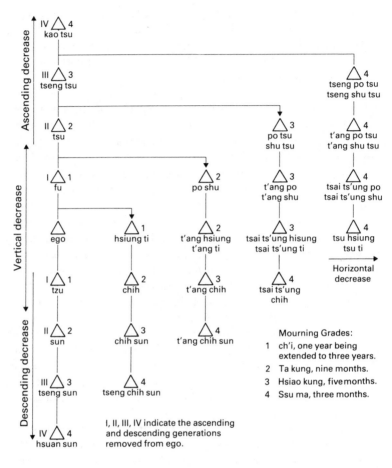

The mourning ritual is not left to the discretion of the mourner's own emotions but he is obliged to mourn in prescribed forms. The mourning grades are codified according to one's precise kinship status. Mourning is worn for the nearest kin for a period of one year (ch'i) as a basic unit. According to 'San fu chüan,' the nearest kin includes three relationships, that is, between father and son, between husband and wife and between brothers. Seeing that the period of one year is extended to three years and decreased to three months, the whole system correlates with the kinship system as shown in this diagram.

Figure 5.1 *Grades of mourning*

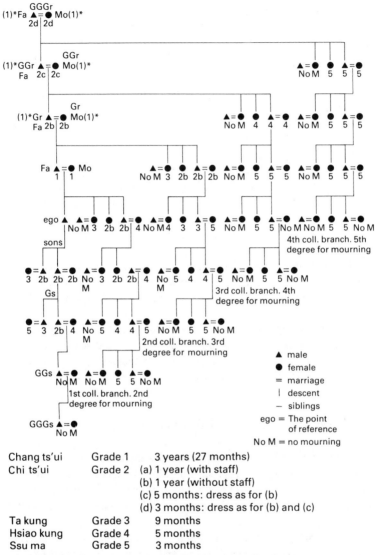

Chang ts'ui	Grade 1	3 years (27 months)
Chi ts'ui	Grade 2	(a) 1 year (with staff)
		(b) 1 year (without staff)
		(c) 5 months: dress as for (b)
		(d) 3 months: dress as for (b) and (c)
Ta kung	Grade 3	9 months
Hsiao kung	Grade 4	5 months
Ssu ma	Grade 5	3 months

Figure 5.2 *The mourning grades of a man towards his agnates within 'fu wu'*

Source: *Ta Ch'ing Lü Li (The Laws of the Ch'ing Dynasty)*

*The figure 1 in brackets against paternal grandparents and great-grandparents and great-great-grandparents indicates that 'ego' was to mourn for them in the first grade if he was the most senior descendant living.

2 The wife wears mourning for her grandparents-in-law for nine months, but they would mourn for her for only three months.
3 The wife wears three months' mourning for her great grandparents-in-law and great-great-grandparents-in-law, but they would wear no mourning for her.
4 The wife and the married daughter of her husband shall mourn for nine months. There are some exceptions as follows:

    (a)   The wife and the aunt of her husband, married or not, shall wear mourning for each other for five months.

    (b)   The wife and the sister of her husband, whether married or not, shall mourn for each other for five months.

    (c)   The wife and her cousin, the child of her husband's uncle, whether married or not, shall mourn for each other for three months.

5 The wife wears mourning for the agnates of the family in which her husband is legally adopted.
6 The wife and the maternal grandparents, the maternal uncle and the maternal aunt of her husband wear the same mourning, that is, three months, while her husband wears mourning for them for a period of five months.
7 The wife wears no mourning for the children of her husband's sister, though the latter wears mourning for five months and vice versa.
8 The wife does not wear mourning for the son of her husband's maternal uncle, maternal aunt or the paternal aunt.

Mourning grades of a married woman for her paternal agnates

That the married woman is not completely alienated from her maternal home is ritually expressed in her mourning obligations. In the event of her marriage, a woman would no longer mourn for her own parents to the same extent as she would were she still a daughter in their house, but she is not entirely freed from mourning obligations towards them. If we compare Figure 5.2 and Figure 5.4 we shall see that marriage noticeably changes a woman's status and relationship towards her own people.[99] The mourning of a married daughter for her paternal agnates and vice versa decreases one grade.
1 The married daughter mourns for her own parents for one year without the staff, while they would wear mourning for her for nine months.

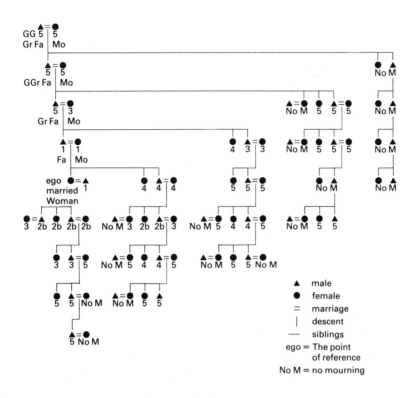

Chan ts'ui	Grade 1	3 years (27 months)
Chi ts'ui	Grade 2	(b) 1 year (without staff)
Ta kung	Grade 3	9 months
Hsiao kung	Grade 4	5 months
Ssu ma	Grade 5	3 months

Figure 5.3 *Mourning grades of a married woman for her husband's agnates*

Source: *Ta Ch'ing Lü Li*, vol. II, pp. 76–82; *Yuan Tien Chang* (*The Laws of the Yuan Dynasty*), vol. XXX, pp. 8a–8b.

2 However, there is no change in her mourning for her own grand-parents, that is, one year without the staff, while they wear mourning for her five months instead of nine months.

3 If the married daughter is repudiated by her husband and returns to her parents, she would mourn for her parents for three years. If she is widowed with no son, she wears mourning for her brother, her un-married sister, and the son or unmarried daugher of her brothers for one year.

4 For a son adopted by her own father she wears mourning for one year; but the adopted son mourns for her for nine months instead of one year.

5 For a married daughter the mourning is reduced by two grades. For example, the mourning between the married daughter and her married sister is five months instead of one year. Between the married daughter and an adopted brother in the other family the mourning is reduced to five months from one year.[100]

Mourning grades of a man and a woman for their mother's agnates and father's sister's children

A man and a woman are bound to mourn for certain of the children of their mother's agnates, such as the children of their mother's brother and mother's sister, and the children of their father's sister. But we should bear in mind that these three cousins fall within the range of prohibited marriage. The extension of grade five includes father's sister's daughter, mother's brother's daughter (chi) and mother's sister's daughter brings these three cousins in theory within the range of pro-hibited marriage.[101]

Mourning grades of a concubine for her master and the latter's agnates

1 A concubine, whether she has children or not, wears three years' mourning for her master and one year for the legitimate wife.

2 A concubine wears one year's mourning insignia for the father and mother of her master, but the latter wear no mourning for her.

3 A concubine having adult children wears five months' mourning for the grandfather and grandmother of her master, but the latter wear no

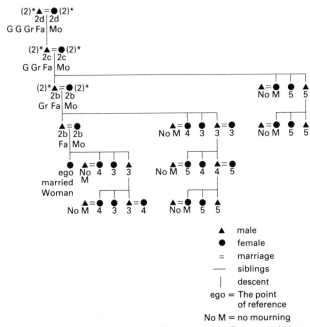

Note: Comparing this Figure, which shows the mourning due from a married woman to her agnates, with Figure 5.3, we can see that marriage reduces a woman's status towards her own agnates.

Chi ts'ui	Grade 2	(b) 1 year (without staff)
		(c) 5 months
		(d) 3 months
Ta kung	Grade 3	9 months
Hsiao kung	Grade 4	5 months
Ssu ma	Grade 5	3 months

Figure 5.4 *Mourning grades of a married woman for her paternal agnates*

Source: *Ta Ch'ing Lü Li*, p. 11a; *Yuan Tien Chang*, 'The Ritual', vol. XXX, p. 7a.

*The figure 2 in brackets against paternal parents and the lineal ascendants above them indicates that 'ego' (married woman) was to mourn for them in the second grade, since she was married.

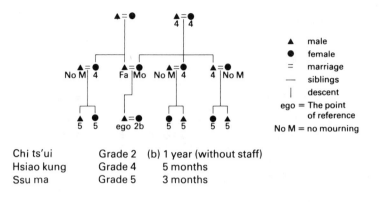

Chi ts'ui	Grade 2	(b) 1 year (without staff)
Hsiao kung	Grade 4	5 months
Ssu ma	Grade 5	3 months

Figure 5.5 *Mourning grades of a man and a woman for their mother's agnates and father's sister's children*

Source: *Ta Ch'ing Lü Li*, vol. II, p. 12b.

mourning for her. But a concubine having no children, or her children being not adult, wears no mourning for the grandfather and grandmother of her master.

4 A concubine wears only one year's mourning for her own natural father and mother, but the latter wear nine months' mourning for her.

5 A concubine's son or unmarried daughter wears three years' mourning for their natural mother, but the latter wears only one year's mourning for them.

6 The wife of a concubine's son wears three years' mourning for the natural mother of her husband, but the latter wears only nine months' mourning.

7 A concubine's son who, in the absence of a legitimate son, becomes an heir by right wears one year's mourning for his natural mother, and she also wears one year's mourning for him. The wife of the concubine's son who becomes an heir wears nine months' mourning for the natural mother of her husband, and the latter wears one year's mourning for her.

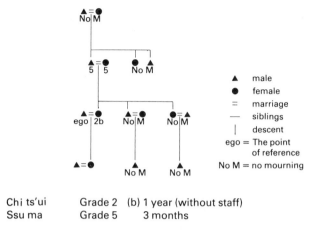

Chi ts'ui   Grade 2   (b) 1 year (without staff)
Ssu ma   Grade 5   3 months

Figure 5.6 *Mourning dress of a man for his wife's agnates*
Source: *Ta Ch'ing Lü Li*, vol. II, 'Mourning Grade Diagram', p. 14a.

8 Male or female, legitimate or concubines' children do not wear mourning for a childless concubine, and the latter wears one year's mourning for male children only. Again, a legitimate wife does not wear mourning for a childless concubine of her father-in-law, but the concubine wears one year's mourning for her if her husband is the first-born son; otherwise, the concubine wears only nine months' mourning.

It is evident from what has been said about the mourning worn for a concubine that she has an inferior status; we have good reasons for this. Differences between a wife and a concubine are conspicuous in the marriage ceremony. The *Li Chi* says that 'betrothal made the woman a wife and that if she went to a man without this ceremony she became a concubine'.[102] 'A concubine,' the *Li Chi* continues, 'was bought, and no ceremony was performed for her entrance into the master's family'.[103]

The word 'concubine' (ch'ieh) means 'to be accepted'.[104] The Chinese do not consider a concubine to be one of her master's relatives. She is addressed by her personal name, and she, like the servants, addresses the head of the family as 'master', and the wife's children as 'young masters'. The wife's children regard her as their father's concubine

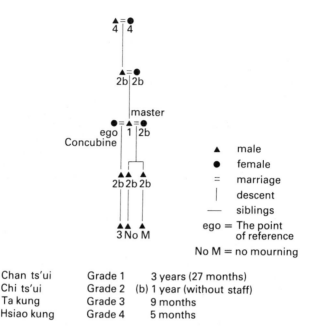

▲	male	
●	female	
=	marriage	
		descent	
—	siblings	
ego =	The point of reference	
No M =	no mourning	

Chan ts'ui	Grade 1	3 years (27 months)
Chi ts'ui	Grade 2	(b) 1 year (without staff)
Ta kung	Grade 3	9 months
Hsiao kung	Grade 4	5 months

Figure 5.7 *Mourning grades of a concubine for her master's agnates*
Source: *Ta Ch'ing Lü Li*, vol. II, 'Mourning Grade Diagram', p. 9b.

(fu ch'ieh), and address her as concubine mother (shu mu) only after she has borne a child. Again the concubine establishes no bond of affection or kinship relationship between the two families. In short, her status is not higher than that of a maidservant.

One may readily raise the question: How do the Chinese conceive of mourning in relation to their social structure? I do not attempt to make a full analysis of the notion of mourning, but only to discuss its nature on the basis of my personal observation. Both the period and fulfilment of mourning are correlated with the actual social relations of kinsmen and their standardized ties of affection. Unlike ancestor worship, mourning is not thought to contribute to the welfare of the spirit of the dead, but it serves to express affection. To other societies than the Chinese the wearing of mourning may be merely a personal expression

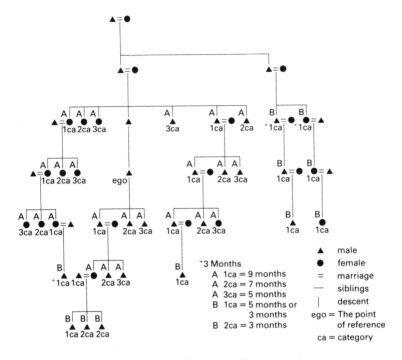

Shang means those who died under age. Three categories:
  1ca those who died between 19 and 16, called chang shang
  2ca those who died between 15 and 12, called chung shang
  3ca those who died between 11 and 8, called hsia chang
The adults of both sexes are:
  1 those of twenty years of age and
  2 those who are married, even if they have not reached the twenty yet.

Figure 5.8 *Three mourning categories for those died under age*
Source: *Yuan Tien Chang*, vol. XXX, 'The Ritual', p. 6b.

of sorrow; to the Chinese it is more than an expression of sorrow at the loss of the beloved relatives; it is a symbol of deprivation of the presence and moral support of the dead, relative and senior. He is gone and left us not merely sorrowing, but helpless and destitute. The mourners are obliged to clothe themselves in sack or hempen cloth to show their bereavement and grief.[105]

Table 5.1 *The mourning grades of a son for three classes of fathers and eight classes of mothers*

A son mourns for:		Period
1	his adopted parents (ssu fu, mu); a son legally adopted by a member of his own family, his paternal uncle	3 years
2	an adopted son for his natural parents (pen shen fu, mu)	1 year without staff
3	foster parents, who took the child abandoned under age	1 year without staff
4	a step-father (tung chü chi fu) the second husband of mother with whom one has gone to live on their remarriage, this step-father has no sons or grandsons	3 months
5	a step-father (pu tung chü fu) with whom one has not gone to live; this step-father has his own sons or grandsons	3 months
6	step-father with whom one has lived, but now has left and a step-father with whom one (son) has never lived	3 months no mourning
7	his re-married mother (chia mu), the mother widow is now re-married	1 year with staff
8	his divorced mother (chu mu), his natural mother but divorced (unmarried)	1 year with staff
9	his step-mother (chi mu) who becomes his father's legal wife by his re-marriage	3 years
10	the principal mother (ti mu), the 'legal wife' of the father as addressed by the son of a concubine	3 years
11	his merciful mother (tzu mu), a father's concubine who after the death of son's own mother and, at the father's direction, brought the son up	3 years
12	his foster, step-concubine (shu) and legal mothers who are repudiated and then remarried	no mourning
13	his step-mother or second mother (kai chia chi mu) who is remarried after her husband dies	1 year without staff
14	the son of a concubine for his natural mother (shing mu)	3 years
15	a son of a concubine wears mourning for a concubine mother who has adult children (shu mu)	1 year
16	his milk mother (ju mu) or wet nurse or a foster-mother, i.e. a concubine who, having lost her own child, nursed the son.	3 months

Source: *Yuan Tien Chang*, vol. XXX, 'The Ritual', p. 7b.

In *Totem and Taboo* Freud related 'mourning customs to the guilty hate the survivors experience as a reaction against the hostile element inevitably present in all close relationships.[106] After death has occurred, it is against this unconscious wish that the reproaches are a reaction.' Although we do not regard Freud's theory as entirely bearing on the notion of mourning among the Chinese, it can be of some help in interpreting their mourning rites. During a funeral procession I have heard mourners in China bewailing the loss of their beloved father and at the same time cursing themselves on the assumption that this misfortune had befallen them on account of their wrongdoing. For example the mourners will exclaim: 'Why did you, dear father, leave us destitute?; what wrong did I do to you as to make you separate from us?; I wish I could go with you; please forgive your unfilial son.' This utterance shows that the mourners have a guilty conscience, not in that they bore ill-will or concealed hostility against the dead father during his lifetime, but that they have a sense of not having lived up to his desire. The inference we can draw from the Chinese attitude in this matter is that they think that they have incurred the displeasure of the dead father.

Moreover, apart from mourning thought of as a spontaneous movement of private feelings wounded by a cruel loss, to weep is a duty imposed, by the corporate group, on the bereft party. It is a ritual attitude which he is compelled to adopt out of respect for custom. It follows that to explain mourning and funeral rites entirely in terms of the emotional comfort they give us is to evade many of the important problems, for instance, the question of why an unloved father – a wastrel – is mourned and buried with the same prescribed ceremony observed for a loved one.

Another important circumstance in mourning rites for the Chinese is that it is an occasion for expressing an individual's social personality by reaffirmation of his social roles. Of equal importance is the way in which mourning and funeral institutions perform a reconciliatory function with whoever has a grudge against the bereaved. During the funeral period of five to seven days the bereaved son is obliged to kowtow to whoever comes to console him. This gesture of great humility shows an apology on the behalf of the dead to those who feel wronged and nurse a grievance. This custom is undoubtedly a kind of mechanism operating to strengthen group solidarity. Again death as the threat of a domestic group, or as the disappearance of those who are near, who are loved, and who have relatives in life is a fact that fundamentally upsets the emotional constitutions of man. In that event mourning rites and funeral ceremonies are of primary significance as a mechanism for expressing and reasserting the sentiments which are most essential to group integration on the occasion of severe emotional strain. Here religious aspects step in, that is, the possibility of communion between the living and the dead. At the death of the father a whole system of mourning and funerary duties devolves on his son. The essence of these duties, seen from the sociological point of view, is that they reaffirm the duties of children towards parents, while from the moral point of view they amount to the religious extension of the ethical rules of conduct as between the members of the family, of the wider kindred group, and of the clan. Later on, the dead father is metamorphosed into ancestorhood and receives seasonal sacrifice. To the unchristian Chinese the ritual of sacrifice to ancestors is essential; on the other hand, in a christian Chinese family, when people commemorate their dead ancestors at graves or carry out memorial services in their churches, there appears a spiritual interaction between the living and the dead of their own family. This extends the family bonds and other social relations entered upon in life to the spirit beyond.

The occasions of ancestor worship

As has been said earlier, the daily life of a family is comparatively regular. Departures from the regularity of daily family life occur about a dozen times in the course of a year on such occasions as festivals, thanksgiving celebrations, ancestor worship and graveyard visiting. While in the ordinary way everyone is busy with his routine, at festivals all are assembled together for the celebrations, enjoying one another's company and renewing friendship, and accordingly the sense of solidarity can be strengthened. Here we are concerned only with the periodic occurrences of ancestor worship and graveyard visiting and renovation. As a rule, special sacrifices are offered to ancestors on the anniversary of their death, and collective offerings for all lineal ancestors are made several times a year. The mode of sacrifice consists of preparing a feast for the spirits, in which foods, incense and paper money are offered. This reflects the prolonged or continuous economic obligations of the young generations towards the dead.

In describing the sacrifices made to ancestors we should start from the beginning of the year. Preparations for the New Year Festival are begun at the beginning of the twelfth month and are quite painstaking.

174

After the twenty-third day of the month there is a house-cleaning, called, 'sao-chen', sweeping the dust. Everything in the house must be cleaned and put in order. The sweeping task embraces the people as well as the gods. A married daughter with her children, are considered outsiders, and may be welcomed with open arms to stay at her parents' home for many months, but they must leave before the twenty-third day. The kitchen god is moved out of the house before its cleaning. The New Year Festival is the great occasion of family reunion and of paying homage to ancestors, and consequently only family members can take part in the New Year's celebrations. This custom, which makes the members of the family feel that they are returning home, helps to reaffirm the wholeness of the family. In the early morning of the New Year's Day the family wake and wash and put on their new clothes; this being done, they gather in the main room to pay homage to their ancestors. The head of the family lights the candles and then three incense sticks, which he holds and raises to his forehead and places in the incense burner. He kneels before the ancestral table and kowtows towards the ancestor scroll. All the males of the family perform the same ritual. When the religious ceremony is over, the family head fires a long string of firecrackers. Women prepare 'chiao-tzu', dumplings. Three bowls of them are put on the ceremonial table as a sacrificial object to the ancestors. Then the junior members greet their elders with: 'kuo nien hao', 'happy New Year'. At sunrise, the men, old and young, go out greeting their relatives and neighbours, from door to door.[107]

In the early morning of the third day, another ancestor remembrance ceremony is carried out. This is called 'sung-tsu', a farewell to the ancestors who are leaving the house.[108]

The Lantern Festival is celebrated on the fifteenth of the first month (Cheng Yueh Shih We) and is the conclusion of the New Year celebration. At this festival – the first full moon – the family will hang a coloured lantern in the ancestral hall, an act called 'hanging the lamp', which symbolizes that 'lamp' (teng) is pronounced like the word 'ting', meaning a man, and has joined the lineage and been recognized as one of its members by the rest of the lineage. The main feature is the making and the distribution of lamps of five colours. Every family makes a number of small round vessels of dough. After these are steamed, wicks are inserted and immersed in peanut oil. In the evening they are lighted in every corner of the house, in the backyard, in the barn and the court, to symbolize brightness and good luck and drive away darkness and bad luck. They also represent the hope for a good crop in the new year.

The origin and history of The Festival of Cold Food (Han shih) is based on the account in *Tso Chuan*.[109] According to *Tso Chuan*, the prince of Chin state had, during his exile, a faithful follower called Chieh Chih-tui. He is said to have been so loyal to the prince that when he was in want of food, Chieh cut flesh from his leg to feed him. When the prince became the duke of Chin state, he rewarded all those who were with him in exile. Unfortunately, the duke forgot Chieh Chih-tui, though he declared that anyone who was forgotten should present himself and be rewarded. Chieh took offence at the remissness of the duke Chin. Later when it occurred to the duke that he had forgotten Chieh, he called on Chieh to make amends. Instead of responding to the duke's call, Chieh vanished with his mother into the immense forest of Mien shan. The duke searched for him for a long time, but he failed in his attempt. In order to drive Chieh out of the forest, the duke gave orders to set fire to it. Chieh and his mother clasped hands about a tree and perished in the flame. Thereafter, in commemoration of their death, fires were forbidden on a fixed day in the third month and food eaten cold.[110] At this festival 'Han Shih', paper pennants were laid on graves of ancestors in the An lu fu district.[111]

Ch'ing Ming is the first great festival after the New Year. It means 'pure' and 'bright'. In this festival, that is, at the beginning of the third month, the bright and warm weather savours of spring. One of the most interesting features is the custom 'sao mu' (visiting, sweeping and repairing graves).[112] On this day, old and young, men and women go to the graves, carrying paper money and food. First, an offering is laid out on the ground or on the stone table in front of the tomb. Now earth is added to the mounds and the dry grass and weeds are wiped out and swept clean. The letters on a tombstone, if any, must be repainted or cleaned. At the same time the members of the family are reminded of the deeds of the ancestors or recently deceased parents.

Another custom on the day of Ch'ing Ming is the wearing of willow branches and evergreen. Women and youngsters wear a thin twig hanging from the hair knot or tie it to their dresses. Willow branches are also inserted between the tiles of the roof and hung above the doors and windows of the house. In North China willow trees are the first to blossom and herald the spring.

The festival 'tuan wu', or the Dragon Boat Festival, is celebrated on the fifth of the fifth month. In this festival a family which has a new-born child must invite the Dragon Boat champion of its own branch and sub-lineage to a banquet called in the lineage 'the Meeting of Gaiety'.

'Tuan Wu' signifies literally the very moment of resistance or opposition between 'yin' - darkness, and 'yang' - light. These two characters 'tuan wu' mean also the solstice of summer, i.e. the fifth of the fifth month, because the spirit of darkness begins to gain ground and level against the 'yang' principle to make it retreat. On this day the members of the family place on a table, before the ancestral tablets, an offering composed of various kinds of meats. This is intended to show respect to the spirits of the ancestors. The *Li Chi* speaks of an offering made in the spring, that is, in the second month, to ancestors when the emperor offered a piece of lamb in the temple of his ancestors.[113] The significant feature of this festival is a Dragon Boat Race. It is to be noted that this custom is very common in Central East and South China. In North China, however, the lack of waterways makes it unpopular.

The custom of the Dragon Boat Race of 'fighting and crossing over' originated in the calling back of Ch'ü Yuan.[114] The scholar and minister, Ch'ü Yuan, during the reign of Ch'u Huai Wang (328–299 BC), attempted, as Ssu-ma Chien wrote, to administer Chu state in the best possible method, but his colleagues showed great jealousy of his undertakings and accused him of disloyalty. When Ch'ü Yuan realized that after listening to false accusations the emperor refused to accept his faithful advice, he drowned himself in the river Mi-lo[115] to bring home the importance of the advice to the emperor. Then the emperor sent a search-party to hunt for Ch'ü Yuan's body, but in vain. He decreed that each year on that day - the fifth of the fifth month - a memorial ceremony should be performed. (The Dragon Boats race up and down the river in pairs as if searching for the body of the drowned officer whom they hope to recover with the assistance of the almighty dragon.)

One of the special dishes prepared for the festival is called 'Tsung-tzǔ' is made of glutinous rice, cut in triangles, wrapped in a strip of bamboo leaves, and boiled overnight. As the legend runs, people threw stones 'tsung-tzǔ' into the river as offerings to and provisions for the drowned scholar.[116]

The custom 'to fight and cross over' emphasizes the importance of the social structure. Yang Si ch'ang points out that the boats belong to clearly defined regions. It often happens that a person whose ancestors have lived in a region associated with a particular boat moves out of this region and lives in a region associated with another boat, but is still considered to be a member of the group to which his ancestors have belonged.[117] The groups associated with the boats are very rigid. A person who was born into a given boat region in a clan group could not renounce his affinity with the group. There is no doubt that the crews of the Dragon Boat Race were the principal representatives of the established group, and accordingly the 'Dragon Boat' fight was engaged between the boat regions and their respective groups. The boat regions are mostly characterized by lineage-village organizations.

Villages can be some distance from each other, but still united by a common ancestor. Yang Si-ch'ang has enumerated the villages related to the boat regions, which are inhabited by a single clan or sub-lineage. For instance, Su Chia Tu, the 'Ferry of the Su families', lying fifteen li (about five miles) east of the capital of the prefecture, has been mentioned in conjunction with the boat regions.[118] Similarly Yü Chia Kang, which suggests a lineage with the clan named 'Yü', was also associated with one of the boats taking part in the ceremony.[119]

In the Dragon Boat Race the 'wu', sorcerer, plays an important role. On the day 'to fight and cross over' in Chang Te Fu, the 'wu' lighted an oil fire for purpose of divination. Fire is conceived of as a symbol of the 'yang' or male principle, and is one of the agents in the 'Wu Hsing' system, and thus a symbol of luck; on the other hand, low black flames, standing for bad luck, are associated with 'yin' or female principle. Drums were beaten to thwart the influence of hostile 'wu' sorcerers. The sound of the drum is the sign of seven days' luck.[120] The sound of drums also played 'guiding' functions, that is, 'shen' - spirits - were guided by the sound of drums. We can assume that the 'shen' thus guided were, in fact, dead ancestors. The 'wu' sorcerer in Chang Te Fu appears to have guided dead ancestors in the performance of the 'to fight and cross over' ceremony. Since a dragon boat was associated with a certain tsu-clan-group, the dead ancestors were no doubt the members of the group and participate in the boat race. In Yüan Men district the boat was welcome, and it is said that 'twenty strangers', most probably dead ancestors, arrived with the welcome boat.[121]

In brief, the 'wu', sorcerer, lighted an oil fire and illuminated the boat so as to guide the dragon boat's crew of dead ancestors. The 'wu' was provided with meat and wine and perhaps made sacrifice to the ancestors. He also walked along the boat from stem to stern scattering grain, and gave each crew member a 'lucky seal', an instrument to ensure the success of the boat race. At the same time the success of the boat race was foretold by divination.[122] The ceremony began with the dragon boat standing by and being told about the arrival of the ancestors and their voyage on the 'jo shui', 'weak water' from the regions of the sunset,[123] that is, from the regions of the setting sun to the world of man. When the flames rose high, the dragon boat set out on the river. The world of living crewmen was ready to participate in the 'to fight and cross over'.

The festival Chi Yueh Chi, took place on the seventh day of the seventh month (in the lunar calendar). According to the myths and legends, there is the fable of Aquila and Vega, known in Chinese mythology as the Herd Boy, living west of the Heavenly River, and the Weaver Girl, who lives east of the Heavenly River, or the Milky Way. The Weaver Girl is the granddaughter of the Emperor of Heaven. She was occupied year by year with her loom, weaving the cloud-embroidered heavenly dress. As a reward, her grandfather, the Emperor of Heaven, married her to the Herd Boy. No sooner did the maiden become a wife than she forsook altogether loom and needle, indulging herself in play. Her grandfather, in great wrath at all this, determined to separate the couple. The girl was then recalled to her natal home east of the Heavenly River. To prevent the lovers from crossing the River secretly, the grandfather ordered the bridge to be removed, and told them that hereafter they were allowed to meet each other only once a year, on the seventh night of the seventh month. But when the lovers kept their tryst, they found it impossible to reach each other because the bridge was gone. So the grandfather – the Emperor of Heaven, ordered myriads of magpies to fly together and, forming a bridge, to support the poor lovers on their wings and backs as if on a roadway of solid land; this bridge is called Magpie Bridge. Later the story was embellished and made more interesting. The legend used to be told to young girls that there was great and rueful sorrow in the annual reunion of the Weaving Girl and the Herd Boy in the seventh month. When they meet, they are thrilled with such joy that they burst into tears; when they realize that their happiness will soon be over, they weep again, this time with sadness. The story goes that the rainy season in North China comes on the seventh day of the month, and it rains almost always on that day.

The story relates the themes of the skill of weaving and embroidering, the love between a boy and a girl, the happiness of having a good husband and the sorrow of losing him. In some parts of China on the seventh night of the seventh month girls give a party to their friends and ask them to offer sacrifices to the Weaver Girl and to pray to her to let them be skilled in weaving and needlework and, especially, to send them a good husband. The story conveys the idea that only girls who are industrious in weaving and housework can win a gift from the Emperor of Heaven: he will marry them to good husbands and grant them a happy and blissful family. The parents make a point of telling their daughters this story which is used to discipline them.

Another appeal of this story is that in the first few years of marriage a young wife is frequently called back to stay with her parents. Although this custom helps the young wife a good deal by reducing the strain of adjusting to a new family, it may be a great hardship to both the husband and wife because of their temporary separation.

Chung Yüan, called also Yü lan Hui, is celebrated on the fifteenth of the seventh month and is the time of special sacrifices. It is said that ancestral spirits return home and visit their living descendants on that day.[124] Every family offers to its ancestors rice, incense, paper money, fruit, wine and meat, and invites relatives to a dinner.[125] In the meantime, presents of lamps, the wick of which is made of woven material drawn up in vegetable oil, are alight along the roads as guides to the hungry ghosts. In the Buddhist temples and on the streets the monks pray for release from punishment.

Chung Ch'iu Chieh, or the Harvest Festival, is celebrated on the fifteenth of the eighth month, and is one of the most joyous and merriest occasions of the year, for then the harvest is ripe and the farmers begin to enjoy their rest after their long and heavy work on the land. It is a harvest festival in which the enjoyment of Heaven's bounty is shared by gods and men. The farmers usually say that, while Ch'i Yueh Shih Wu, the fifteenth of the seventh month, is for ghosts, the Chung Ch'iu Chieh is for men. There is no religious significance attached to the festival; it is simply a holiday. The specially prepared meal is 'moon cake', made of wheat flour and brown sugar, and stuffed with sweets and fruit shreds. The moon cake weighs from half a catty to two catties (Chinese weight). The people do not make the cake themselves, but buy it in the market town bakeries.[126] The following prayer is uttered to the full moon:[127]

Thy nature is effulgent, transparent without spot;
Thou, the icy-wheel in the milky way along the heavenly street,
A mirror always bright; 100,000 classes all receive thy blessings.

Within the first ten days of the eleventh month it is said that all the graves are open,[128] the sons and grandsons visit them and uproot dry grasses and offer wine and meal.[129]

Tung Chih, the Winter Solstice

In Tung Chih every family prepares a special dish as an offering to his ancestors.[130]

The La Pa Chieh, the Festival of the Eighth of the Twelfth Month

This is also called Chia Ping Day and occurs annually on the eighth day of the twelfth month and is the festival of the eight ch'a or pa ch'a: that is, the spirits which give protection against locusts or grasshoppers, and the hunters. The eight (pa) categories of beings or genii help to ripen good harvests. The Hunters' Festival originated in the hunting period of Chinese civilization. Hence, La Pa Chieh seems to commemorate the gods of husbandry and the gods of hunting. The special food for this day is called La Pa Chou (like oatmeal), a gruel of eight different cereals and dates, symbolizing the variety of the harvest. On this day sacrifices are offered to ancestors.

Ch'u Hsi, New Year's Eve

Ch'u Hsi is called 'Tz'u Tsao', the Farewell offering to the Kitchen God.[131] It is the occasion when the Kitchen God and Goddess are courteously entertained and happily sent off to report the family life to the Supreme Ruler of Heaven. In the evening the God and Goddess are offered four dry dishes, one of which is a sweet made of sticky millet or rice. Paper money is burnt and incense sticks are lighted. Fodder is put in the courtyard as provisions for the horses of the God and Goddess. The sweet is made of glutinous rice to glue the lips of the God and Goddess together so as to prevent them speaking ill of the family. A picture representing the Door God and paper money of five colours[132] are hung on the door as a preparation for the New Year Festival.[133] In the stillness of the night, sacrifices are offered to the ancestors.

Why do the Chinese cleave to the tradition of celebrating festivals for many thousands of years? In the light of what has been said above we can gather that the Chinese are expected carefully to attend to funeral rites of parents and follow them, when gone, with due sacrifices.

Many annual festivals are associated with land and harvests, the former having been bequeathed to living descendants by their ancestors. It is not surprising to see such an association because China is predominantly an agricultural society; it is on the land that people depend for their livelihood. Correlated with this productive system are the obligation to perform periodic sacrifices to ancestors and the taboo against selling land and houses. The continuity of land-holding which the ancestors bequeathed to their descendants is an expression of filial piety.

Recreational aspects of the social life in the Chinese kinship system

The routine of everyday family life and annual festivals together present a lively picture of life. The family is a constituent unit of the lineage, whereas the individual is the component unit of the family. Although each individual is endowed with the potentiality of self-development, his personality will be moulded in conformity with the culture in which he happens to be placed by his birth. Family culture exerts the most direct and the most powerful influence in shaping the personality of an individual. Thus any particular type of individual personality is patterned according to what the special culture of a lineage and special family traditions have provided for. Recreational activities offer an opportunity not only for relaxation from muscular and nervous tension after hard work, but also for reinforcement of the social ties among the participants.

In the household domestic gatherings take place as a rule in the evening when the daily toil ends. This gathering serves greatly to strengthen the family bonds and develop an intimate sense of a defined 'we' feeling.

Farm work affords periodic respites. Men use these intervals to enjoy themselves in teashops,[134] which are in the towns as well as in the centre of the villages. Both in the day and in the evening many teashops are found open to welcome people who care to come to sip to and chat. One can also see a group of three to five men squat near some street corner and talk, while smoking pipes. At the informal gatherings they usually discuss topics such as crops, selling and buying of land. Again local affairs and stories of the old days and exciting events colour their conversations. Occasionally some women appear in the teashops, mostly to look for their men. Women spend most of the intervals in their work visiting relatives and neighbours, attending their children, and sometimes in playing cards with their friends. In winter many women go to weave in the neighbourhood where there are available looms. Their conversation tends to turn on their daughters-in-law.

The evening gatherings of the domestic groups, the congregation of people in the teashops, and the frequent visits among the relatives and neighbours during the rest periods are informal and spontaneous. Although they are different from the festivals and formal communal gatherings, they also serve to reinforce the local ties among the people. We now proceed to a description of some recreational activities which is not meant to be exhaustive, but which represents the general pattern of these activities.

Gambling

Gambling in traditional as well as contemporary China is a common practice that is theoretically condemned, but is tolerated by public opinion. To my knowledge, no villages have imposed taboos on gambling, but many cautious members of the community realize that its practice will endanger their fortune and thus only indulge in it at Chinese New Year holidays. In most parts of China people enjoy three days of free gambling every year. They begin on the first day of the first moon and end up on the night of the third day. During this entire period all ages can be seen sitting in the gambling dens staking their luck at the gambling tables. Women are tabooed from attending any gambling dens and from mixed gatherings with men in public places. But they also regale themselves and their friends by playing cards in their houses. Hsu describes the gambling game in the West Town as follows:

> Until 1943 three gambling dens did a thriving business. They were open nightly and sometimes daily. One was in the home of a police detective; another was in the home of the headman of a pao; the third was located in one of the clan temples. In the first den were gathered middle-aged and younger people who went in for big stakes which in 1943 often ran into five figures. In the second den were gathered players of all age levels who went in for smaller stakes. In the third place were gathered younger people only, and the stakes ran about the same as in the second den. The game played always included 'ma chiang' and poker. All visitors, whether they played or were just by-standers received free hospitality, food, drink and a pipe of opium if so desired.

Yang Ke Play

On the basis of local tradition, songs for the farmers to sing while they were planting the rice fields were written by the poet Su Tung-p'o (AD 1036-101) when he was the magistrate in Ting Hsien, Hopeh province, North China. The Chinese call these songs 'yang ke', or planting songs. There is no evidence of how the yang ke moved from the rice fields on to the local stage, how the original simple group songs were made into plays, or how the singers changed from blue-clad farmers into actors in costume performing for the amusement of the people in annual festivals. In Peking yang ke referred to the parade through the streets where actors stand on three or four foot stilts. The chief actor, playing the part of a monk, led the procession through the crowds by swinging a long stick in front of him. Other features consist of a regular group, a bearded man, a woman, a grandmother, a young man, a butterfly girl, a painted face, a stupid boy and his wife, military and civil attendants. The group sang, played on the drum and gongs, made jokes and amorous remarks, and amused the crowd by their whimsical swinging actions. In North China, for example, in Shantung province, the walkers on stilts of the yang ke used to take part in the entertainment of visitors at the temple fairs.

In the New Year's and Lantern Festivals, the spring and autumn, the temple fairs 'miao hui', and after the harvest, the yang ke was performed. The players or performers sang songs in a falsetto voice which could regularly be heard in Chinese singing. The stories of the plays can be classified into six different categories; boy and girl; filial piety and chastity; husband and wife; mother-in-law and daughter-in-law; humorous; and miscellaneous.

The category of boy and girl is reflected in the Chinese moral principle that as there are no two saddles for a good horse, a good woman does not have two husbands; the plays also make clear that women like to marry men who will be scholars and become officials.

The Chinese lay special emphasis on filial piety as an ineluctable obligation. A filial daughter would sacrifice her honour if necessary to secure an opportunity to avenge the death of her parents.

Between husband and wife, the former exercises authority and discipline over the latter. If she fails to give birth to male issue, she will permit her husband to take a concubine in order to have a son. Some plays show that the husband even has the power to sell his wife.

As soon as a girl marries, she must leave her own family and become a member of her husband's. His mother-in-law possesses complete power over her daughter-in-law. A daughter-in-law has no rights to any freedom of her own as long as her mother-in-law lives. Thus a daughter-in-law is depicted as hoping that her mother-in-law will die very soon.

In the episode when spirits take on human form and carry on work and romance, and when a wife bullies her husband and forces him to kneel with a brick or lamp on his head as punishment for gambling or when she has a hen-pecked husband, the 'yang ke' has an opportunity to insert much more good-humoured teasing and broad jokes.

The miscellaneous group of 'yang ke' involves local stories borrowed from the local stage and local humorous jokes. The following play is illustrative.[135] This play tells how Wang Su-chen's sister had to suffer maltreatment at the hands of her mother-in-law and sister-in-law. After her marriage, a girl was sold to her husband's family, she had no freedom and was virtually enslaved. All she could do was to yield to the caprice of her mother-in-law. A daughter-in-law would look forward eagerly to a visit to her parents' home. She had to request such a visit from her mother-in-law, and if such leave were granted, she dared not outstay her leave. She married at eighteen: a daughter-in-law could not help suffering each day, grinning and bearing a harsh oppression and patiently waiting for the death of her mother-in-law. After many years of subjugation, if she lived, she, the daughter-in-law, would herself become the mother-in-law.

The Village Home of Wang Su-chen

WANG SU-CHEN (enters)
    Since my little sister came home,
    I have not sent her back to her
    mother-in-law's across the river.
    Seeking her I go.
    One li, two li, three li, passing
    by four houses, five houses, six
    pavilions, seven pavilions, eight flowers, nine
    flowers, nine flowers, ten
    flowers - -
    I am Wang Su-chen.
    Let me ask her the exact length
    of the leave of absence her mother-
    in-law gave her.
    Sister!
    Where are you?
    Lo! There she comes

SISTER (enters)
> Hearing my brother's call, I go out
> to meet him, asking:
> 'Elder Brother, pray what are
> your orders?'

WANG
> Be seated, Sister!
> I wish to talk to you.

SISTER
> Thank you, Brother!
> I am listening.

WANG
> How many days did your mother-in-
> law say you could stay here with me?

SISTER
> Ten days, Brother.

WANG
> How many days have you already
> stayed with me?

SISTER
> Nine days already.

WANG
> Little Sister, I am thinking of sending
> you back to your mother-in-law's
> home.
> What do you say?

SISTER
> Really?
> No, Brother - - no!
> Brother - -

WANG
> Sister, I am sorry.
> But I must.

SISTER

    That is to kill your sister - - Ah!

(sings)

    Hearing that Elder Brother must
    send me back to my mother-in-law,
    I cannot stop my tears that flow
    incessantly, swift as shuttles - -

WANG

    Little Sister, do not grieve, do not shed tears; your Elder Brother
    is to go with you. Let me go and saddle the horse.

SISTER (sings)

    In the front parlor the little maiden is left alone.
    Her Elder Brother has gone to saddle a horse.
    She enters the embroidery chamber to change her dress.
    The little maiden is changing her dress, preparatory to leaving for
    her mother-in-law's home.

. . . .

A Country Road

SISTER (sings)

    The little maiden has mounted the horse; her Elder Brother is
        carrying her packages,
    The little maiden rides ahead, ahead - -

WANG

    Tell me, tell me, Little Sister, tell me what lies heavy in your
        heart?

SISTER (sings)

    Good Elder Brother, your sister will unbosom her grief to you.
    Our father was Squire in this district.
    He promised a family in Chang-tzu p'o, Hopei province, that they
        would have me as their daughter-in-law.
    He died soon thereafter, when I was still very young.
    When I reached the age of eighteen, I was married into the family -
        as contracted . . . .
    I pray not live, but to die soon.

. . . .

WANG (sings)
>I blame the go-between woman who lied. I blame her. I hate her.
. . . .

>Listen to your brother's advice and do not think of death.
. . . .

SISTER (sings)
>The little maiden whips the horse to cross the bridge.
. . . .

WANG (sings)
>Elder Brother and Younger Sister have both crossed the bridge.
. . . .

Home of Sister's Mother-in-law
WANG (sings)
>Sister, here we are in front of your mother-in-law's house.
>Let me help you to dismount.

SISTER (sings)
>I dismount.

WANG (sings)
>Here is your package, Sister.
>When you go in you must ask after your mother-in-law's health, say, 'How do you do', to your sister-in-law.
. . . .

SISTER (sings)
>I want to ask my brother to come in and have some lunch, but do not dare . . . .

WANG (sings)
>Thank you, but I am neither hungry nor thirsty.
. . . .

>I am going directly home.
>Goodbye - - goodbye. (exits)

SISTER (sings)
>Ah me!
>In front of this cruel gate I am left alone, and I must not stand here too long.
>The ugly daughter-in-law cannot avoid meeting her mother-in-law.
>Now I go to meet my fate. (exits)

The present section has made two points clear.

(1) The foregoing presentation of games and recreational activities has been intended to show that the relationship of 'friendship' is established by kinship or by membership of a lineage or clan. But two or more boys or girls belonging to lineages different from one another, and thus more or less strange, are brought into friendship by their games; they are played to a certain extent in a spirit of antagonism, though socially controlled and regulated. When they grow up they enter upon a regular association, which provides the channel for a kind of commerce between the groups to which they belong. In American families parents often arrange a birthday party for their children and invite the latter's playmates as a preliminary to forming friendships; this corresponds to the way in which young Chinese boys and girls are brought into a friendship relationship through engaging in competitive games.

There is a distinction between what are called 'friendship' relations and what are called relations of 'solidarity' established by kinship or by membership of a lineage or clan. Friendship is conceived of as the relationship set up between persons or groups on the basis of a regular contact through games or plays, though they are in competition or rivalry. This is where Radcliffe-Brown's theory of friendly rivalry is relevant. He said that 'a component of the relationship between groups is a certain amount and kind of opposition, meaning by that term socially controlled and regulated antagonism; social relations of friendly rivalry are of considerable theoretical importance'.[136]

In the light of Radcliffe-Brown's theory the playing of competitive games is an expression of friendship in which there is an appearance of antagonism, controlled conventional rules. Thus, those who participate in the games follow the conventional rules and take winning and losing for granted; at all events, it is only a game. Bateson has elaborated this theory further to prove it important for psychotherapy.[137] In his article 'culture' in the *Encyclopedia of Social Sciences*, Malinowski has pointed out that recreation does not merely 'lead man away from his ordinary occupations'; it also contains 'a constructive and a creative element'. He has said further that innovations are 'allowed to filter in through the activities of recreation'. He has noted that some types of play have a different character, being 'entirely non-productive and non-constructive', such as round games, competitive sports, and secular dances, but they 'play a part in the establishment of social cohesion'.[138] The social implications of games are important. Where individual play tends to make the person self-sufficient, group games and play increase his dependence on his partners and thus strengthen group solidarity and co-operation.

(2) The 'yang ke' plays were of outstanding importance as they vividly pictured the rural family life or the life the rural people were living. There can be no doubt that yang ke plays and songs laid bare what people felt about their weal and woe.

Love-making on the stage was decidedly an emotional release for the crowd. While there was inevitably some vulgarity and a considerable taint of sex in yang ke, the plays did not exert a harmful influence. The most important feature in yang ke plays is the joking scene. According to Hsü Meng-ling, the system, construction and dialogue of these songs and plays clearly express joking relationships. In the rustic plays in Yün Nan province two performers swing to and fro and sing while they dance so that their movement is graceful and glamorous.[139] We can also see that a man and a woman shake hands and embrace each other, that a father kisses his daughter in public, husband and wife make love, daughters-in-law speak in jest with their mothers-in-law and even concubines make fun of their masters. The joking relationship under such circumstances is in opposition to a conventional relation; there is privileged disrespect and freedom or even licence, and the parties are not to take offence at the disrespect under such extenuating circumstances. In ordinary times people who are related by common membership of a domestic group, a lineage or a clan, each of which has been defined in terms of the whole set of socially recognized rights and obligations, must observe what is a customary pattern of behaviour, etiquette or morale. Thus in making jests with her mother-in-law, the daughter-in-law will commit a breach of family code and filial obligations and is subject to a legal sanction. For it is a breach of 'li' - a moral principle - as well as of law.

In studying the Chinese kinship system we find it is necessary to distinguish the different relatives with reference to the kind and degree of respect that must be paid to them. One of the principles is that a person is bound to show great respect to the relatives belonging to the first ascending generation, for instance, the father. Since the father has authority as well as the rights of exercising discipline over his son, he imposes upon him constraints; it follows that a joking relationship between them is ruled out. If we ask why Chinese society has the social structure that it has, the only answer lies in its history and its cultural pattern.

Notes

1 The nature and the development cycle of the Chinese family

1 'Kin' means consanguineal relatives or persons descended from a common ancestor; 'kith' are relatives not connected by kin ties, or one's friends by vicinity or neighbourhood. *African Systems of Kinship and Marriage*, ed. A. R. Radcliffe-Brown and D. Forde, Oxford, 1960, p. 14.

2 'Generation' means social order based upon genealogical ranking, while kinship implies a biological classification based on birth, R. Firth, *We, the Tikopia*. London, 1936, p. 248.

3 The character 'Chia' is composed of two parts: symbolizing house and pigs. Among Chinese farmers each family feeds at least one pig. This is needed not only for meat but also for manure. *Shu Wen Chieh Tzu*, vol. 7, p. 2a in *Ssu Pu Ts'ung Kan* (see Glossary).

4 The term 'chia', family, used by Chinese social anthropology refers to the procreative unit and embraces, like the Jewish mishpacha, all members of the same household, such as parents, young children, and sometimes grown-up unmarried children; all the members stand under one head or 'pater familias' and must have the same surname, as in India, Greece and Rome. J. F. McLenna, *Studies in Ancient History*, London, 1876, p. 217. In terms of the kinship system, first, the family 'chia' or dwelling, referring to clan relatives of an older generation than 'ego'; it also refers to the relatives of the generation of, but of higher status than, for instance, older brother 'hsiung'; secondly, 'shê', household, applies to the clan relatives of the same generation of, but of lower status than, ego, for example, a younger brother 'ti'. It principally applies to the relatives of the first descending generation, and sometimes to all descending generations; third, 'hsiao', minor, junior, small, is pre-

fixed to the terms for clan relatives of a lower generation than ego, primarily in reference to one's own children or grandchildren. Note that the depreciated modifiers used for 'my own family' or 'my own clan' are not used for relatives of a different clan name. Fêng Han-yi, *The Chinese Kinship System*, Cambridge, Mass., 1948, p. 15.

5 The strictly reproductive functions which are attributed to the nuclear family group are distinguishable from the activities connected with the production of food and shelter in the domestic group for assuring continuity with society at large.

6 J. A. Barnes, 'Seven Types of Segmentation', *The Rhodes-Livingstone Journal*, no. 17, 1955. Barnes's terminology differs from Fortes's. Barnes conceives of both segmentation and fission as processes, the former being the process by which any social group becomes subdivided internally and yet retains its own unity and cohesion, the latter being the process by which a social group is divided into two or more distinct groups, so that the original group disappears as a social entity.

7 M. Fortes, 'Time and social structure: an Ashanti study', in *Social Structure: Presented to A. H. Radcliffe-Brown*, ed. M. Fortes, New York, 1962, p. 60.

8 In social anthropology the term 'joint family' is commonly used as it best expresses family organization. On the other hand, the term 'large family' might be taken to describe the size rather than the organization of the family.

9 We learn that in the Chin dynasty (AD 265–420) Han Yüang-chang and his brothers lived in the same household until they were toothless. Tao Ch'ien (AD 365–427) *Tao Yüang Ming Chi*, 8, 2a; *Ssu Pu Ts'ung Kan* also is reported in *Hou Han Shu* that Fan Chung's (AD 22) family property was kept undivided for three generations. Fan Yeh, *Hou Han Shu*, 32, 1a; Ts'ai Yung (AD 159–92) held his family property in common for three generations so that he and his uncle and cousins were honoured by their neighbours for their righteousness. *Hou Han Shu*, 90, 2 and 2b, *Ssu Pu Pei Yao*. Again, Chinese history records a large household of twenty generations. A certain Hsü family in the Sung dynasty had 781 members. Ouyang Hsüan, *Sung Shih*, vol. 456, p. 3a in *Ssu Pu Pei Yao*; *Ibid*., p. 4a and 6a. The largest family ever known is the Ch'ên family which had 3764 members and had maintained its unity for almost four hundred years. See Fang Hsüan-ling, *Chin Shu*, 91, 4a, *Ssu Pu Pei Yao*.

10 J. J. L. Duyvendak, trans., *The Book of Lord Shang*, a classic of

the Chinese School of Law, London, 1928, p. 15.
11 *Shih Chi*, vol. 5, 'The Record of Ch'in', p. 186 in *SSu Pu Pei Yao*.
12 Mabel Ping Hua-li, *The Economic History of China*, New York, 1921, pp. 173, 174, 176.
13 The same dwelling may include some individual elementary families. For example, three married brothers living with their wives and children in a compound set up their own family.
14 The general pattern of houses and living in rural areas remained unchanged until the Communists came into power; yet by no means all the dwellings conform strictly to the pattern described above.
15 *Notes and Queries on Anthropology*, Committee of The Royal Anthropological Institute of Great Britain and Ireland, London, 1960, p. 64.
16 D. H. Kulp, *Country Life in South China*, New York, 1925, p. 148.
17 Cornelia Spencer, *The Land of the Chinese People*, London, 1947, p. 15.
18 A 'compound' alone is an enclosure containing a row of houses or flats. For example, a factory or a military barrack is a compound, since it needs several houses for different functions. In China a so-called compound family consists of several brothers carrying on daily activities in common. On the death of their father, the sons inherit the property jointly, but they may refrain from dividing and separating. As has already been observed, the compound family is equivalent to the joint family. Furthermore, in the compound family the members are classed according to the degree of descent from a common ancestor, and are arranged in a genealogical table, each generation occupying a room in the house according to its position in the table. G. Jamieson, 'The history of adoption and its relation to modern wills', *China Review*, vol. XVIII, pp. 137–46.
19 A lineage consists of all the descendants in one line of a particular person through a determinate number of generations. *Notes and Queries on Anthropology*, London, 1960, p. 88. The terms 'hsing' and 'shih' stand for clan and lineage on the basis of the meaning of these two characters 'hsing' and 'shih', the latter being a branch lineage of the former. The 'hsing' is a large and widespread common descent group, while the 'shih' denotes a corporate group living in physical proximity.
20 English terms are used in Figure 1.6 in a close approximation to Chinese terms merely for exposition purposes.
21 Apart from being an economic unit, the family is a communal group, sharing the same cooking stove, and eating together. Several cooking stoves mean separate family units.

22　E. E. Evans-Pritchard, *The Nuer*, Oxford, 1940, p. 192.

23　*Ibid.*, p. 195.

24　*Pai Hu Tung*, vol. VIII, 'Clans and kindred', p. 6a in *Ssu Pu Ts'ung Kan.*

25　Tsung-t'ung Li, *The History of Ancient China*, vol. II, Taiwan – Formosa Chinese Culture Press, 1952, p. 213 Robert W. Williamson, *The Social and Political System of Central Polynesia*, vol. 3, Cambridge, 1924, p. 138.

26　O. Lang, *Chinese Family and Society*, New Haven, Yale University Press, 1946, p. 20.

27　The commentary that nine generations of lineal descendants bear the same surname is read in *Shang Shu. Shang Shu Chu Shu*, vol. 2, p. 5a, in *Ssu Pu Pei Yao.*

28　G. Jamieson, *op. cit.*

29　Pan Kwang-tan, *The Family System and Gens and Clan,* in *She Hui Hsueh Chieh*, vol. IX, 1936, p. 92.

30　Hu Hsien-chien, *The Common Descent Group in China and Its Functions*, New York, 1948, p. 97.

31　Sze-ma, a horse-keeper, marshal, minister for war is descended from the count of Ch'eng; its original name was Ch'eng (Pih-Ch'eng), the capital of the earldom of Pih. The first man to bear the name was Hsiu-fu, who lost his fief during the reign of the emperor Suan. *Kuo Yü*, vol. 80, 'Ch'u', part 2, p. 3a in *Ssu Pu Ts'ung Kan.*

32　Liu Hui-chen Wang, *The Traditional Chinese Clan Rules*, New York, 1959, p.4.

33　Creel's argument that the terms 'hsing' and 'shih' stand for clan and lineage respectively is sensible and cogent on the basis of the meaning of these two characters 'hsing' and 'shih'; the latter being a subdivision or branch of the former. The 'hsing' is a large and loose 'common descent group', while the 'shih' denotes, in the sense of Max Weber's terminology, a 'corporate group'. This group, which may act corporately, must live in the same area. The basis of their group attachment is lineage, not clan, membership. H. G. Creel, 'The beginning of bureaucracy in China: the origin of the Hsien', *Journal of Asian Studies*, vol. 18, no. 22, February 1964, p. 168.

34　*Kuo Yü* mentions seven cases of marriage between members of the same hsing surname. This was a breach of the exogamic principle and was severely condemned as a serious crime. *Kuo Yü*, vol. 2, 'Chou', part 2, pp. 2b–3a in *Ssu Pu Ts'ung Kan.*

35　The term 'tsu' has the connotation that the clan groups are branched out over a wide area and they no longer remain in one single organization, though each branch still recognizes others as perhaps descended from a remote ancestor. For example, the surname 'chao' is found in Hopeh (province) in North China as well as in Fukien (province) in South China.

36 Liu Hui-chen Wang, *op. cit.*, p. 4.

37 Whether or not Chinese society passed through a prior matrilineal stage has not been documented. Granet and Kuo Mo-jo have submitted some evidence which is, however, suggestive rather than conclusive.

38 *Jih Chih Lu Chi-Shih*, vol. 2, p. 26 in *Ssu Pu Pei Yao*. Clans may be localized or dispersed and may or may not form corporate groups.

39 Where a surname has two distinct origins, persons of the same surname may inter-marry on the condition that their line of ancestry can be traced from the separate stock, i.e. of the same surname but of a different ancestry. On the other hand, families of the same ancestry have branched off under a different name and cannot inter-marry. For instance, 'hsú' and 'Hsǔ', both pronounced 'hsu', were one family until the reign of Yung Cheng (AD 1723–36). Persons having these names cannot inter-marry. H. A. Giles, 'Family Names', *Journal of the North China Branch of the Royal Asiatic Society*, vol. XXI, 1887, p. 284.

40 The term 'traditional China' refers to the society that existed before its rapid disintegration in the process of modernization during the last few decades and until the overthrow of the Ch'ing dynasty.

41 An affective clan is a much narrower group, the members of which can trace their common ancestor and observe exogamy and the ceremonial mourning.

42 M. Fortes, *The Web of Kinship among the Tallensi*, London, 1940, p. 14.

43 The Chinese surname (Hsing) is composed of two characters meaning 'woman' and 'born' ('shing', beget). Chinese etymologists explain that the surname was originally the mother's name only. In ancient times eight noble surnames have 'nü' (woman or female) part, such as kiang, chi, wei, yao and ssu. *Tso Chuan Chu Shu*, vol. 4, 'Duke ying' p. 6b and 7a, *Ssu Pu Pei Yao*. See *Hsue-Hai Leh Pien*, p. 2b. In the *Annals of the Bamboo*, ancient rulers, Hwang-ti, Chen-ti, Che-ti, Chuen-hsü, Yao, Shun had their parentage recorded not in the name of their father, but in that of their mother. See *The Annals of the Bamboo*. Chu shu Chi Nien T'ung Tsing, vols. I–II, ed. Hsu Wen-ching, commentary by Shen Yüeh, 1750. The character 'hsing' was explained by the most famous of Chinese etymologists, Hsǔ shen, who lived in the first century of our era, to be 'that with which a man is born'. In relation to the word 'hsing' there is a well-known book, *A Hundred Family Names*. This was a

collection of family names taken from the *T'u yüan chi*, a sort of miscellany, and was collected by an old scholar of Hang-Chow at the beginning of the Sung dynasty (AD 960–1278). It was in the period when Chao Ch'ien was the governor of Chekiang province. Hence, 'Chao' is the first name on the list and 'Ch'ien' the second. The third, 'Sun', was the name of Chao Ch'ien's favourite, and the fourth, 'Li', was that of the ruler of Nanking (p. 356). (These follow the great clan names of the empire in a rhythmical arrangement). The book, *A Hundred Family Names*, contains more than one hundred names, that is, 408 single or monosyllabic names, and 30 double or disyllabic names, making a total of 438 in all (p. 355). According to the general lexicon published two centuries ago under the auspices of the emperor K'ang Hsi, we find no less than 1,678 characters mentioned as family names, making a grand total of 1,854. See H. A. Giles, *Historic China and Other Sketches*, London, 1882, pp. 355–7. Chao Ch'ien's capital was Hang-Chow, where the old scholar dwelt to make this compilation. The surname 'Chao' is the surname of the founder of the Sung dynasty.

44 *Erh Ya Chu Shu*, vol. IV, 'Shih Ch'in', pp. 9a–9b, *Ssu Pu Pei Yao*. The word 'sheng' means that the male 'ego' refers to his sister's son by the word 'chu'. The combination of the character 'sheng' (birth) and 'chu' (exit). Also ego's maternal uncle speaks of his sister's son as 'sheng'. Hence sheng means birth, while 'chu' means that in marrying out to another male the sister gives birth to children.

45 The character 'sun', grandchild, means 'posterity'. *Erh Ya Chu Shu*, vol. IV, 'Shih Ch'ing', p. 8b, in *Ssu Pu Pei Yao*.

46 'Piao' means 'outside' or 'external'; the father's sister's, mother's sister's, and mother's brother's descendants are all addressed with the same term, 'piao'. The descendants of father's and of mother's sister and brother, though they are consanguineal relatives of distinct affiliations, are all non-clan relatives, and so the merging in the term 'piao' is understandable. See Fêng Han-yi, *The Chinese Kinship System*, Cambridge, Mass., 1948, p. 36–7.

47 Ego's 'kin' all together form ego's kindred.

48 *Li Chi Chu Shu*, vol. 33, 'The Mourning', vol. 21, p. 5b in *Ssu Pu Pei Yao*.

49 *Ibid.*, 33.

50 *T'ung Tien*, vol. 95, pp. 8a–12a.

51 The term 'piao' means 'outside' or 'external'. The descendants of father's sister, 'ku piao', and of mother's sister, 'yi piao' and mother's brother, 'chiu piao', though consanguineal relatives of distinct affiliation, are all non-clan relatives and are the three first-degree 'piao' relationships of the Chinese kinship system.

52 A Rygaloff, 'Deux points de nomenclature dans les systèmes chinois de parenté', *L'Homme*, November–December, 1962, pp. 55–8.
53 M. Granet, *La polygénie sororale et la sororat dans le Chine féodale*, Paris, 1920, p. 10.
54 *Li Chi Chu Shu*, vol. I, ch. I 'Chü Li', part 1, pp. 10b, 12a–12b, in *Ssu Pu Pei Yao.*
55 Lin Yueh-hua, *The Golden Wing*, 1948, ch. XII; Su Sing-ging, *The Chinese Family System*, New York, 1922, p. 37.
56 Matthew, I: 1–16.
57 *Hou Han Shu*, vol. 97 'Wai Ch'i', pp. 6a and 6b in *Ssu Pu Pei Yao.*
58 Wang Min-sheng, *Shih Ch'i Shih Shang Chüe*, vol. 86, Shanghai, p. 924.
59 Ch'an Sun Wu-Chi, *T'ang Lü Shu Yi*, vol. 14, 'Hu Hun', pp. 297–8, *Ts'ung Shu Chi Cheng.*
60 Wang Min-sheng, *Shih Ch'i Shi Shang Chüe*, 86, p. 924. 'Their marriages were the most gross violation of relationship of humanity'.
61 Each 'ching' ('well') consists of a square divided into nine plots. The eight exterior plots are allotted to eight families, while the central plot is shared by them all and cultivated in common. The 'ching' is dug in the centre, but within the limits of each 'ching' four roads are opened. The 'ching tien' is the system of land tenure and distribution made to eight families and rented from the government. Rent is paid by labour on the central plot with reversion to the government on death or disability.
62 This Figure was drawn by the author.
63 'The Chinese Roots', the *China Review*, vol. 13, July 1884–June 1885, pp. 387–401.
64 Martin Yang, *A Chinese Village*, Taitou, Shantung province, London, 1948, p. 244 f.
65 In the feudal period under the Chou dynasty (*c.* 1100–246 BC), the clan began to develop into economic families. At the end of the feudal period the 'village community' which was composed of neighbours, non-clansmen, began to appear. In imperial times, ownership of land was established, and most of the land in villages inhabited by one or several clans belonged to individual economic families, and not to the clans, K. A. Wittfogel, 'Foundation and stages of Chinese economic history', *Zeitschrift für Sozialforschung*, IV, no. 1, Paris, 1935, p. 44.
66 Fei Hsiao-tung, *Peasant Life in China*, London, 1939, pp. 98–9.
67 Residence means that the members of a joint family of two or three generations may live under the same roof or in a separate household, i.e. scattered over different households, the latter reflecting the elasticity of a joint-family system. The expression

'under the same roof' must be understood in a broad sense, as, for example, a stretch of flats in a compound, a camp-fire group, or a military barrack which requires several house structures to lodge different functional activities. F. Keesing, *Cultural anthropology*, New York, 1958, p. 271.

68 Mai Huei-ting, *The Problem of Reforming the Chinese Family System*, Shanghai, 1929, p. 51.

2 The family in kinship structure

1 A marriage between persons of the same surname has been taboo from the time of the Chou dynasty (1100–256 BC). *Li Chi Hsün Tsuan*, vol. I, 'Chü li', p. 12a in *Ssu Pu Pei Yao*.

2 Vocatives are used for addressing relatives direct in person. They are limited to relatives of higher generations than ego, and to those of the same generation but of higher age status.

3 *Li Chi Chu Shu*, vol. 28 'Nei Zei', p. 6a in *Ssu Pu Pei Yao*.

4 *Li Chi Hsün Tsuan*, vol. 12 'Nei Zei', p. 10b in *Ssu Pu Pei Yao*.

5 W. Lloyd Warner, *The Black Civilization*, New York, 1964, p. 60.

6 Tsung fa, a product of Chinese feudalism in the Chou dynasty, is a system in which the clan is organized to the extent that the inheritance of rank and feudal fiefs and the rules of sacrifice are defined.

7 Ssu-ma Ch'ien, *Shih Chi (Historical Records)*, vol. 87, p. 9a in *Ssu Pu Pei Yao*.

8 *Pai Hu Tung*, vol. 4, p. 5a in *Ssu Pu Ts'ung Kan*.

9 *Hou Han Shu*, vol. 67, 11a–b.

10 *Ibid.*, vol. 67, p. 16a in *Ssu Pu Pei Yao*.

11 A. F. P. Hulsewe, *Remnants of Han Law*, vol. I. Introductory Studies and Annotated Translations of Chs 22 and 23 of the *History of the Former Han Dynasty (Sinica Leidensia)*, vol. IX, Leiden, 1955, pp. 88–9.

12 *Hsiao Ching Chu Shu (The Book of Filial Piety)*, part 2, ch. 11, 'Wu Hsing', p. 2a in *Ssu Pu Pei Yao*.

13 *Chou Li Chu Shu*, vol. 10, p. 12a in *Ssu Pu Pei Yao*.

14 *Wei Shu*, vol. 111, p. 10b in *Ssu Pu Pei Yao*.

15 *T'ang Lü Shu Yi*, vol. I, p. 16 in *Ts'ung Shu Chi-Ch'eng*, vol. 106. The ten offences are: plot of rebellion, plot of great insubordination, plot of treason, odious insubordination, monstrous crime, great irreverence, disobedience, disorder, disloyalty and internal disorder, or intimate promiscuity or incest.

16 *T'ang Lü Shu Yi*, vol. 22, p. 504 in *Ts'ung Shu Chi-Ch'eng*, vol. 106.

17 Yüan Hsing, *Ta Ch'ing Hsien Hsing Hsing Lü*, pp. 202, 206.

18 *T'ang Lü Shu Yi*, 22, 9b; *Sung Hsing Tung*, 22, 9a; *Ta-Ch'ing Lü Li*, 28, 59a.

19 *Ibid.*, 28, 60b.
20 *Ibid.*, 30, 81a.
21 *Hsing An Hui Lan*, 44, 5a–6a.
22 *Ibid.*, 44, 5a–6a.
23 Ssu-ma Kuang, *Ssu-ma Shih Shu Yi*, vol. 4, p. 41, in *Ku Ching Tu Shu Chi Ch'eng*, vol. 40.
24 T. Addison, *Chinese Ancestor Worship*, Shanghai, 1925, pp. 50 ff.
25 The two-thousand-year stability of the Chinese family rests no doubt on the basis of the strong urge to have children, borne or adopted. To fail in this duty is to the Chinese to undermine one of the principles on which their society is based.
26 Fei Hsiao-tung, *Peasant Life in China*, London, 1939, p. 74.
27 M. Freedman, *Lineage Organization in South-Eastern China*. London, 1958, p. 28.
28 In a wealthy family the strong father who exerts a strict control over his children will bring about a conflict between himself and his sons; these stand together in opposition to their father. Again, the father may live in luxury and extravagance in dissipation of family property. Finally, the father is likely to take concubines who can give birth to children; as a result, many children will have only a tiny share in family property when it is divided.
29 *Chun Chiu Tso Chuan*, vol. 25, 'Duke Chao', pp. 18a–b in *Ssu Pu Pei Yao*.
30 Tso Hsueh-Chin, *The Dream of the Red Chamber* (*Hung Lou Mêng*), ch. 22, pp. 395–7, Peking, 1953.
31 Lee Shu-chin, 'China's traditional family', *American Sociological Review*, vol. 18, June 1953.
32 Freedman, *op. cit.*, p. 90.
33 'Nü erh' is colloquial and used both by parents and daughter. When the daughter writes to her parents, only 'nü' is used in referring to herself.
34 *Shih Ching Chu Shu*, vol. 11, 'Hsiao ya', 'Ssu Kan', p. 6b in *Ssu Pu Pei Yao*.
35 *Tso Chuan*, collection of Chinese history and philosophy, vol. 18, 'Hsiang Kung', p. 6b, in *Ssu Pu Pei Yao*.
36 *Li Chi Chu Shu*, vol. 27, ch. 12 'Nei Tze', p. 6a, *Ssu Pu Pei Yao*, vol. 23.
37 *Ibid.*, vol. 8, 'Nei Zeh', p. 286 in *Ssu Pu Pei Yao*.
38 *Ibid.*, p. 29b.
39 *I Li* (*The Book of Rites*), vol. 6, p. 2a.
40 *Li Chi Chu Shu*, vol. 2, p. 8a, in *Ssu Pu Pei Yao*.
41 *Tso Chuan*, vol. 15, 'Duke Hsiang' (571–540 BC), pp. 2a–b in *Ssu Pu Pei Yao*.
42 *Ibid.*, vol. 2, 'Duke Huan', pp. 21a–21b in *Ssu Pu Pei Yao*.

43 Ssu-ma Ch'ien, *Shih Chi*, vol. 32, p. 86 in *Ssu Pu Pei Yao*.
44 *Chin Ku Ch'i Kuan*, Peking, ch. 26, pp. 489–513.
45 Florence Ayscough, *Chinese Women, Yesterday and Today*, Boston, 1937, pp. 219 ff.
46 *Pai Hu Tung*, vol. 9, p. 4b.
47 The words 'chia t'zu' symbolize the kindness of the mother, while 'chia yen' represents the dignity and austerity of the father. The universal vocative of mother is ma or ma ma. Yü Yen, *Hsi Shang Fu T'ang*, I. 2a. Niang, used as a vocative for the mother, was first noticed during the fourth and fifth centuries AD. Li yen shou, *Nan Shih*, 44, 5a and 5b and *Pei Shih* 64, 13b and 14a, Tung Wen Publisher.
48 *Li Chi Chu Shu*, vol. 32 'Piao Chi', p. 6b, in *Ssu Pu Pei Yao*.
49 A pact of feudal times described the inequality of boys and girls in the royal family: 'The sons are put to sleep on couches, clothed in robes, have a sceptre to play with, while the daughters are put to sleep on the ground, clothed in wrappers; they will have tiles to play with.'
50 *Li Chi*, vol. 8, 'Nei Zeh', in *Ssu Pu Pei Yao* edition, vol. 5, p. 28b.
51 An arrow hanging on the door symbolizes the destiny of the new-born boy in carrying arms. A handkerchief or serviette means that the new-born girl performs the duty of maintaining the cleanliness and neatness of the house.
52 Tufts are left on the top of temples above the fontanel and the rest of the hair is shaved. These passages treat of the children in a family of the upper classes.
53 *Translations China Branch Royal Asiatic Review*, 1853–4, p. 31.
54 C. Alabaster, 'The new law of inheritance', *China Review*, vol. V, July 1878 to June 1879, p. 194.
55 Granet propounded the hypothesis that the sororate was an institution during the feudal period. He elaborated relevant data to buttress his theory of sororate and levirate which suggested survivals of an early group marriage. *La polygynie sororale et le sororat dans la Chine féodale*, Paris, 1920, p. 80.
56 *Kung Yang Chu Shu*, vol. 8, 'Duke Chuang', p. 1a in *Ssu Pu Pei Yao*.
57 *Ibid*.
58 *Shih Ching Chu Shu*, vol. I, ch. 3, 'Chiao mu', p. 7b in *Ssu Pu Pei Yao*.
59 *Li Chi*, 'Tan Kun', p. 63a. The mother of Poi Yü was repudiated, but he observed mourning for the divorced mother.
60 *Ibid*., 'Chiao Te Shing'; in her youth, the woman follows her father; after his death she follows her eldest son, and after marriage she follows her husband.

61 *Ibid.*
62 F. Hsu, 'Observations on cross-cousin marriage in China', *American Anthropologist*, vol. 47, no. 1, January–March 1945, pp. 83–103.
63 Pai Hu Tung, vol 9, pp. 13b–14a in *Ssu Pu Ts'ung Kan*, section 4; *T'ung Tien*, compiled by Tu Yu, *Wan You Wen K'u*, edn. 1896.
64 G. Jamieson, 'Translations from the General Code of Laws of the Chinese Empire', *China Review*, vol. 10, July 1881–June 1882, p. 83.
65 According to *Shu Wen*, 'ko' does not mean older brother, but it refers to 'to sing' or 'song'. Ko, first used from sixth to the eighth centuries AD means father; in the ninth and tenth centuries AD, 'ko' became an addressing or vocative for older brother. See *Kai Yü Ts'ung K'ao* by Chao I, AD 1727–1814; edited 1790. When an older brother or sister refers to the younger brother, the term 'hsien-ti' is used; at present, simply 'ti' is used.
66 *Chiu T'ang shu*, vol. 64, pp. 4a–5b in *Ssu Pu Pei Yao*.
67 Fong Mong-lung, and Ling Mon-chu, *Chin Ku Ch'i Kuan*, Shanghai, 1933, ch. 34, pp. 957, 961–7.
68 *Li Chi Hsün Tsuan*, vol. 7 'Tseng Tzǔ Wen', p. 5b in *Ssu Pu Pei Yao*.
69 The term 'joking relationship' means a relation between two persons in which one is by custom permitted and in some cases required to make fun of the other, who is in turn, however, required not to take it amiss. The joking may be verbal, or include horseplay or elements of obscenity. This is Chinese custom.
70 Tso Hsueh-ching, *The Dream of the Red Chamber*, Peking, 1953, ch. 33, pp. 397–9.

3 Filial piety and kinship

1 A common saying.
2 Meng Chia of the Tang dynasty, 'Words of a Travelling Son'.
3 In Egypt a special yearly fête was known as the reunion of the relations of the deceased at which offerings were made at the 'mastaba' or tomb and the visitors spoke to the deceased and burned incense before his statue. See François Lenormant, *Histoire ancienne de l'Orient jusqu'aux guerres modiques*, Paris, 1881–8, vol. III, p. 241.
4 Luke, 14: 26.
5 The Chinese philologists divide a great many characters into two great classes: the wen, simple 'figures' and the tsu, compound 'letters'. The figures are subdivided into hsiang or hsiang-hsing, that is, imitative drafts, and chih-shih, indicative symbols. The compound 'letters' are subdivided into hui-i, logical aggregates, in

which all parts have a meaning, and into hsing-sheng or hsieh-sheng, phonetic complexes, in which one part has a meaning, while the other points out the pronunciation.

6 *Lun Yü*, vol. 1, ch. 2 'Wei Cheng', pp. 10b-11a in *Ssu Pu Pei Yao*.

7 The concept of filial piety is not Confucian, though Confucius accepted it unreservedly, but is a concept anterior to him. W. J. Clennel, *The Historical Development of Religion in China*, London, 1917, pp. 25 ff. The canon of filial piety had existed in some form in the third century BC, but it did not develop into its present form until the fourth century, when the Confucians attached extreme importance to piety (hsiao) towards living parents. The doctrine of filial piety prevailed since the time of the sage emperor Shun (2255-205 BC) who was selected by emperor Yao (2357-255 BC) to be successor to the empire largely due to his extraordinary filial piety. See Cheng T'ien-hsi, *China Moulded by Confucius*, London, 1947, p. 166.

8 *Chung Yung*, ch. 18, p. 11a and 11b in *Ssu Pu Pei Yao*.

9 *Lun Yü*, vol. 1, ch. 1, 'Hsueh Erh', p. 3a in *Ssu Pu Pei Yao*.

10 *Hsiao Ching Chu Shu*, vol. 1 'Kai Tsung Ming Yi', p. 1b in *Ssu Pu Pei Yao*.

11 This is clearly in accord with the statement of St John the Divine that Christianity is essentially a religion of filial piety. E. R. Hughes, *The Comparative Study of Chinese Philosophy and Religion* Oxford, 1935, pp. 20-1.

12 Herbert A. Giles, *Civilizations of China*, London, 1911, p. 70: 'Confucius taught virtue for virtue's sake, and not for the hope of reward or fear of punishment; he taught . . . filial piety as the basis of all happiness in the life of the people'.

13 *Luther's Work and the Word of God* by W. H. Anderson, the author of *What Sort of Man was Martin Luther?* London, 1883, Part II, p. 150.

14 The word 'jen', when referring to 'righteousness', is reminiscent of benevolence, i.e. love of mankind accompanied with the desire to promote man's morality and happiness, but often it means also perfect virtue of which benevolence is a constituent part. 'Jen', the amelioration of family relationship, works for strengthening the position of governor. According to C. P. Chao's statistics, in the *Lun Yü* there are fifty chapters dealing with 'jen', and the word 'jen' has been used one hundred and five times. C. P. Chao, *Ku-Tai Ju-Chia Che-Hsueh Pi Ping* (*A Critique of Ancient Confucian Philosophy*), p. 127.

15 *Lun Yü*, ch. 1, 'Hsieh Erh', p. 26 in *Ssu Pu Pei Yao*.

16 *Moh Tzŭ*, vol. 4, 'Chien Ai', part III, p. 11a in *Ssu Pu Pei Yao*.

17 Confucius said that 'one who cares little for what is the more important to him and at the same time cares much for what is less important is a case that has never existed', *Ta Hsueh* (*The Great Learning*). These passages mean that he who holds little affection for those with whom he is bound up by a natural tie and sets an excessive affection for others to whom he is not obliged acts from selfish motives rather than from true benevolence.

18 Hsieh Yu-wei, 'Filial Piety and Chinese Society', *Philosophy East and West*, vol. X, 1961, p. 57.

19 In the T'ang dynasty (AD 618–906) Tzŭ-lang, a native of Kiang-ling of Kiangsu province, was a very wealthy businessman. He left his home and his old mother in search of officialdom. Although he possessed great wealth, he left his mother stranded and was unconcerned about her afflictions under social turmoil and political agitation. He lived in luxury and debauchery in the capital city. After a few years he returned home and found his whole village destroyed so that he could hardly recognize it. His brother was killed and his sister had been raped. After inquiries made over a few days and a search, he found his mother and one of her servants, both starving, in one of the dilapidated temples. When he saw his mother, he held her to him in a warm embrace. He said he was elevated to a higher rank. 'What rank did you obtain?' asked his mother. 'The governor of the province', he said. Then he served his mother to her heart's content. Fong Mong-lung and Ling Mong-chu, *Chin Ku Ch'i Kuan*, ch. 40, pp. 758–89. Peking 1957.

20 'Li' (conduct) is a body of rules or conventions which existed prior to the laws passed and which served to govern the conduct of men, especially educated men, and formed, in old days, the rules which governed the regulations between the states. The Chinese regard 'li' as their cultural heritage and hold Confucius to be the man who was the guardian of 'li'. In this sense, 'li' as ceremony may correspond to English constitutional convention as ceremony.

21 Chang Wing-tsi, *Religious Trends in Modern China*, New York, 1953, p. 253.

22 Fung Yu-lan, *Hsin Li Hsueh*, Shanghai, 1947, p. 127.

23 *Ibid.*, pp. 301–2.

24 Chang Wing-tsi, *op. cit.*, p. 254.

25 Fong Mong-lung and Ling Mong-chu, *op. cit.*, ch. 3, p. 40.

26 This points out that he was an orphan in his infancy and had been brought up under his grandmother's gentle care.

27 This is a collection of ancient essays.

28 Straws symbolize, in ancient times, posthumous profusion of gratitude.

29 *Li Chi*, vol. 14, ch. 24 'Tze Yi', pp. 13b and 14b in *Ssu Pu Pei Yao*.
30 *Hsiao Ching Chu Shu*, vol. 1 'Kai Tsung King Yi', p. 3b in *Ssu Pu Pei Yao*.
31 There is a mutual dependence between the sovereign of the state and the people. Local leaders are the intermediaries between the rulers and their subjects. Although the emperor is presumably appointed by Heaven, his kingship or tenure of office depends upon the will of the people. As the family is a microcosm of the state, filial devotion and loyalty (*fides*) is a replica of filial piety towards the parents.
32 C. T. Lewis and C. Short, 'Pietas', *Latin-English Dictionary*, Oxford, 1880, p. 1374.
33 E. R. Hughes and K. Hughes, *Religion in China*, London, 1950, p. 50. *The Book of Odes, The Book of History, The Book of Changes*, and *I Li* may be taken as the old testament of Confucius. *The Analects* record Confucius's sayings and those of his disciples, *The Book of Mencius* (Mêng Tzu 372-289 BC) and *The Book of Filial Piety* and *Chung Yung* form the new testament of Confucius.
34 By undertaking a journey, sons and parents are separated. If it is of long duration, say overnight, the sons incur an obligation to send their parents a message lest they should be worried. The destination which has been given to parents must not change, otherwise the parents must be informed again. In case of the parents calling the sons back, the latter must return at once. In short, filial piety rests on parental and filial mutual attachment to each other.
35 *Lun Yü*, vol. 1, ch. 2 'Wei Cheng', pp. 10b-11a in *Ssu Pu Pei Yao*.
36 Hu Shih, 'Confucianism', *Encyclopedia of the Social Sciences*, vol. IV, New York, 1931, pp. 198-9.
37 *Lun Yü*, vol. 2, ch. 4, 'Li Jen', pp. 14a-14b in *Ssu Pu Ts'ung Kan*.
38 *Lun Yü*, ch. 4, 'Li Jen', p. 14b in *Ssu Pu Ts'ung Kan*. According to Chu Hsi, in serving his parents a son may remonstrate with them, but gently; should they punish him, he does not allow himself to murmur. It is better to displease parents by remonstrating with them than to see them offend clans or community by their living a bad life. *Li Chi*, 'Nei Tze', p. 11a.
39 *Hsiao Ching Chu Shu*, vol. 7, ch. 15, 'Chien Cheng', ('The duty of correction'), in *Ssu Pu Pei Yao*.
40 *Lun Yü*, vol. 7, ch. 13, 'Tzu Lu', p. 5a in *Ssu Pu Pei Yao*.
41 *Chun Chiu Tso Chuan (The Spring and Autumn Annals)* digested under the four seasons of every year. *Tso Chuan*, 'Duke Yin', vol. I, pp. 3a and 3b. Duke Yin was the first of the twelve dukes, and his rule extended from 721 to 711 BC.
42 Tan Hsuan Tsung or Tang Ming Huang, i.e. the Bright emperor. The

title of the first part of the emperor's reign (713–40) was K'ai Yuan. That of the second portion was Tien Pao.

43 *Lun Yü*, vol. I, ch. 1, 'Hueh Erh', p. 4a in *Ssu Pu Pei Yao*. Practical love for children without limit and the illness of children are a worry to parents. According to Chu Hsi, the superior man draws his attention to what is radical. That being established, all practical courses naturally develop. Filial piety and fraternal submission – are they not the root of all benevolent actions? Filial piety is the root of benevolence, while the nature of benevolence is the root of filial piety and fraternal submission. Benevolence is nature, whereas filial piety and fraternal submission refer to practice. The nature embraces four virtues: benevolence, justice, rites and faithfulness. But benevolence is inherent in love. No love is greater than love for parents. So filial piety and fraternal submission are the root of benevolence.

44 M. Granet, *Danses et Légendes de la Chine ancienne*, Paris, 1959, p. 246 n.

45 *Ta Hsüeh (The Great Learning)*, p. 2b in *Ssu Pu Pei Yao*.

46 *Shu Ching*, 'Chou Shu', vol. 5, 'Ts'ai Chung Chih Ming', in *Ssu Pu Pei Yao*, vol. 1, under the title 'Shang Shu', p. 35. Commentary by Ts'ai Shen.

47 The Three Kingdoms or three States into which the Han empire was divided are called Wei, Shu and Wu. Each leader claimed himself to be the legal heir of the Han empire and resorted to all possible means to establish himself as the emperor. Intrigue, imposture, tyranny and bloodshed, which the author, Lo Kuan-Chung, painted vividly and embellished in strong colours, have elicited the unfading interest of readers.

48 Shih Nei-an, *Shui Hu chuan (All Men Are Brothers)* a thirteenth-century novel, trans. P. Buck, London, 1957, vol. 24, ch. 70.

49 *Ibid.*, ch. 42, p. 673.

50 *Ibid.*

51 *Shu Ching*, 'Chou shu', vol. 5, p. 35. Commentary by Ts'ai shen.

52 *Mêng Tzu Chu Shu*, vol. 7, 'Li Lou', part I, p. 2b in *Ssu Pu Pei Yao*. According to Chu Hsi, the original duty is to love parents. Elsewhere he stated that filial piety is connected with loyalty towards sovereign and obedience to superiors. Upright personal behaviour ensures family harmony as well as social order.

53 *Ibid.*

54 Arthur H. Smith, *Chinese Characteristics*, London, 1892, p. 183.

55 Yü Kuan-ying, *Yueh Fu Shih Hsüan*, Peking, 1954. The Mu-lan poem appears also in *Han Hsüeh T'ang Ts'ung Shu* vol. 19, p. 126.

56 *Pai Hu Tung*, vol. 8, 'Clan-names and Personal names', p. 8b, the

meaning of 'fu' (father) and of 'tzŭ' (male and female) in *Ssu Pu T'sung Kan*.

57 Kung Yeh Chang was one of Confucius' disciples and married his daughter (tzŭ).

58 *Lun Yü*, ch. 5 'Kung Yeh Chang', vol. 3, p. 1a in *Ssu Pu Ts'ung Kan*.

59 *Ibid.*

60 *Mêng Tzu Chu Shu*, 'Wang chang', part 1, pp. 10b and 11a in *Ssu Pu Pei Yao*.

61 *Mêng Tzu Chu Shu*, vol. 6 'Teng wen Kung', part 2, p. 2b in *Ssu Pu Pei Yao*.

62 This ode praises the dependence of brethren on one another and the beauty of brotherly harmony. According to Mao's commentary, in addition to the happy union of wife and children, like the music of lutes and harps, there must be the harmony of brethren, and then the wife and children can be regulated and happy. The relationship of husband and wife was not in ancient times among the five relationships because the union of brothers comes from Heaven, while that of husband and wife from man. *Lun Yü*, ch. 14, p. 8b in *Ssu Pu Pei Yao*.

63 Chu Hsi offered a similar interpretation of the same passage. Complacence and happiness result in the concord of husband and wife, and the harmony of brothers. From wife, and children and brothers parents are reached; this illustrates how from what is low we ascend to what is high. *Ibid.*, p. 106.

64 *Li Chi*, vol. 15, ch. 27, 'Ai Kung wen', vol. 5, p. 5b in *Ssu Pu Pei Yao*.

65 *Chung Yung*, ch. 19, 'Ai Kung wen', p. 12b in *Ssu Pu Pei Yao*.

66 Chu Hsi stated: 'Knowledge (chih) is required to select the detailed way of fulfilling duty, magnanimity (jen), unselfishness of the heart is necessary in pursuance of the duty, and energy (yung) means the perseverence of carrying it on'. I also endorse the comments of Ch'eng Ho: 'The singleness is simple sincerity on which the rest of work dwells', i.e. singleness of the soul in the apprehension and fulfilment of the duties of the 'mean' (chung), which is attainable by watching over one's self, when he remains alone.

67 Mencius – *Mêng Tzu Chu Shu*, vol. V, 'T'eng wen kung', part 1, p. 2a in *Ssu Pu Pei Yao*. *Shu Ching*, 'Kao Tao mo'; from Heaven are the social arrangements, several duties; to us it is given to enforce those five duties and thus we have the five courses of generous conduct, i.e. five relations: sovereign–minister, father–son, brothers, husband–wife and friends.

68 *Li Chi*, vol. 8, ch. 11 'Chiao te hsing', p. 13b in *Ssu Pu Pei Yao*.

69 Genesis, III: 16.
70 Exodus, XX: 12 Deuteronomy, V: 16; Matthew, XV: 4; Matthew, XIX: 19; Ephesians, VI: 2.
71 *Li Chi Chu Shu*, vol. 27, ch. 12, 'Nei Tze', p. 5a in *Ssu Pu Pei Yao*, vol. 23. Pai Hu Tung, 0, p. 3b. According to Ch'eng Ho's commentary, this passage means the commands of parents-in-law.
72 *Li Chi Chu Shu*, vol. 27, ch. 12, 'Nei Tze', pp. 5a–5b in *Ssu Pu Pei Yao*, vol. 23.
73 *Kung Tzu Chia Yü (The Table Talk of Confucius)*, 9, p. 2b in *Ssu Pu Ts'ung Kan*, vol. 96.
74 *Hou Han Shu* vol. 114, 'Lieh Chuan', vol. 74 'Lieh Nü Chuan', pp. 2a–3b.
75 *Han Ch'i Shu*, vol. 39, 'Lieh Chuan', 20 'Liu Hsuan', p. 46.
76 *Li Chi Chu Shu*, vol. 27, p. 6a in *Ssu Pu Pei Yao*.
77 Chou Mi, *Ch'i Tung Yeh Yü*, vol. I, pp. 18a–19b in *Hsüeh Chin T'ao Yuan*; Shen Te-chien, *Ku Shih Yüan*, vol. 4, pp. 1a–4a in *Ssu Pu Pei Yao*.
78 Pauline privilege is the privilege conceded by St Paul (I Cor. 7: 15) to a partner in a heathen marriage to contract a new marriage on becoming a Christian if the other partner (non-Christian) wishes to put serious obstacles in the way of the convert's faith and practice (G. H. Joyce S. J. *Christian Marriage*, London, 1933, ch. xi).
79 *Mencius*, 'Wang Chang', vol. 9, part I, p. 1b in *Ssu Pu Pei Yao*.
80 Oliver Goldsmith, *The Traveller*, London, 1958.
81 Shen Te-chien, *Ku Shih Yüan* vol. IV, 'Han Shih', in *Ssu Pu Pei Yao*, trans. F. Ayscough, *Chinese Women, Yesterday and Today*, Boston, 1937, pp. 250–62.
82 Ch'ien Yuan is the primal male element identified with Heaven.
83 *Ta Hsueh (The Great Learning)*, ch. I, p. 2b in *Ssu Pu Pei Yao*. In the viewpoint of Chu Hsi, heart (hsin) is the lord of the body; thought is sent forth by heart. It is the metaphysical part of our nature, that is, all that is embraced under the terms of mind or soul, heart or spirit. This is conceived of as being quiescent; and it is activated. We have thoughts and purposes related to what affects the heart.
84 *Hsiao Ching (The Book of Filial Piety)*, ch. 9 'Shing Chih', p. 9b. Confucius attached great importance to filial piety so that it carries an absolute power in the life of sons. The same homage which must be paid to the supreme ruler should equally be shown to one's father.
85 *Lun Yü*, vol. 2 'Li Jen', p. 15a in *Ssu Pu Ts'ung Kan*.
86 *Han Fei Tzŭ*, vol. 19, p. 6b (20 vols).

4 Ancestral rituals and kinship

1 *Structure and Function in Primitive Society*, Chicago, 1962, p. 163.
2 J. J. M. de Groot, *The Religious Systems of China*, Leiden, 1892–1910, vol. IV, book II, 'On the Soul and Ancestral Worship', part I, 'The Soul in Philosophy and Folk Conception – Duality of the Human Soul', pp. 3–5. He derives the concept of the soul from the *Li Chi*, 'Chi I', p. 9b in *Ssu Pu Pei Yao*, vol. 5.
3 *Li Chi*, ch. 24, 'Chi I', vol. 14, p. 10a in *Ssu Pu Pei Yao*, vol. 5.
4 J. MacIntyre 'Jottings from the Book of Rites, part 1, "Ancestor Worship" ', *China Review*, vol. VII, July 1878–June 1879, p. 291.
5 *Li Chi Chu Shu*, vol. XXI, 'Li Yün', p. 5b in *Ssu Pu Pei Yao*.
6 J. Goody, *Death, Property and Ancestors*, London, 1962, p. 199.
7 *Lun Yü* vol. 6, ch. 11, 'Hsien chin', p. 2b and 3a, *Ssu Pu Pei Yao*.
8 *Lun Yü*, vol. 2, ch. 3. 'Pa-yi', p. 4a in *Ssu Pu Pei Yao*.
9 *Li Chi*, vol. 8, 'Tan Kung', p. 17a in *Ssu Pu Pei Yao*, vol. 5.
10 *Chan Kuo Ts'e, The Strategy of Warring States*, vol. 4, pp. 8b–9a in *Ssu Pu Pei Yao*. The queen, Ching Hsüan, was the mother of Chao Hsian; her maiden name was Pan, and she was born in Ch'u State, in *Ssu Pu Pei Yao*.
11 Many of the Confucianists boldly deny the existence of a soul separated from the body. Chinese statements turn the doctrine of rewards and punishments into ridicule because at death the whole man is dissolved or dispersed and returned to earth, or water or air.
12 It should be kept in mind that this idea represents a common view of Chinese scholars and it accords with the positive statement of Wang Chung quoted above. Again such a view has a very important bearing upon the meaning and purpose of sacrifice to the dead.
13 *The Analects of Confucius*, vol. II, ch. 3, 'Pa Yi', p. 4a. *Lun Yü (The Analects of Confucius)*.
14 Boüinais and A. Paulus, *Le culte de morts dans le céleste Empire et l'Annam*, Paris, 1893, pp. 9ff.
15 *Li Chi*, 'Chü Li', p. 23b in *Ssu Pu Pei Yao*, vol. V.
16 J. Addison, *Chinese Ancestor Worship*, Shanghai, 1925, p. 35 f.
17 *Ibid.*, p. 14.
18 August Boeckh, *Encyklopädie und Methodologie der Phologischen Wissenschaften*, Leipzig, 1886, p. 422.
19 A. Maspéro, *Les religions Chinoises: Mélanges posthumes sur les religions et l'histoire de la Chine*, Paris, 1950, p. 130. The Buddhists in China believe in the punishment of bad spirits in a separate state; this produces the paradoxical idea of wicked ancestors who are themselves suffering punishment, being able to help their descendants on earth.

20 J. Legge, *The Religions of China – Confucianism, Taoism described and compared with Christianity*, London, 1880 pp. 189 f.
21 A. Ford, *Yang Chu's Garden of Pleasures*, London, 1912, 'Introduction', p. 7 f.
22 L. Giles, *Taoist Teachings*, London, 1912, p. 32.
23 H. A. Giles, *Chuang Tzu*, London, 1889, p. 86.
24 Wang Ch'ung in A. Ford, *Lung Heng*, part I, London, 1911, pp. 346 f.
25 'Hun', a yang principle, is composed of two characters: 'kuei' and 'yung'; 'p'o', a ying principle, is composed also of two characters: 'kuei' and 'pai'. This combination represents the sound of 'hun' and 'p'o', that is, when we pronounce 'kuei' and 'hun' together, we have the sound 'hun'. The same refers to the derived sound 'p'o' from two characters: 'kuei' and 'pai'. Kuan Ying Tzu says: 'man becomes "kuei" after death. "Hun" stands for "feng" (wind) and "feng" for "mu" (wood): "pai" stands for "ch'i" (air) and "ch'i" for "chin" (gold); wind being light ascends on high, while gold, a solid and weighty metal, descends to earth'. See *Hsüeh Hai Lei P'ien*, 'Chen Chai Wei Yen', pp. 4b–5a.
26 A. Forde, *Lung Heng*, part I, p. 191 f; part II, p. 369 f.
27 Sir E. B. Tylor, *Primitive Culture*, London, 1913, vol. II, p. 118.
28 F. L. K. Hsu, *Under the Ancestors' Shadow*, London, 1949, p. 240.
29 *Ibid.*, p. 244.
30 A. Maspéro, *op. cit.*, p. 130.
31 D. C. Graham, 'Folk Religion in South-West China', *Smithsonian Miscellaneous Collection*, November 1961, vol. 142, no. 2, p. 218.
32 D. Kulp, *Country Life in South China*, New York, 1925, p. 306.
33 It would appear that a man who died with a grievance can still take vengeance even after he has been despatched to the community of the ghosts by the mortuary rites.
34 Fei Hsiao-tung, *Peasant Life in China*, London, 1939, p. 78.
35 J. T. Addison, *op. cit.*, p. 14.
36 M. Freedman, *Lineage Organization in Southeastern China*, London, 1965, p. 86.
37 *Tso Chuan*, vol. 6, – 'Duke Chao', pp. 38a–38b.
38 *Tung Chou Lieh Kuo*, vol. 4, ch. 13, p. 12a and ch. 15, p. 5b.
39 In Chinese reckoning, if a man dies with a legitimate grievance in his heart, his ghost would take vengeance, causing sickness or other misfortune ending in death; it is impossible to make peace with the dead.
40 Leo Wieger, *Folk-Lore*, Hsienhsien county province, Imprimerie de la Mission Catholique, 1909, Case 208.
41 Freedman, *op. cit.*, p. 90 n.

42 Hsu, *op. cit.*, pp. 229, 241.
43 Yüan Mei, *Sui Yüan Sui Pi*, 'Hsin Ch'i Hsieh', vol. 6, pp. 5a and 5b.
44 Lee Shu-chin, 'China's Traditional Family', *American Sociological Review*, vol. 18, June 1953: 'If a wife is barren, her husband is obliged to take a concubine'. A concubine serves to procreate male children, but her status can never equal that of a wife, p. 275.
45 Ancestral halls are erected by individuals or several branches of a family of the same surname and much display is made in ornamentation. Family temples are built by wealthy families and are detached from other dwellings and open to the street for the accommodation of other branches of the family. Sometimes in spacious mansions one room is set apart for the purpose.
46 According to Po Hu tung, in spring the sacrifice is called 't'zu', in summer 'yüeh', in autumn 'ch'ang', in winter 'cheng'. *Pai Hu Tung Shu Cheng*, vol. 12, p. 8b, 6 vols.
47 *Ibid.*
48 *Chinese Repository*, vol. XVIII, July 1849, no. 7, part 4.
49 It is on this wooden tablet that the name of the recipient of rites is written, and his title, birth and death dates. It consists of a rectangular piece of wood set in a base and covered with a case, which is removed during the ceremony. As a rule, a friend well versed in calligraphy is invited to write the name of the ancestor on the tablet.
50 'The Worship of Ancestors among the Chinese': A notice of the *Chia-Li- Tieh-Shih Chi-Cheng*, Collection of Forms and Cards used in Family Ceremonies, *Chinese Repository*, *op. cit.*, p. 381.
51 After the ratification of the Covenant at Sinai the Jewish people asked; Why should we not have made an image of Yahweh? At their petition Aaron manufactured an image, a golden bull, symbolizing Yahweh. Throughout the Orient the bull was an accepted symbol of divinity. Upon his return from Sinai, Moses in holy wrath smashed the tablets upon which the Decalogue was written. P. Heimisch, *History of the Holy Testament*, trans. W. G. Heidt St Paul, Minnesota, 1950, pp. 93–4.
52 Legge contends that while the worship is performed, the tablet is supposed to be occupied by the ancestral spirit interested in the service; at the conclusion the spirit returns to his own place.
53 J. Jackson, *Ancestral Worship*, Centenary Missionary Conference, no. 7, Shanghai, 1907, p. 16.
54 *Ibid.*
55 *Ibid.*
56 *Chinese Repository op. cit.* The prayer is taken from the *Chia-Li Tieh-Shih Chi-Cheng – Collection of Forms and Cards used in Family Ceremonies.*

57 Hsu, *op. cit.*, p. 45.

58 J. J. M. de Groot, *The Religious System of China*, Leiden, 1897, vol. III, p. 1017.

59 C. H. Plopper, *Chinese Religion Through the Proverb*, Shanghai, 1926, p. 123.

60 Hsu, *op. cit.*, p. 47.

61 The 'virtuous' people are those who excel in filial or fraternal conduct and those who have made contributions to common funds.

62 Hu Hsien-chin, *The Common Descent Group in China and Its Functions*, New York, 1948, p. 36.

63 George W. Botsford, *A History of Rome*, New York, 1901, pp. 214–15.

64 J. H. Bradley, *Form and Spirit*, London, 1951, p. 66.

65 Hu Hsien-chin, 'The Judiciary Powers of the Tsu', in *The Common Descent Group in China and Its Functions*, pp. 53 f.

66 *Lun Yü (The Analects of Confucius)*, vol. 1, ch. 2 'Wei Cheng', pp. 6b–7a in *Ssu Pu Pei Yao*.

67 Ch'en Ku-yüan, (ed.) *The History of the Chinese Laws*, Shanghai, 1934, p. 56.

68 Pan Ku, *Han Shu*, vol. 58 'Yi Kuan', p. 9b in *Ssu Pu Pei Yao*.

69 Fan Yeh, *Hou Han Shu*, vol. 78, Lieh Chuang 'T Ying Shao', p. 11b, *Ssu Pu Pei Yao*. The Annals of the State of Lu, where Confucius was born, are said to have been written by the sage himself.

70 *Han Fei Tzŭ*, vol. 19, p. 4a in *Ssu Pu Ts'ung Kan*.

71 *Lun Yü – (The Analects of Confucius)* vol. 12, p. 46 in *Ssu Pu Pei Yao*.

72 *Hou Han Shu*, vol. 76, Lieh Chuang, 'Ch'en Ch'ung', p. 8a in *Ssu Pu Pei Yao*.

73 Fung Yu-lan, *Hsin Li Hsüeh (New Rational Philosophy)*, Shanghai, 1947, p. 143.

74 This coincides with what Dr Yang thinks of ancestor worship. He contends that 'the Chinese do not worship their ancestors in the way that gods are worshipped, and ancestor worship should not be interpreted in a religious way'. Martin Yang, *A Chinese Village*, London, 1948, p. 90. I suspect that the shortcomings of Yang's statement consist in ruling out or ignoring the entrenched customs of ancestor cult among the illiterate Chinese. The matter should not be left there without further consideration. Various implications should be laid bare lest one should be misled.

75 Leviticus, IV: 9, VII, 14.

76 Henry Hubert and M. Mauss, *Sacrifice, Its Nature and Function*, trans. W. D. Halls. London, 1964, pp. 2–3.

77 J. Legge, *The Religion of China*, London, 1880, pp. 93–4.

78 *Shih Ching* (*The Book of Odes*), vol. 17, 'Ta Ya', Ode 'Chi Tsui', p. 7b in *Ssu Pu Pei Yao*.

79 *Ibid.*

80 *Li Chi*, vol. XIV, ch. 24, 'Li I', p. 5b in *Ssu Pu Pei Yao*, vol. 5.

81 *Ibid.*, pp. 1a–2b. So filial piety taught by ancient kings required that the eyes of the son should not forget the looks of his parents, nor his ears their voices.

82 *Hsün Tzu*, vol. 13, ch. 19 'Li Luan', pp. 24b–25a in *Ssu Pu Ts'ung Kan*.

83 Chan Wing-tsi, *Religious Trends in Modern China*, New York, 1953, p. 245.

84 *Li Chi*, vol. 24, 'Li I', pp. 8b, 9b–10a in *Ssu Pu Pei Yao* edition.

85 I am of the opinion that in Chinese ancestor rites there are the individual's status as a social person, rank, lineage, ceremonies, and ritual with which social structure and culture correspond. As ritual is a symbol, it makes the social structure real; the rite has a symbolic function for the sacrificer as political, religious, educational and moral leader of a group.

86 J. Goody, 'Religion and ritual', *British Journal of Sociology*, vol. 12, 1961, pp. 162–3. Dr Leach considers ritual a 'pattern of symbols', referring to the 'system of socially approved proper relations between individuals and group', *Ibid.*

87 *Lung Lü Chu Shu* (*The Analects of Confucius*), vol. I, 'Hsiao Erh', p. 4a in *Ssu Pu Pei Yao*.

88 I need to call attention to Moist utilitarianism which regards the performance of sacrifices as meaningless. Mo Tzŭ says: 'To hold that there are no spirits and learn sacrificial ceremonies is like learning the ceremonials of hospitality when there is no guest or making fish nets when there are no fishes'. *Mo Tzŭ*, 'Kung Meng', p. 19b; *Mo Tzŭ*, trans. Mei Yi-pao, London, 1929, p. 236.

89 Hu Shih, *The Chinese Renaissance*, Haskell Lectures, Chicago, 1933, p. 79.

90 The moral code of this religion is physical, intellectual, and moral amelioration with the view of becoming increasingly for the service of others. John H. Bridges, *Illustration of Positivism*, Chicago, 1915, pp. 222–3.

91 James Jackson. *Ancestral Worship*, Centenary Missionary Conference no. 7, Shanghai, 1907, p. 11.

92 *Ibid.* The ancestor worship is reckoned as the bond which brings about group cohesion and 'we'-feeling. The descendants have the aversion to dishonour their ancestor.

5 Various aspects of social life in the Chinese kinship system

1 In North China there is no markedly large-scale clan village. By marriage, wives belong to their husband's clan.
2 *Li Chi Chu Shu*, vol. 47, ch. 24 'Tze Yi', p. 2a in *Ssu Pu Pei Yao*, vol. 24.
3 *Meng Tzŭ Chu Shu*, 'Li Lou', part 2, p. 13b, *Ssi Pu Ts'ung Kan*.
4 *Hsing-An Hui-Lan*, vol. 1, p. 74 a.
5 *Ibid*., vol. I, p. 73b.
6 *Li Chi Chu Shu*, vol. 51, ch. 30 'Fang Ki', p. 9b in *Ssu Pu Pei Yao*, vol. 24.
7 Sung Lien, *Yüan Shih*, vol. 103, pp. 11a, 13, 3b–4a.
8 *Ibid*.
9 *T'ang Lü Shu Yi*, vol. I, p. 18b; *Sung Hsing Tung*, vol. I, p. 10b; *Ming Lü Li*, vol. I, p. 5a; *Ch'ing Lü Li*, vol. 4, p. 19a.
10 *T'ang Lü Shu Yi*, vol. 12, p. 5a; *Sung Hsing Tung*, vol. 12, p. 7a; *Ming Lü Li*, vol. 4, p. 25b; *Ch'ing Lü Li*, vol. 8, p. 53a–53b.
11 *T'ang Lü Shu Yi*, vol. 12, p. 5a; *Sung Hsing Tung*, vol. 12, p. 7b.
12 *Ming Lü Li*, vol. 4, p. 26a; *Ch'ing Lü Li*, vol. 8, p. 53a.
13 Huang En-t'ung, *Preface to Ta Ch'ing Lü Li An Yü*, Hai Hsien Kuan Ts'ang Pan edition, 14 vols. Also see Yang Hung-lieh, *The History of the Development of Chinese Laws*, Shanghai, no date, 2 vols, vol. I, p. 6.
14 *Li Chi Chu Shu*, vol. V, ch. 15 'Sang fu hsiao chi', p. 3a in *Ssu Pu Pei Yao*, vol. 32.
15 *Ibid*.
16 As has been said earlier, all brothers have equal claims to their father's estate. When they begin to assert their individual rights, which tend potentially to pull the component elementary family apart, the division of the family is impending.
17 Su Sing-ging, *The Chinese Family System*, New York, 1922, pp. 51–2.
18 Illegitimate children whose father is known but who are legitimized by a subsequent marriage or who are adopted and the children of a prostitute (Tsa chung, bastards) are illegitimate; they are under the power of the mother whose surname they bear.
19 C. Alabaster, 'The New law of inheritance', *China Review*, vol. V, July 1876 to June 1877, p. 194.
20 According to the Ch'ing Code, the family property descends directly to a son or an adopted heir after his father's death. If the son is not yet grown, his mother can manage the property on his behalf until he comes of age. A widow who remarries is prohibited from taking either the family property or even her dowry with her. Both remain with the family.

21 Sir H. Maine, *Ancient Law*, Oxford, 1959, pp. 150–1. The rights and obligations which attach to the deceased head of the house will attach, without breach of continuity, to his successor; in point of fact, they will be the rights and obligations of the family, and the family has the distinctive characteristic of a corporation.

22 M. Fortes, 'Some Reflections on Ancestor Worship in Africa', in *African Systems of Thought*, Oxford, 1965, p. 139.

23 *Kung Yang Chu Shu*, vol. I, 'Duke Yin', pp. 9b–10a in *Ssu Pu Pei Yao*, vol. 28.

24 Ssu-ma Ch'ien, *Shih Chi*, vol. 33 'The Feudal State of Lu', pp. 9a–10a in *Ssu Pu Tsing Kan*.

25 *Ibid.*, vol. XL 'The Feudal State of Ch'u', pp. 16a–16b.

26 *Ibid.*, vol. XL, p. 6b.

27 *Ibid.*, vol. XL, p. 16b.

28 *Ta Ming Ling*, *The Law of the Ming Dynasty* (*Ming Lü Li*).

29 The adopted person must cast his lot with the new family if he wants a share in the family property. He cannot wait until his share accrues, and bring it back to his native family. In other words, the share taken from his adoptive father must not pass to the general estate of his natural father.

30 In contrast to Hindus, among whom the right to inherit a dead man's property is exactly co-extensive with the duty of performing his obsequies, the descendants in China are strictly bound to abide by the term fixed for mourning and to perform the sacrificial ceremonies at the ancestral temples and at the graves. See *The Analects of Confucius*. The coffin has to be buried in the native soil, and there the funeral ceremonies are properly performed. If the funeral rites are not properly performed by the proper person, no relationship is thought to be established between the deceased and his son surviving him. The law then does not apply and thus no one can inherit the property of the family. On the other hand, the onerous nature of the funeral duty cannot be denied. In 1878 when the father of Fong Chun-kuang, a former Custom Officer of Shanghai, died, he went as far as Kansu province in the north-west of China to fetch the coffin and bring it to Canton, his native province, for the burial. The rough and arduous voyage, in which multifarious ceremonies had to be performed, so exhausted the dutiful son that he succumbed to the invincible difficulties; his brother took his place and continued the voyage. P. G. von Möllendorff, 'The family law of the Chinese', *Journal of the China Branch of the Royal Asiatic Society*, New Series, vol. XXVII.

31 Sir H. Maine, *Ancient Law*, London, 1917, p. 106. 'Let there be careful attention to perform the funeral rites to parents and let them

be followed when long gone with the ceremonies of sacrifice',
vol. 1, 'Hsiao I', p. 4a in *Ssu Pu Pei Yao*.

32 *Ibid.*, p. 105.
33 *Ibid.*, p. 106.
34 P. G. von Möllendorff, *op. cit.*, pp. 182–3.
35 Notes and Queries in the *China Review*, vol. XIII, p. 119.
36 In adopting a son-in-law, the parents are enabled to have the services
 of their own daughter all their life – a rare privilege. Because whoever is adopted is entitled to the division of family property, many
 people with little property prefer to adopt a son-in-law. Again the
 adopted son-in-law is treated as a natural son, but the children of
 the third generation revert to his original clan name; customarily
 one male child is set apart to continue the line of the wife's clan.
37 P. G. Möllendorff, *op. cit.*, p. 133.
38 M. G. Mitchell-Innes, 'Adoption', *China Review*, vol. XIV, July
 1885–June 1886, p. 204.
39 *Ibid.*, pp. 202–203.
40 It may be that such a lapse of time without much change in social
 structure is inconceivable to the Western mind, accustomed as it
 is to change and prone to confound movement with progress. See
 H. P. Wilkinson, *The Family in Classical China*, Shanghai, 1926, p.47.
41 Lin Yueh-hua, *I-Hsü*, pp. 11–12. These ideas are derived from Lin
 Yueh-hua.
42 *Hou Han Shu*, vol. 106, p. 15a in *Ssu Pu Pei Yao*.
43 Liu Hsü, *Chiu T'ang Shu*, vol. 185, 'Lieh Chuan', vol. 135, p. 9a in
 Ssu Pu Pei Yao.
44 The character 'lao', old man (see the Glossary) refers to 'mao',
 meaning hair and beard. The top part of the character, 'lao', means
 a man, while the lower part, Mao', symbolizes a venerable or septuagenarian old man whose hair and beard, 'mao', change and grow
 white.
45 Chen Han-seng, *The Present Agrarian Problem in China*, Shanghai,
 1933, pp. 1–14.
46 Chen Han-seng, *Agrarian Problems in Southernmost China*,
 Shanghai, 1936, p. 37.
47 Y. K. Leong and L. K. Tao, *Village and Town Life in China*, London,
 1915, pp. 35–6.
48 Daniel H. Kulp. *Country Life in South China*, New York, 1925,
 p. 111.
49 Lin Yueh-hua, 'An Enquiry into the Chinese lineage village from the
 viewpoint of anthropology', in *She Hui Hsüeh Chieh*, 1936, no. 9.
50 Yang, *op. cit.*, pp. 190–1.
51 Kulp, *op. cit.*, pp. 93–6.

52 Sidney D. Gamble, *Ting Hsien, A North China Rural Community*, New York, 1954, p. 159. Ting Hsien is a town only about forty miles from the writer's village.

53 This Village Protection Organization is still vivid in my memory. My grandfather provided this group with our front yard, while we lived in the backyard, being separated by a wall.

54 Lin Yueh-hua, *op. cit.*, p. 6. The 'pao chia' system was descanted upon by Wang An-shih (1021–86) during the Sung dynasty. *Sung Shu* by Shen Yo, vol. 327, Shanghai, 1977, p. 10544.

55 Fei Hsiao-tung, *Peasant Life in China*, London, 1939, p. 112.

56 Liu Hsing-t'ang, 'The structure of kinship groups in Fukien,' *Shih Huo* (in Chinese), vol. 4, no. 8, 1936, p. 42.

57 Yang, *op. cit.*, pp. 174–5.

58 Literati are not people of an exclusive class, being placed far above the other classes of people. Not being an hereditary class, they may be drawn from all classes of society; they may join the festivals, but may also guide the common people to indulge in more intellectual games. Y. K. Leong and L. K. Tao, *op. cit.*, pp. 113–14.

59 Hu Hsien-chin, *The Common Descent Group in China and its Functions*, New York, 1948, pp. 27f.

60 Freedman, *Lineage Organization in South-Eastern China*, London, 1958.

61 Yang, *op. cit.*, p. 181. Chen Han-seng (*op. cit.*, p. 37) indicates that the so-called strong branches of the clan supply the effective 'clan' officers.

62 Freedman, *op. cit.*, p. 69.

63 Lin Yueh-hua, *op. cit.*, p. 9.

64 According to ancient tradition the autumn rites were performed in commemoration of distant ancestors, while the spring rites in the memory of the founding ancestor. It is written in *Tung Tien*, 'Ancient kings formulated ritual of sacrifice in four seasons to the effect that a filial son could express his affection for his relatives and remember them'. See *T'ung-tien* vol. 49, 'Rites 9', pp. 1a–1b.

65 Kulp, *op. cit.*, p. 147.

66 This custom reflects the function of exogamy by which the legal and ritual ties are created from the movement of a woman from her natal or original family to her husband's.

67 Among the Tallensi when a child is a minor, a father's agnatic cousin may act in 'loco parentis' if the father's nearer male agnates are not available; but this is a position of 'trusteeship' rather than of full paternal authority. Fortes, *op. cit.*, p. 146.

68 According to Cheng Hsüan, 'tsung' is 'family stock' referring to the paternal uncle who is in charge of the small tsung. See *Shang Shu Chu Shu*, vol. 4, pp. 6b–7a in *Ssu Pu Pei Yao*.

69 Mao Ch'i-ling, *Ta Hsiao Tsung T'ung-Shih,* p. 9b; Ch'eng Yao-tien *Tsung Fa Hsiao Chih,* p. 1a.
70 *Pai Hu Tung,* vol. 8, p. 5b in *Ssu Pu Ts'ung Kan,* vol. 130, sect. 4. *Li Chi Chu Shu,* vol. 5 'Chü li', p. 11b in *Ssu Pu Pei Yao,* vol. 22.
71 J. J. de Groot, *Les fêtes annuellement célébrées à Emoui – Étude concernant la religion populaire des chinois* in *Annales du Musée Guimet,* vol. 11 and 12, Paris, 1886, p. 19.
72 *Ibid.,* pp. 552 f.
73 Hu Hsien-chin, *op. cit.,* p. 32.
74 Chen Han-seng, *op. cit.,* p. 41.
75 Leong and Tao, *op. cit.,* p. 25.
76 Yang, *op. cit.,* pp. 140–1.
77 Fortes, *op. cit.,* p. 137.
78 Alfred Loisy, *Essai historique sur le sacrifice,* Paris, 1920, p. 1.
79 According to Wang Kuo-wei, the character 'li' is synonymous with 'fung', which symbolizes sacrificial vessels. Traditionally, in offering sacrifice to the supreme god and to the ancestors, people used to offer two pieces of jade contained in a vessel. The character 'fung' is derived from two pieces of jade, and a bean 'tou' represents a 'vessel of jade'. Yang Yung-kuo *The History of Ancient Chinese Thought,* Hong Kong, 1962, p. 10.
80 *Ch'eng Shih I Shu,* vol. II, pp. 2a, 3a, vol. XXV in *Ssu Pu Pei Yao,* vol. 280. 'Li' is moral because it is the completion of 'jen', goodness. Fung Yu-lan, *Hsin Li Hsüeh,* Shanghai, 1947, p. 294.
81 Hu Shih, 'Shou Ju', in *Lung Hsüeh Chin Chu,* vol. I, pp. 19, 24, 94.
82 Chêng chen, *Ch'ao Ching Ch'ao Wen Chi* – Collected Works of Chêng chen, AD 1806–64, in *Ch'ing Tai Hsüeh Shu Ts'ang Shu.*
83 Hu Hsien-chin, *op. cit.,* p. 17.
84 *Li Chi Chu Shu,* vol. 34, 'Ta Ch'uan', p. 7b in *Ssu Pu Pei Yao.*
85 F. L. K. Hsu, 'The problem of incest taboo in a North China village', *American Anthropologist,* vol. 42, no. 1. January–March, 1940, p. 123 n.
86 *Li Chi Chu Shu,* vol. XXXII, 'San Fu hsiao ki', p. 3b in *Ssu Pu Pei Yao.*
87 *Ibid.,* 'Ta Chuan', p. 4b.
88 Virtually the period of three years' mourning terminates within 25 months, definitely within 27 months. In the eastern mode of speaking of time, 'three years' means to say that it extends into the 'third' year. For instance, a child not being more than six months old is said to be two years old; a little cross-questioning shows that he has been born towards the end of the previous year, that he has lived in two years, and thus has been spoken of as two years of age. See *Li Chi,* 'San nien wen', vol. 58, pp. 3a–4b.
89 'Chan' means 'unhemmed'. A mourning apparel is made up of two

parts: the superior part is called 'ts'ui', and the lower part 'shang'. The border or edge and hem-line of the apparel is unhemmed; a piece of cloth, seven inches square is sewn down the collar and hung in front of the chest. This symbolizes the lament of the son. Another piece of cloth six inches in length and four inches in width is sewn in front of the left lapel, having on both sides an open collar and the lapels under the armpits, and hung down like swallow tails so that they can cover the edges of the lower part of the funeral or mourning apparel, i.e. the trousers. *Ta Ch'ing Lü Li.* The waist cord is made up of hemp, and two pieces of cord are twisted together; the end of two pieces is loose or unfastened, and the end of their junctures is tied up by thin cords.

90 The period of three years is, according to *The Analects of Confucius*, a universal rule of all under Heaven, and mentioned in *Li Chi*, 'San nien wen'. In fact, this custom was certainly not universal in later dynasties. In *Mencius*, vol. V, 2b, the peoples of the Tent protested that even in the State of Lu, the Confucian native state, none of the former princes practised it. A. Waley, *The Analects of Confucius*, London, 1945, p. 215a.

91 Ku Yen-wu, *Jih Chih Lu* (Ching I Chai Ts'ang edn), vol. 5, p. 33b.

92 *Hsüeh Hai Lei Pien*, ed. Ts'ao Jung with additions by T'ao Yüeh, Shanghai, 1920, vol. 2, p. 2b.

93 *Li Chi Chu Shu*, vol. XXXII, p. 4b; *I Li Chu Shu*, 'Sang fu', vol. XI, p. 3a. Chia Kung-yen comments on the *I Li* passage (4b–5a) as follows: 'Bamboo is round, resembling Heaven; inside and outside it has joints, resembling the son who inwardly and outwardly grieves, and it does not change throughout the four seasons, just as the son mourns for his father throughout the cold and hot seasons without changing'. 'Tung' means also 't'ung' (similar), that is, in the heart of the son the mother is the same as the father.

94 *Pai Hu Tung*, vol. IV, p. 5b.

95 According to *The Book of Ritual*, if the father still lived, the sons wore only one year's mourning for their mother; if the father died, they wore three years' mourning for their mother. In the first year of his reign, 'Shang Yüan' (*c*. AD 647), the emperor Kao Tsung of the dynasty T'ang, granted the request of his concubine Wu Tze-tien for decreasing three years' mourning for the mother notwithstanding the father was still alive. See *Chiu T'ang Shu*. Also the emperor Tai-tsu of the Ming dynasty, on the occasion of the death of his concubine, Sun-she, enjoined Sun Ling, the academician, to write a book of filial piety titled *Hsiao Tze lu* and decreed that the children of either a legitimate mother or concubine were obliged to wear three years' mourning for their mother even if their father was still alive. See *Ming Shih*, vol. 60, pp. 226–28a.

96   *Ta Ch'ing Lü Li Hui Chi Pien-Lan*, Hupeh Yen Chü edition, 1872, vol. 2, p. 3b.
97   *Ibid.*, vol. II, p. 6a.
98   Chao I *Kai Yü Tsing Kao*, vol. 32, Shanghai, 1957, p. 673.
99   As a married woman is incorporated into her husband's family, her own natal family has no clear-cut rights to interfere in her affairs. Any intervention on the part of the wife's own kinsmen would involve them in unbearable embarrassment.
100 *Ta Ch'ing Lü Li Hui Chi Pien-Lan*, vol. II, pp. 11b–12a.
101 In the T'ang Code it says: 'There is a prohibition of cross-marriage.' *T'ang Lü Shu Yi*, vol. I, pp. 14, 2b. According to the 'Ming' Code, 'whoever contracts marriage with a cross-cousin, must be punished by 80 strokes.' See *Ming Lü Chih Chieh*, vol. 6, p. 17a. The Ching Code enforces the prohibition of cross-cousin marriage with the clause: 'A man cannot marry the children of his aunt on the father's side, or of his uncle or aunt on the mother's side because though they are of the same generation, they are within the fifth degree of mourning.' Later it was permissible, in the interest of the people, to marry the children of a paternal aunt or of a maternal uncle or aunt. *Ta Ching Lü Li.*
102 *Li Chi Chu Shu*, vol. 28 'Nei Zse', p. 11b in *Ssu Pu Pei Yao*, vol. 23.
103 *Li Chi Chu Shu*, vol. 2 'Ch'ü Li', part 1, p. 8a in *Ssu Pu Pei Yao*, vol. 22.
104 *Pai-Hu T'ung*, 9, 16a, in *Ssu Pu Ts'ung Kan* vol. 130, sect. 4.
105 Mourning dress must be colourless, i.e. white or plain garments because any colour other than white is reckoned by the Chinese as a sign of joy and happiness. Dr Yang is of the opinion that the white mourning cloth is the most obvious sign of lamentation. M. Yang, *A Chinese Village: Taitou*, London, 1948, p. 86.
106 S. Freud, *Totem and Taboo*, London, 1950, p. 66. 'It is only neurotics whose mourning for the loss of those dear to them is still troubled by obsessive self-reproaches, the secret of which is revealed by psycho-analysis as the old emotional ambivalence.'
107 *Ku Chin Tu Shu Chi Ch'eng* (*The Great Chinese Encyclopaedia*), compiled by Chen Ming-lei. This enormous work has 10,000 volumes, providing a comprehensive survey of all that was best in the literature of the past, dealing with every branch of knowledge. It is a direct descendant of *Yü lan*. The scheme of the work had been conceived and formulated by the emperor Kang Hsi of the Ch'ing dynasty, and Chen Men-lei was the man chosen to carry it into execution. He completed this stupendous work officially, and the first printed edition appeared in 1726. A new edition was published after 1862, and a further edition a little

reduced in size, appeared in the years 1885–8. In reference to the New Year Festival, see VI: vol. 1130, 'Feng Hsu', p. 1b.

108　*Ku Chin Tu Shu Chi Ch'ng*, VI: 1120, p. 4a.

109　*Tso Chuan*, vol. 6, 'Duke Hsi', p. 13b in *Ssu Pu Ts'ung Kan*.

110　In China the Taoist philosophy taught people not to accept worldly compensation for a good deed. If they refuse a high reward, their virtue will be much exalted.

111　*Ku Chin Tu Shu Chih Cheng*, VI: 1142, 'Feng Hsu', p. 2a.

112　*Ibid.*, VI: 1120 and 1259, 'Feng Hsu', p. 1b.

113　*Li Chi*, vol. V, ch. 6, 'Yu Ling', p. 6a in *Ssu Pu Pei Yao*.

114　*Ku Chin Tu Shu Chi Ch'eng*, II: 51, p. 3a.

115　Yang Si-ch'ang has elaborated on a version from *Ti Li Chi*, the geographical section of *Sui Shu*, History of the Sui dynasty, and said that Ch'ü Yuan was drowned in the river 'Mi-lo' on the full moon of the fifth month. The people of this region ran after him and when they reached the Tung T'ing Lake, they could not see him. The lake was too large, but their boat was too small to cross over. Then they sang the following words: 'With what can we cross the lake? Being as it is, let us, drumming and paddling, return fighting; let us meet at the pavilion.' *Ku Chin Tu Shu Chi Cheng*, II: 51, p. 5a.

116　The legend of tsung-tzu is that the people of Chang Sha district saw the spirit of Ch'ü Yuan and were told that 'tsung tzu' were swallowed by dragons. Hereafter the people tied 'tsung tzu' with varicoloured treads in order to frighten dragons.

117　*Ku Chin Tu Shu Chi Ch'eng*, II: 51, p. 7a.

118　'Su' is the surname of the families.

119　*Ku Chin Tu Shu Chi Ch'eng*, II: 51, 4a, 66, 7a.

120　The drums are pots covered with a 'shen mien' – 'spirit face' or figure. *Ching Ch'u Sui Shih Chi*, VI: 1204. 'Shan sh'uan', vol. 3, p. 9b. In Suei Yang district there was a custom on New Year's Day called 'nao cien' – the tumult of the New Year, when children were let loose with bamboo crackers, gongs and drums. Drums were played the previous night: 'In the still of the night, "Chi" sacrifices are made to ancestors. The sound of drums and fire crackers give reverence.' *Ibid.*, vol. VI: 1120, 'Feng Hsu', pp. 4a, 5b.

121　*Ibid.*, VI, 'Tsi mia', vol. 2, p. 1a.

122　The milfoil and the tortoise-shell are used for divination. 'Kuei' – tortoise-shell – means 'chiu', long-lasting. 'Shih' – milfoil – means 'chi'i', aged. Liu Hsiang in *I Hsi Tz'u I* says that 'by their great ages the tortoise becomes a "genius," i.e. ling, and the milfoil, a spirit-shen'.

123 'Jo shui' or 'weak water' is a cosmic river. In the *Shang Hai Ching*
     it is said that the source of the 'jo shui' is at the foot of the jo shu
     (tree), that is, the tree of the sunset. See B. Karlgren, 'Legends and
     cults in ancient China', *Bulletin of the Museum of Far Eastern
     Antiquities*, no. 18, Stockholm, 1949, pp. 204f.
124 *Ku Chin Tu Shu Chi Ch'eng*, VI: 1249, 'Feng Hsu', p. 5.
125 *Ibid.*, VI: 1130, 'Feng Hsu', p. 1.
126 According to *Shen I*, at the full harvest moon in the eighth month
     each family lights incense made into a vase with gift flowers as
     an offering.
127 H.C. du Bose, *The Dragon, Image, and Demon, or Three Religions
     of China*, London, 1886, p. 69.
128 *Ku Chin Tu Shu Chi Ch'eng*, VI: 1249, 'Feng Hsu', p. 5.
129 *Li Chi*, vol. 24, 'Ch'i I', pp. 5a–5b in *SSu Pu Pei Yao*. 'When he
     [the superior man] treads on the dew which has descended as
     hoar-frost he cannot help a feeling of sadness . . . . In spring when
     he treads on the ground wet with the rains and dews that have
     fallen heavily he cannot avoid being moved by a feeling as if he
     were seeing his departed friend.'
130 *Ku Chin Tu Shu Chi Ch'eng*, VI: 1120.
131 There is some reason to believe that the Hearth God or Kitchen
     God was once regarded as an anonymous ancestor of the family.
     though nowadays this relationship is neglected. Reginald F.
     Johnston, *Lion and Dragon in Northern China* London, 1910;
     Ku Chin Tu Shu Chi Ch'eng, VI 1130; 'Feng Hsu', p. 1.
132 Five colours are: red, yellow, green, white and black.
133 *Ibid.*, vol. 6, p. 1120, p. 4.
134 The beverage 'tea' (ch's) first appears in *Erh Ya*, vol. III, 'shih
     mu' (explanation of plant), p. 7a. The commentary is given by
     Kuo pu. *Ssu Pu Ts'ung Kan*, 'Ching pu' (ritual). 'chia' is a bitter
     tea and bears leaves in winter, which is boiled and drunk. We
     name 'tea' what is picked in the morning, and 'ming' the tender
     leaf or leaf buds of tea picked in the evening.
135 Chinese village plays based on Franklin C.H. Lee and Chang
     Shih-wen, *The Ting Hsien Yang Ke Hsüan*, ed. Sidney D. Gamble,
     Amsterdam, 1970.
136 A.H. Radcliffe-Brown, *Structure and Function in Primitive So-
     ciety*, Chicago, 1952, p. 112. He said that 'the universities of
     Oxford and Cambridge maintain a certain relation by competing
     regularly in rowing, football, etc. In North-West America one group
     would call in a friend group to erect a totem-pole for them.
     In Potlatch, among the Kwakiutl, there is competition or rivalry
     in the exchange of valuable.'

137 G. Bateson, 'A History of play and fantasy', *Psychiatric Research Report*, 2, American Psychiatric Association, 1954, pp. 39–51.

138 B. Malinowski, 'Culture', *The Encyclopedia of the Social Sciences*, New York, 1931, pp. 621–45.

139 Han Ten Play, 'Two visits to sister', cited by Hsū Mêng-Ling, *The History of Drama and Plays in Yün Nan Province*. The National University of Yün Nan Press, 1949, pp. 86–8.

Glossary

Wade System	Hanyu Pinyin	
Cha T'ou Pu	Zha Tou Bu	紮頭布
Ch'a	Cha	茶
Chan Kuo	Zhan Guo	戰國
Chang Shang	Zhang Shang	長殤
Chan Li	Zhan Li	戰慄
Chan Ts'ui	Zhan Shuai	斬衰
Ch'ang	Chang	嘗
Chao Ch'ien	Zhao Qian	趙錢
Chao Hsian	Zhao Xiang	昭襄
Che Kiang	Zhe Jiang	浙江
Chen Ch'ung	Chen Chong	陳寵
Cheng	Zheng	鄭，成，燕
Ch'eng	Cheng	程
Ch'eng Fu	Cheng Fu	成服
Ch'eng Chi	Cheng Ji	承繼
Ch'eng Ling-shen	Cheng Ling-sheng	程廩生
Ch'eng Yao-tien	Cheng Yao-tien	程瑤田
Chi	Ji	祭

In the character 'chi' 祭, 夕 symbolizes a piece of flesh or meat, the offering; ' ㄑ ' represents a hand, and ' 示 ' stands for a ghost. The character 'chi' indicates that sacrifice is a gift offered by worshippers to the spirit or ghost of the ancestors.

Chi Mu	Ji Mu	繼母
Chi Pieh	Ji Bie	繼別
Ch'i	Chi	氣，齊
Ch'i Ts'ui	Chi Shuai	齊衰
Ch'i Tung Ye Yü	Chi Dong Ye Yu	齊東野語
Ch'i Yueh Shih Wu	Chi Yue Shi Wu	七月十五
Çhia	Zhia	家，價
Chia Ping	Zhia Ping	嘉平
Chia Tzu	Zhia Ci	家慈
Chiang Shih	Jiang Shi	姜詩
Chiao	Jiao	教
Chiao Chung-ch'ing	Jiao Zhong-qing	焦仲卿
Chiao Tzu	Jiao Zi	餃子
Chieh	Qie	妾
Chieh Chih-tui	Jie Zhi-tui	介之推
Chieh Tsung Tzu	Jie Zong Zi	接宗子
Chien Yuan	Qian Yuan	乾元
Chih	Zhi	支
Chin	Jin	晉
Chin Ku Ch'i Kuan	Jin Gu Qi Guan	今古奇觀
Chin Shu	Jin Shu	晉書
Ch'in	Qin	秦
Ching	Jing	井
Ching Pu	Jing Bu	經部
Ching Tai Hsüeh Shu Ts'ang Shu	Qing Dai Xue Shu Cong Shu	清代學術叢書
Ching Tien	Jing Tien	井田
Chiu	Zhiu	舅，九
Chiu Piao	Zhiu Biao	舅表
Chou	Zhou	周
Chou Shu	Zhou Shu	周書
Chou Li Chu Shu	Zhou Li Zhu Shu	周禮注疏
Ch'ou Lan	Chou Lan	仇覽
Chu	Zhu	主，朱，竹

Chu	Ju	聚，矩
Chu Hsi	Zhu Xi	朱熹
Chu Shu Chih Nien	Zhu Shu Ji Nien	竹書紀年
Ch'u Mu	Chu Mu	出母
Ch'u	Chu	楚
Ch'u Huai Wang	Chu Huai Wang	楚懷王
Chü Jen	Ju Ren	舉人
Ch'ü Yuan	Qu Yuan	屈原
Chüan	Quan	勸
Ch'uan	Chuan	傳
Chuang Tzu	Zhuang Zi	莊子
Chün	Jun	君
Ch'un Ch'iu	Chun Qiu	春秋
Ch'un Ch'iu Chüe Yü	Chun Qiu Jue Yi	春秋決議
Chung	Zhong	中
Chung Ch'iu Chieh	Zhong Qiu Jie	中秋節
Chung Yuan	Zhong Yuan	中元
Erh Ya	Er Ya	爾雅
Erh Ku Tu Shu	Er Gu Du Shu	二谷讀書
Fah	Fa	發
Fang	Fang	房
Fan Chung	Fan Zhong	樊重
Fen	Fen	分
Fong Mêng-lung	Feng Meng-long	馮夢龍
Fu	Fu	父
Fu Ch'in	Fu Qin	父親
Fung	Fong	豐
Hai Hsien Kuan Ts'ang Pan	Hai Xian Guan Cang Ban	海仙館藏版
Han	Han	漢
Han Shih	Han Shi	寒食
Han Wei Ts'ung Shu	Hai Wei Cong Shu	漢魏叢書
Hang Chou	Hang Zhou	杭州
Ho Hsün	He Xun	賀循

225

Hsi Shang Fu T'an	Xi Shang Fu Tan	席上腐談
Hsia	Xia	夏
Hsia Shang	Xia Shang	下殤
Hsiang	Xiang	鄉
Hsiang Chang	Xiang Zhang	鄉長
Hsiang Ch'i	Xiang Qi	象棋
Hsiang Tuan	Xiang Tuan	鄉團
Hsiao	Xiao	孝

The character 'hsiao' 孝 is composed of two ideograms: the ideogram '尹' means 'old' and the other '子' is a child. The character 'hsiao' means filial piety, that children should show to their old parents. 耂 means that, as a cane a child supports his old parents when they walk.

Hsiao Ching	Xiao Jing	孝經
Hsiao Kung	Xiao Gong	小功
Hsiao Tsung	Xiao Zong	小宗
Hsiao Tze Lu	Xiao Ci Lu	孝慈錄
Hsieh	Xie	謝
Hsien	Xian	顯
Hsüeh Erh	Xue Er	學而
Hsin Li Hsueh	Xin Li Xue	新理學
Hsing	Xing	姓
Hsing Shih	Xing Shi	姓氏
Hsiu Fu	Xiu Fu	休父
Hsiung	Xiong	兄
Hsiung Ti	Xiong Di	兄弟
Hsü	Xu	許，徐
Hsü Mêng-ling	Xu Meng-ling	徐夢麟
Hsü Wen-ching	Xu Wen-jing	許文靖
Hsüeh Hai Lei Pien	Xue Hai Lei Bian	學海類編
Hsü Kuang-ch'i	Xu Guang-qi	徐光啟
Hsü Shen	Xu Shen	許愼
Hsuan Sun	Xuan Sun	玄孫
Hsüeh Chin T'ao Yuan	Xue Jin Tao Yuan	學津討原
Hu	Hu	戶

Hu Shih	Hu Shi	胡適
Huang En-t'ang	Huang En-tan	黃恩彤
Huan	Hun	魂
Hui Shang Tz'u T'ang T'u	Hui Shan Ci Tang Tu	惠山祠堂圖
Hui	Hui	諱
Hui Ti	Hui Di	惠帝
Hwa Mu-lan	Hua Mu-lan	花木蘭
Hwang	Huang	黃
I Fu	Yi Fu	義服
I Kuan	Yi Kuan	倪寬
I Li	Yi Li	儀禮
Jen	Ren	仁
Ju	Ru	儒
Ju Mu	Ru Mu	乳母
Jih Chi Lu	Ri Zhi Lu	日知錄
Jih Hsia Chiu Wen Kao	Ri Xia Jiu Wen Kao	日下舊聞考
Jo Shui	Rao Shui	弱水
Kai Chia Chi Mu	Gai Jia Ji Mu	改嫁繼母
Kai Yü Ts'ung K'ao	Gai Yu Ceng Kao	陔餘叢考
K'ang Hsi	Kang Xi	康熙
Kang Hsi Tzu Tien	Kang Xi Zi Dian	康熙字典
Kao Tzu	Gao Zi	告子
K'ao	Kao	考
Ko Ko	Ge Ge	哥哥
Ku	Gu	姑
Ku Piao	Gu Biao	姑表
Ku Chin Tu Shu Chi Ch'eng	Gu Jin Du Shu Zi Cheng	古今讀書集成
Ku Shih Yuan	Gu Shi Yuan	古詩源
Ku Yen-wu	Gu Yen-wu	顧炎武
Ku Yi	Gu Yi	姑姨
Kuan Chung	Guan Zhong	管仲
Kung Yang Chu Shu	Gung Yang Zhu Shu	公羊注疏

Kuo Nien Hao	Guo Nien Hao	過年好
Kuo Pu	Guo Pu	郭璞
Kuo Ssu	Guo Si	過嗣
Kuo Yü	Guo Yu	國語
Kung	Gong	公
Kung Ye Chang	Gong Ye chang	公冶長
Kuan Ti	Guan Di	關帝
Kwei	Gui	閨，鬼

The character 'kwei' 閨 consists of two ideograms: the ideogram 'kwei' 圭 is a jade, while the ideogram 'men' 門 a door in which a piece of jade, that is, a woman is secluded and dwells. The Chinese have much respect for a woman's purity and, confining her in the house, makes her flawless-like jade.

The character 'kwei' 鬼 ghost is the symbol of 歸 a return. 'Kwei' 鬼 means 'manes' returning into the ultimate dwelling, peace and reality. The deceased, becoming a 'kwei' 鬼 become dependent on their former family for offerings and libations.

La Pa Chieh	La Ba Jie	臘八節
Lan Chih	Lan Zhi	蘭芝
Lang	Lang	郎
Lao	Lao	老

The character 'lao' 老 means a septuagenarian old man; it is composed of two ideograms: the upper ideogram 耂 stands for hair, while the lower one 匕 refers to change, that is, the stage when the old man's hair turns white.

Lao Tai Tai	Lao Tai Tai	老太太
Lao Tzu	Lao Zi	老子
Li	Li	例
Li Chi	Li Ji	禮記
Li Chih-tsao	Li Zhi-zao	李之藻
Li Mi	Li Mi	李密
Lie Tzu	Lie Zi	列子
Lieh Nü Chuang	Lie Nu Zhuang	列女傳
Ling Mêng-ch'u	Ling Meng-chu	凌夢初
Liu	Liu	劉
Liu Huan	Liu Huan	劉獻

Lu	Lu	魯
Lu Hsin	Lu Xin	魯迅
Lung	Long	龍
Lung Heng	Lun Heng	論衡
Lung Hsüeh Chin Chu	Lun Xue Jin Zhu	論學近著
Lung Wei Mi Shu	Lun Wei Mi Shu	龍威秘書
Ma Chiang	Ma Jiang	麻將
Mai Hui-t'ing	Mai Hui-ting	麥惠庭
Mao	Mao	七
Men	Men	門
Men Fa	Men Fa	門閥
Meng Lan	Meng Lan	孟蘭
Miao Hui	Miao Hui	廟會
Mien Shan	Mien Shan	綿山
Mi Lo	Mi Lo	汨羅
Ming	Ming	茗
Mo Tzu	Mo Zi	墨子
Mu	Mu	母
Nan Ch'i Shu	Nan Qi Shu	南齊書
Nei	Nei	內
Nei Hsiung Ti	Nei Xiung Di	內兄弟
Nou Yang-chien	Nou Yang-jian	獳羊肩
Nü Erh	Nu Er	女兒
Pa Pa	Ba Ba	爸爸
Pai	Pai	派
Pai	Bai	拜
P'ang	Pang	潘
Pao Chia	Bao Jia	保甲
Pao Fu	Bao Fu	報服
Pen Shing	Ben Sheng	本生
Pen Shing Fu, Mu	Ben Shen Fu, Mu	本生父，母
Pi	Pi	妣
Piao Hsiung Ti	Biao Xiong Di	表兄弟
Pieh Tzu	Pie Zi	別子

Po	Bo	柏
P'o	Po	魄
Po Ts'u	Po Cu	迫促
Pong Sheng	Peng Sheng	彭生
Pu Tung Chü Chi Fu	Bu Tong Ju Ji Fu	不同居繼父
Sao Chen	Sao Chen	掃塵
San Shang Fu	San Shang Fu	三殤服
Sang Fu	Sang Fu	喪服
Sang Fu Chuan	Sang Fu Zhuan	喪服傳
Sang Fu Hsiao Chi	Sang Fu Xiao Ji	喪服小記
Shan	Shan	繕
Shang	Shang	殤
Shang Ch'en	Shang Chen	商臣
Shang Shu	Shang Shu	尙書
Shang Yang	Shang Yang	商鞅
She	Shi	諡
Shê	She	舍
She Hui Hsüeh Chieh	She Hsui Xue Jie	社會學界
Shen	Shen	神
Shen Hsiang	Shen Xiang	神像
Shen Mien	Shen Mien	神面
Shen Wei	Shen Wei	神位
Shen Yi	Shen Yi	神翼
Sheng	Sheng	甥
Shih	Shi	仕
Shih Mu	Shi Mu	釋木
Shih Tzu	Shi Zu	世族
Shih Chi	Shi Ji	史記
Shih Hou	Shi Hou	石厚
Shih Ch'i Shih Shang Chüe	Shi Qi Shi Shang Que	十七史商榷
Shih Tseuh	Shi Cu	石碏
Shing Mu	Shing Mu	生母
Shou Ju	Shou Ru	說儒

Shou Wen Chieh Tzu	Shou Wen Jie Zi	說文解字
Shu	Shu	叔
Shu Mien	Shu Mien	庶民
Shu Mu	Shu Mu	庶母
Shou Wen	Shou Wen	說文
Shui Hu Chuan	Shui Hu Zhuan	水滸傳
Ssu Fu, Mu	Si Fu, Mu	嗣父，母
Ssu-ma Chao	Si-ma Zhao	司馬昭
Ssu-ma Shih	Si-ma Shi	司馬師
Ssu-ma Yu	Si-ma You	司馬攸
Ssu Pu Pei Yao	Si Bu Bei Yao	四部備要
Ssu Pu Ts'ung Kan	Si Bu Ceng Kan	四部叢刊
Su Chia Tu	Su Jia Du	蘇家渡
Su Tong-p'o	Su Dong-po	蘇東坡
Sun	Sun	孫
Sung	Song	宋
Sung Kung-ming	Song Gong-ming	宋公明
Sung Lien	Song Lien	宋濂
Sung Tong	Song Dong	悚動
Sung Tsu	Song Zu	送祖
Sung Tzu	Zong Zi	粽子
Ta Ch'ing Lü Li Hui Chi Pien Lan	Da Jing Lu Li Hui Ji Bien Lan	大清律例彙輯便覽
Ta Ch'ing Lü Li	Da Jing Lu Li	大清律例
Ta Chuan	Da Zhuan	大傳
Ta Hsiao Ts'ung T'ung Shih	Da Xiao Zong Tong Shi	大小宗通釋
Ta Kung	Da Gong	大功
Ta Tsung	Da Zong	大宗
Tan Kung	Tan Gong	檀弓
Tan Mien	Tan Mien	袒免
T'ang	Tang	堂
T'ang Chih Sun	Tan Zhi Sun	堂姪孫
T'ang Chung Tsung	Tang Zhong Zong	唐中宗

T'ang Hsiung Ti	Tang Xiong Di	堂兄弟
T'ang Lü Li	Tang Lu Li	唐律例
Tao Ch'ien	Tao Qian	陶潛
Tao Tsai Men	Dao Ta Men	倒踏門
Teh	De	德
Teng	Deng	燈
Ti	Di	弟
T'i	Ti	悌
Ti Ching Ching Wu Liao	Di Jing Jing Wu Lue	帝京景物略
Ti Li Chih	Di Li Zhi	地理志
Ti Mu	Di Mu	嫡母
Ti Pao	Di Bao	地保
Tieh	Die	牒，爹
Tien	Tien	田
Tien Ho	Tien He	天河
Tien Pao	Tien Bao	天寶
Ting	Ding	丁
T'ing	Ting	庭
Ting Hsien	Ding Xian	定縣
Ting Lan	Ding Lan	丁蘭
Tou	Dou	豆
Tsai Chi	Cai Ji	蔡姬
Tsai Chung Chih Ming	Cai Zhong Zhi Ming	蔡仲之命
Tsai O	Zai E	宰娥
Tsai Ts'ung Ti	Cai Cong Di	再從弟
Tsai Yung	Cai Yong	蔡邕
Ts'ao Jung	Cao Rong	曹溶
Tseng Tsan	Zeng Cen	曾參
Tseng Tsu	Zeng Zu	曾祖
Tsi T'ang	Ci Tang	祠堂
Tseng	Zeng	贈
Tso	Zuo	佐
Tso Chuan	Zuo Zhuan	左傳

Tso I	Zuo Yi	祚裔
Ts'ou	Cou	湊
Tsu	Zu	族
Ts'u	Cu	蹙
Tsu Chang	Zu Zhang	族長
Tsu Jen	Zu Ren	族人
Ts'un Chang	Cun Zhang	村長
Tsung	Zong	宗
Tsung Ch'in	Zong Qin	宗親
Tsung Fa Hsiao Chi	Zong Fa Xiao Ji	宗法小記
Ts'ung Mu Hsiung Ti	Cong Mu Xiong Di	從母兄弟
Ts'ung Mu Tzu Mei	Cong Mu Zi Mei	從母姊妹
Tsung Tsu	Cong Zu	宗族
Tu Yu	Du You	杜佑
Tuan Wu	Duan Wu	端午
Tung Chih	Dong Zhi	冬至
T'ung	Tung	桐
T'ung Chü Chi Fu	Tung Ju Ji Fu	同居繼父
T'ung Tien	Tung Tien	通典
Tzǔ Tsao	Ci Zao	辭竈
Tzǔ	Zi	子
Tzu Ch'an	Zi Chan	子產
Tzu Kung	Zi Gong	子貢
Tzu Lu	Zi Lu	子路
Tzu Mei	Zi Mei	姊妹
Tzu Shang	Zi Shang	子上
T'zu	Si	祠
Wai	Wai	外
Wai Hsiung Ti	Wai Xiong Di	外兄弟
Wai Shing	Wai Sheng	外甥
Wai Sun	Wai Sun	外孫
Wai Tsu	Wai Zu	外祖
Wan	Wan	完
Wan Yu Wen K'u	Wan You Wen Ku	萬有文庫

233

Wang	Wang	王
Wang An-Shih	Wang An-Shi	王安石
Wang Chung	Wang Chong	王充
Wang Kuo-wei	Wang Guo-wei	王國維
Wang Tsu	Wang Zu	望族
Wei	Wei	魏
Wei Chi	Wei Ji	韋機
Wen Chiang	Wen Jiang	文姜
Wei Chou-fu	Wei Chou-fu	魏醜夫
Wen Wang (King Wen)	Wen Wang	文王
Wu	Wu	巫
Yang	Yang	陽，楊
Yang Hung-lieh	Yang Hong-lie	楊鴻烈
Yang Yung-kuo	Yang Yung-guo	楊國榮
Yang Ke	Yang Ke	秧歌
Yang Nü	Yang Nu	養女
Yang Tzu	Yang Zi	養子
Yen	Yen	嚴
Yin	Yin	隱
Yin Kung	Yin Gong	隱公
You Kuai Lu	You Guai Lu	幽怪錄
Yü Chia Kang	Yu Jia Gang	漁家港
Yü Lan Hui	Yu Lan Hui	盂蘭會
Yü Tai Hsin Yung K'au I	Yu Tai Xin Yong Kao I	玉台新詠考異
Yuan Tien Chang	Yuan Dien Zhang	元典章
Yueh	Yue	禴
Yueh Fu Shih Hsian	Yue Fu Shi Xuan	樂府詩選
Yun Mêng	Yun Meng	雲夢
Yung	Yong	勇永
Yung Lo	Yong Le	永樂
Yung Jui	Yong Rui	庸芮

Bibliography

Addison, J. T., *Chinese Ancestor Worship, A Study of its Meaning and Relations with Christianity*, Shanghai, 1925.

Alabaster, C., 'The new law of inheritance', *China Review*, vol. V, July 1876 to June 1877.

Anderson, W. H., *Luther's Work and the Word of God*, London, 1883.

Ayscough, F., *Chinese Women, Yesterday and Today*, Boston, 1937.

Ball, J. Dyer, 'Sin', *The Encyclopedia of Religion and Ethics*, vols XI, and XII, New York, 1951.

Barnes, J. A., 'Seven types of segmentation', *The Rhodes–Livingstone Journal*, no. 17, 1955.

Bateson, G., 'A history of play and fantasy', *Psychiatric Research Report*, 2, American Psychiatric Association, 1954.

Boeckh, A., *Encyklopädie und Methodologie der Philologischen Wissenschaften*, Leipzig, 1886.

du Bose, H. C. *The Dragon, Image and Demon, or Three Religions of China*, London, 1886.

Botsford, G. W., *A History of Rome*, New York, 1901.

Boüinais and A. Paulus, *Le culte des morts dans le céleste Empire et l'Annam*, Paris, 1893.

Bradley, H. H., *Form and Spirit*, London, 1951.

Bridges, John H., *Illustrations of Positivism*, Chicago, 1915.

Butler, John H., 'Preface', *Fifteen Sermons*, London, 1856.

Chan Kuo-ts'e, *Records of the Warring States*, Chin dynasty.

Chang Wing-tsi, *Religious Trends in Modern China*, New York, 1953.

Ch'ang-sun Wu-chi, *T'ang Lü Shu I*, (*Commentary on the Penal Code of the T'ang Dynasty*) (Imperial Code), AD 653.

Chang Lo-lin and T'ung Chi-yeh, in *Hsüeh Hai Lei Pien* ed. Ts'ao Jung with additions by T'ao Yüeh, Shanghai, 1920.

Chao Chi-pien, *Ku Tai Ju Chia Che Hsüeh Pi Ping*, (*A Critique of Ancient Confucian Philosophy*).

Chao Wei-pang, 'The Ting Hsien Play', *Folklore Studies*, vol. 3, 1944.

Chavannes, E., *Les mémoires historiques*, Paris, 1901.

Chen Han-seng, *The Present Agrarian Problem in China*. Shanghai, 1933.

Chen Han-seng, *Agrarian Problems in Southernmost China*, Shanghai, 1936.

Ch'en Ku-yüan, *The History of the Chinese Laws*, Shanghai, 1934.

Chen Ming-lei, *Tu Shu Chi Ch'eng*, Imperial Encyclopaedia, AD 1120.

Ch'en Shou, *San Kuo Chih* (*History of the Three Kingdoms*), AD 220–80, Chin dynasty *c.* AD 290.

Chêng Chen (ed.), *Ch'ao Ching Ch'ao Wen Chi* (*Collected Works of Chêng Chen*), 1806–1964.

Cheng T'ien-hsi, *China Moulded by Confucius*, London, 1947.

Ch'êng Shih I Shu, (*Posthumous Writings of the Chêng Brothers*), ed. Chu Hsi, 11th century.

Chinese Recorder, XVIII, 1886.

Chinese Repository, vol. XVIII, July 1849, no. 7 art. 7.

Ching Ch'u Sui Shi Chi, (*Annual Folk Customs of the States of Ching and Chu*).

Chiu T'ang Shu (*Old History of the T'ang Dynasty*), by Liu Hsü.

Chou Hung-hsiang, *The Imperial Records of the Shan and Yin Dynasties*, Hong Kong, 1958.

Chou Li Chu Shu (*Record of the Rites of the Chou Dynasty*), former Han dynasty, Compilers unknown.

Chou Mi, *Ch'i T'ung Yeh Yü* (*Rustic Talks in Eastern Ch'i*), Yuan dynasty, *c.* AD 1290, in *Ssu Pu Pei Yao*.

Chu Shu Chi Nien (*The Bamboo Books*) (Annals), Chou dynasty, *c.* 195 BC, writers unknown, Taiwan, 1970.

Ch'ü T'ung-tsu, *Law and Society in Traditional China*, Paris, 1961.

Chu Y-tsun, *Jih Hsia Chiu Wen Kao* (*Daily collection of Past Events*).

Chun Chiu Tso Chuan (*Spring and Autumn Annals or Records of Spring and Autumn*), 722 and 481 BC, writers unknown.

Chung Yung (*The Doctrine of the Mean*), Chou dynasty, 4th century BC, by Kung Chi.

Clennel, W. J., *Historical Development of Religion in China*, London, 1917.

Creel, H. G., 'The Beginning of Bureaucracy in China: The Origin of the Hsien', *Journal of Asian Studies*, vol. 18, no. 22, February 1964.

Doolittle, J., *Social Life of the Chinese*, London, 1868.

Duyvendak, J. J. L., *The Book of Lord Shang*, a classic of the Chinese school of Law, London, 1928.

Edkins, J., 'Literature of Ancestral Worship in China', *Academy*, vol. 28, 19 September, 1885.

Bibliography

Erh Ya, (*Literary Expositor*) (dictionary) enlarged and commented on
c. AD 300 by Kuo P'u.

Evans-Pritchard, E.E., *The Nuer*, Oxford, 1940.

Fan Sheng and Cheng Chen, 'The Origin of Hsiang Ch'i in China', in
Collection of the Chinese History of Physical Culture, Peking, 1957.

Fang Hsüan-ling, *Chin Su* (*History of the Chin Dynasty*), AD 265 to 419.

Fei Hsiao-tung, *Peasant Life in China: A Field Study of Country Life in
the Yangtze Valley*, London, 1939.

Fêng Han-yi, *The Chinese Kinship System*, Cambridge, Mass., 1948.

Feng Mêng-ling, *Hsing Shih Heng Yen* (*Stories to Awaken Men*), c. AD
1640.

Firth, R., *We, the Tikopia: A Sociological Study of Kinship in Primitive
Polynesia*, London, 1936.

Fong Mong-lung and Lin Mong-chu, *Chin Ku Ch'i Kuan* (*Strange Tales
New and Old*), Shanghai, 1933.

Forde, A., *Yang Chu's Garden of Pleasures*, London, 1912.

Fortes, M. 'Time and social structure: an Ashanti study', in *Social
Structure: Presented to A. R. Radcliffe-Brown*, ed. M. Fortes. New
York, 1962.

Fortes, M., 'Some reflections on ancestor worship in Africa', in *African
Systems of Thought*, Oxford, 1965.

Freedman, M., *Lineage Organization in Southeastern China*, London,
1965.

Freud, S., *Totem and Taboo*, London, 1950, reprinted 1965.

Fung Yu-lan, *Hsin Li Hsüeh* (*New Rational Philosophy*), Shanghai,
1947.

Gamble, S. D., *Ting Hsien, A North China Rural Community*, New
York, 1954.

Gamble, S. D. (ed.), *Chinese Village Plays*, Amsterdam, 1970.

Giles, H. A., *Historic China and Other Sketches*, London, 1882.

Giles, H. A., 'Family Names', *Journal of the North China Branch of the
Royal Asiatic Society*, vol. XXI, 1887.

Giles, H. A., *Chuang Tzǔ*, London, 1889.

Giles, H. A., *Civilizations of China*, London, 1911.

Giles, L., *Taoist Teachings from the Book of Lieh Tzu*, London, 2nd
edn, 1947.

Goldsmith, O., *The Traveller*, London, 1858.

Goody, J., *Death, Property and the Ancestors*, London, 1962.

Goody, J., 'Religion and ritual', *British Journal of Sociology*, vol. XII,
1961.

Graham, D. C., 'Folk religion in south west China', *Smithsonian Miscellaneous Collection*, vol. 142, no. 2., 1 November 1961.

Granet, M. *La polygénie sororale et le sororat dans la Chine féodale*,
Paris, 1920.

237

Granet M., *Danses et légendes de la Chine ancienne*, Paris, 1959.

de Groot, J. J. M., *The Religious System of China*, 6 vols, Leiden, 1892-1910, vol. IV, book II, 'On the Soul and Ancestral Worship'.

de Groot, J. J. M., *Les fêtes annuellement célébrées à Emoui – Étude concernant la religion populaire des chinois in annales du Musée Guimet*, vols. 11 and 12, Paris, 1886.

Han Fei Tzu, The Book of Master Han Fei, Chou dynasty early 3rd century BC, by Han Fei; trans. Liao Wen-kuei.

Heimisch, P., *History of the Holy Testament*, trans. W. G. Heidt, St Paul, Minnesota, 1950.

Hou Han Shu (*History of the Late Han Dynasty*), AD 25–220, by Fan Yeh.

Hsiao Ching, (*The Classic of filial piety*), 1st century AD, by Tseng Shen, trans. de Rosny.

Hsieh Yu-wei, 'Filial piety and Chinese society', *Philosophy East and West*, vol. X, 1961.

Hsu, F. L. K., *Under the Ancestors' Shadow: Chinese Culture and Personality*, London, 1949.

Hsu, F. L. K., 'The problem of incest taboo in a North China village', *American Anthropologist*, vol. 42, no. 1, January–March 1940.

Hsu, F. L. K., 'Observations on cross-cousin marriage in China', *American Anthropologist*, vol. 47, no. 1, January–March 1945.

Hsü Mêng-ling, *The History of Drama and Plays in Yün Nan Province*, National University of Yun Nan Press, 1949.

Hsü Sheng, *Shou Wen Chieh-tzu*, (*Analytical Dictionary of Characters*), later Han dynasty *c.* AD 121.

Hsü Wen-ching (ed.) *The Annals of the Bamboo Books* in *Han Wei Ts'ung Shu*, 80 vols, 1952.

Hsüeh Hai Lei Pien, ed. Ts'ao Jung with additions by T'ao Yüeh, Shanghai, 1920.

Hsün Tzu, The Book of Master Hsün, Chou dynasty, *c.* 240 BC by Hsün Ching.

Hu Hsien-chin, *The Common Descent Group in China and Its Functions*, New York, 1948.

Hu Shih, 'Confucianism', *The Encyclopedia of the Social Sciences*, New York, 1931, vol. IV.

Hu Shih, *The Chinese Renaissance*, Haskell Lectures, Chicago, 1933.

Hu Shih, 'Sho Ju', in *Hu Shi Lung Hsüeh Chin Chu*, vol. I, Shanghai, 1935.

Huâng En-tung, Preface to *Ta Ch'ing Lü Li An Yü*, Hai Hsien Kuan Ts'ang Pan edition.

Hubert, H. and Mauss, M., *Sacrifice, Its Nature and Function*, trans. W. D. Halls, London, 1964.

Huc, l'Abbe, *Christianity in China, Tartary and Tibet*, London, 1858.

Hughes, E. R., *The Comparative study of Chinese Philosophy and Religion*, Oxford, 1935.

Hughes, E. R. and Hughes, K., *Religion in China*, London, 1950.

Hulsewe, A. F. P. *Remnants of Han Law*, vol. I, 'Introductory Studies and Annotated Translation of Chapters 22 and 23 of the History of the Former Han Dynasty', *Sinica Leidensia*, vol. IX, Leiden, 1955.

I Ching, (*The Classic of Changes* or *Book of Changes*), Chou dynasty with former Han dynasty additions. Compilers unknown, trans. R. Willhelm and J. Legge.

I Ching, (*Book of the Spiritual and Strange*) 4th Century AD, by Tung Fan-shou.

I Li (*The Personal Conduct Ritual*) (One of the Three Rituals with Li Chi and the Chou Li), Ch'in and Han dynasties, based on Chou dynasty material, by Kaothan Sêng.

Jackson, H., *Ancestral Worship*, Centenary Missionary Conference, no. 7, Shanghai, 1907.

Jamieson, G., 'The history of adoption and its relations to modern wills', *China Review*, vol. XVIII.

John G., 'The Ethic of the Chinese with Special Reference to the Doctrine of Human Nature and Sin', *Journal of the North China Branch of Royal Asiatic Society*, vol. II, no. 1, September 1860.

Johnston, R. F., *Lion and Dragon in Northern China*, London, 1910.

Joyce, G. H., *Christian Marriage*, London, 1933.

Kai Yü Ts'ung K'ao, by Chao I, 1790, in *Shou K'ao T'ang Ou Pei Ch'uan Shu*.

Karlgren, B., 'Legends and cults in ancient China', *Bulletin of the Museum of Far Eastern Antiquities*, no. 18, Stockholm, 1949.

Keesing, F., *Cultural Anthropology*, New York, 1958.

Ki Jun-shu, *Yü Tai Hsin Yung K'ao I*, Shanghai, 1937. An inquiry into Text and Discrepancies in 'The Jade Table Anthology of Modern Ballads'.

Ku Shih Yuan (*The Origin of Ancient Poems*), compiled by Shen Te-chien.

Ku Yen-wu, *Jih Chih Lu* (*Daily Additions to Knowledge*), Ch'in dynasty, AD 1673.

Kulp, D. H., *Country Life in South China*, New York, 1925.

Kung Yang Chu Shu (*Master Kung Yang's Commentary on the Spring and Autumn Annals*), attributed to Kung Yang Shou.

K'ung Tzu Chia Yü, (*The Table Talk of Confucius*), later Han dynasty, 3rd century AD, (ed.) Wang Su.

Ku Chin Tu Shu Chi Ch'eng, compiled by Chiang T'ing-hsi and others, Shanghai, 1884.

Kou Yü, Discourses on the ancient feudal States: Late Chou, Chin and former Han dynasties containing early material from ancient written records. Writers unknown.

Lee Shu-ching, 'China's traditional family', *American Sociological Review*, vol. 18, June 1953.

Lenormant, F., *Histoire ancienne de l'Orient jusqu'aux guerres modiques*, Paris, 181–8.

Legge, J., *The Religions of China - Confucianism, Taoism described compared with Christianity*, London, 1880.

Levenson, J. R. *Confucian China and its Modern State*, London, 1958.

Lewis, C. T., and Short. C., 'Pietas', *Latin–English Dictionary*, Oxford, 1880.

Li Chi (The Records of Rites), Former Han dynasty, *c.* 70–50 BC.

Li Tsung-t'ung, *The History of Ancient China*, 2 vols, Formosa, 1952.

Lieh Tzu (The Book of Master Lieh), AD 380, by Lieh Yü-k'ou.

Li Yen-shou, *Nan Shih, Pei Shih*, Tung Wen Publisher.

Lin Yueh-hua, 'An enquiry into the Chinese Lineage–village from the viewpoint of anthropology', *She Hui Hsüeh Chieh*, no. 9, 1936.

Lin Yueh-hua *I-hsü*, 1936.

Lin Yueh-hua, *The Golden Wing, A Sociological Study of Chinese Familism*, London, 1948.

Liu Hsiang, *I Hsi Tz'u I*.

Liu Hsing-t'ang, 'The structure of kinship groups in Fukien', *Shih Huo*, vol. 4, no. 8, 1936.

Liu Hsü, *Chiu T'ang Shu (Old History of the T'ang Dynasty)*, AD 618 to 906.

Liu Hui-cheng, Wang, *The Traditional Chinese Clan Rules*, New York, 1959.

Liu Tun-chêng, *Peking Architecture and Technology Survey*, Peking, 1947.

Liu T'ung and Yü I-cheng, *Ti Ching Ching Wu liao (Descriptions of Things and Customs at the Imperial Capital)*, Ming dynasty AD 1638, by Liu T'ung.

Loisy, A., *Essai historique sur le sacrifice*, Paris, 1920.

Lü Shih Ch'un-ch'iu (Master Lü's Spring and Autumn Annals) (compendium of natural philosophy), Chou (Ch'in) dynasty 239 BC, by Lü Pu wei.

Lun Yü (The Analects of Confucius), *c.* 465–450 BC, compiled by the disciples of Confucius.

MacIntyre, J., 'Jottings from the Book of Rites', Part I, 'Ancestor Worship', *China Review*, vol. VII, July 1878–June 1879.

McLennan, J. F. *Studies in Ancient History*, London, 1876.

de Mailla, M. 'Histoire générale de la Chine', *The Annals of China*, vol. IV, 1699.

Main, H. Sir, *Ancient Law*, Oxford, 1959.

Malinowski, B., 'Culture', *The Encyclopedia of the Social Sciences*, New York, 1931.

Mao Ch'i-ling, 'Ta Hsiao Tsung T'ung Shih', in *Mao Hsi-Ho Hsien-Sheng Ch'uan-Chi*.

Maspero, A., 'Les religions chinoises', *Mélanges posthumes sur les religions et l'histoire de la Chine*, Paris, 1950.

Meadows, T. T., *Desultory Notes on the Government and People of China and on the Chinese Language*, London, 1847.

Mei Huei-ting, *The Problem of Reforming the Chinese Family System*, Shanghai, 1929.

Mencius or *Mêng Tzǔ* (*The Book of Master Mêng* (Mencius)), Chou dynasty, *c.* 290 BC, by Mêng Kho. trans. by J. Legge, Hong Kong, 1861.

Mêng Tzǔ Chu Shu (*Exegesis of the Book of Master Mêng*), in *Ssu Pu Pei Yao*.

Ming Lü Li (*The Statute or Law of the Ming Dynasty*), Peking, 1908.

Ming Shih (*History of the Ming Dynasty*), AD 1368–1643, by Chang T'ing-yü, 1739.

Mitchel-Innes, M. G., 'Adoption', *China Review*, vol. XIV, July 1885– June 1886.

von Möllendorff, O. G., 'The family law of the Chinese', *Journal of the China Branch of the Royal Asiatic Society*, new series, vol. XXVII, 1892–3.

Moh Tzǔ (including Mo Ching), (*The Book of Master Mo*), Chou dynasty (4th century BC), by Moh Ti (and disciples).

Nan Ch'i shu (*History of the Southern Ch'i Dynasty*), AD 479–501.

Niu Song-ju, *Yu Kuai Lu*, Record of things Dark and Strange in Lung Wei Mi Shu.

Notes and Queries on Anthropology by a Committee of the Royal Anthropological Institute of Great Britain and Ireland, London, 1960.

Ou Yang Hsuan, *Sung Shih* in *Ssu Pu Pei Yao*.

Pai Hu Tung (*Comprehensive Discussions at the White Lodge*), later Han dynasty, *c.* AD 8. Pan Ku.

Pai Hu Tung Shu Cheng.

Pan Kuang-tan, 'The family system and gens and clan', in *She Hui Hsüeh-Chieh* vol. IX, 1936.

Ping Hua-li, M., *The Economic History of China*, New York, 1921.

Plopper, C. H., *Chinese Religion through the Proverb*, Shanghai, 1926.

Radcliffe-Brown, A. R., *Structure and Function in Primitive Society*, Chicago, 1952.

Radcliffe-Brown, A. R., and Forde, D., *African Systems of Kinship and Marriage*, Oxford, 1960.

Rygaloff, A., 'Deux points de nomenclature dans les systèmes chinois de parenté', *L'Homme*, October–December 1967.

Shang Hai Ching (*Classic of Mountains and Rivers*), writers unknown.

Shang Shu, (greater commentary on the Shang Shu chapters of the historical classic), by Fu Sheng.

Shih Ch'i Shih Shang Chüeh by Wang Ming-sheng.

Shih Chi (*Historical Records*), former Han dynasty, *c.* 90 BC, by Ssu-ma Ch'ien.

Shih Ching (*Book of Odes*), (ancient folksongs), Chou dynasty, 9 to 5 BC, fifth century, tr. J. Legge, Oxford, 1879.

Shih Nei-an, *Shui Hu Chuan* (*All Men are Brothers*), 4 vols; thirteenth-century novel, trans. P. Buck, London, 1957.

Shu Ching, (*Book of Documents*), (historical classic), writers unknown, trans. J. Legge, Oxford, 1879, trans. W. H. Medhurst, Shanghai, 1846.

Smith, A., *Chinese Characteristics*, London, 1892.

Spencer, C., *The Land of the Chinese People*, London, 1947.

Ssu-ma Ch'ien, *Su Shih Chi.*

Ssu-ma Kuang, *Ssu-ma Shih Shu Yi.*

Sui Shu, History of the Sui Dynasty, AD 581–617, by Wei Chêng *et al.*

Sung Hsing Tung, The Penal Code of the Sung Dynasty, vol. I. p. 106.

Sung Lien, *Hsiao Tzu Lu.*

Sung Shih (*History of the Sung Dynasty*), AD 960–1277, by Ouyang Hsüen.

Su Sing-ging, *The Chinese Family System*, New York, 1922.

Ta Ch'ing Lü Li (*The Statue or Law of the Ch'ing Dynasty*), 1646.

Ta Ming Ling (*The Code of the Ming Dynasty*).

T'ang Lü Li (*The Statute or Law of the T'ang Dynasty*).

T'ang Lü Shu Li (*Explanation of the Meaning of the Code of T'ang Dynasty*).

T'ao Ch'ien, *T'ao Yüan Ming Chi, The Collected Works of T'ao Yüan Ming or T'ao Ch'ien.* Ssu Pu Ts'ung Kan edition.

Tjan Tjoe Som, (trans.) *Pai Hu Tung (The Comprehensive Discussions in the White Tiger Hall*), 2 vols. Leiden, 1949–52. *Translations of the China Branch of the Royal Asiatic Society Review*, 1853–4.

Ts'ao Jung, *Hsüeh Hai Lei Pien*, The Ocean of Scholarship fooled by category. Shanghai, 1920.

Tso Chuan (*Spring and Autumn Annals*), 430–250 BC, by Tso Chiu ming.

Tso Hsueh-Ching, *The dream of the Red Chamber*, Peking, 1972.

T'ung Tien (*Comprehensive Institutes*) (reservoir of source material on political and social history), T'ang dynasty, AD 812, by Tu Tu.

Tung Chou Lieh Kuo, vol. IV, *The Romance of the States of Eastern Chou.*

Bibliography

Tylor, E. B., *Primitive Culture*, London, 1913.

Waley, A. (Trans.), *The Analects of Confucius*, London, 1945).

Wang Ch'ung, *Lung Heng (Discourse weighed in the Balance)*, AD 82 and 83, trans. A. Forde, London, 1911.

Wang Min-sheng, *Shih Chi Shih Shang Chüeh.*

Warner, W. L. *The Black Civilization*, New York, 1964.

Wei Shu (History of the Northern Wei Dynasty), AD 386–550, by Wei Shou.

Wells, S., *The Middle Kingdom*, 2 vols, London, 1883.

Weiger, L., *Folk-lore*, Hsien hsien (county), Hopei, China, Imprimerie de le Mission Catholique, 1909.

Wilkinson, H. P., *The Family in Classical China*, Shanghai, 1926.

Williamson, R. W., *The Social and Political Systems of Central Polynesia*, 3 vols, Cambridge, 1924.

Wittfogel, K. A., 'Foundation and stages of Chinese economic history', *Zeitschrift für Sozialforschung*, vol. IV, no. 1, 1935.

Yang Hung-lieh, *The History of the Development of Chinese Laws*, 2 vols, Shanghai (no date).

Yang Jung-kuo, *The History of Ancient Chinese Thought*, Hong Kong, 1962.

Yang, N., *A Chinese Village: Taitou, Shantung Province*, London, 1948.

Yü Kuan-ying, *Yueh Fu Shih Hsüan*, Peking, 1954.

Yü Yen, *Hsi Shang Fu T'ang*. Old fashioned table talk.

Yuan Hsing, *Ta Ch'ing Hsien Hsing Lü (The Criminal Law in Force in the Ch'ing Dynasty)*.

Yüan Mei Sui Yüan Sui Pi.

Yuan Shih (The History of Yuan Dynasty), AD 1206–1367, Ming dynasty c. AD 1370, by Sung Lien et al.

Yuan Tien Chang (The Laws of the Yuan Dynasty).

Index

Evans-Pritchard, E. E., 19
Exogamy, 34

Family, 17, 18, 132–3; compound,
17, 193; economic, 16–17;
joint, 11; nuclear or elementary, 8–9; orientation, 40–1;
procreation, 40–1; property,
49; stem, 9–10
Fang sub-lineage, 17
Farmhouse, 8
Father: adoptive, 41; and daughter,
51–3; natural, 41; and son, 41–
8
Fei Hsiao-tung, 3, 15, 37, 151
Feng Shui – geomancy, 120
Filial impiety, 75–6
Filial piety, 42, 44, 49, 71–94,
202; ancestor worship, 79,
124–5, 127–30; Christianity,
72, 91, 93, 99; Greeks, 72;
Jen, 74, 77; Romans, 72; and
state, 78, 79, 81–3; Semitic
people, 72; three grades, 78
Fortes, M., 3
Fortune, R., 4
Freedman, M., 3
Freud, S., 173
Fu character, 43
Funeral rites, 132

Gambling, Ma Chiang, 183
Generation, 17, 29–31, 33, 191
Gens, 8
Girls, status of, 50–2
Goody, Jack, 4
Grandparents and grandchildren,
67–70
Great Learning, 98

Herd Boy, 179
Homestead, 15
Household, 15–16, 38, 192
Hsiao, piety, 72, 226
Hsiao Ching, 79
Hsing, 194
Hu Hsien-Chin, 3
Hun, 104, 209

Husband and wife, 57–61, 75,
91, 93

Illegitimacy, 213
Inequality of boy and girl, 200
Inheritance, 49, 139–40

Jen, 202
Joking relations, 67, 69, 201
Jo shui, weak water, 221
Ju Chiao, 121

Kai kou, 6
Kin, 7–8
Kinship, 41, 46, 134; and ancestor worship, 101, 130; family
graveyards, 120; and religion,
153; and succession and inheritance, 139, 140
Kitchen god, 221
Kulp, D. H., 3, 15–16, 147, 149,
154
Kwei character, 51, 102–3, 209,
228
Kwei, 228

Land, 10, 133
Lantern Festival, 175
Lao, old, 228
La Pa Chieh, 181
Leach, E., 4
Legalized incest, 58
Li, 43, 74–5, 124, 158, 203, 217
Li Mi, 77–8
Lineage, 17, 19–21, 26, 37, 193
Lin Yueh-hua, 36, 38–9, 147, 151,
153

Maine, Sir Henry, 139, 140
Malinowski, B., 6, 189
Marriage: age, 42; cross-cousin,
31, 59, 219; function, 59
Memorialism, 130
Milfoil, 220
Milk name, 6
Milky Way, 179
Mills, W., 3
Moist utilitarianism, 212